"This is a terrific book, rich with anecdotes and logic. Capon makes sense of all of the marketing clutter by integrating the insights of the world's best marketers into a series of simple rules. These rules become the manifesto for market leaders and those who want to become one. This is the best marketing book I've read in a long time."

—REED HOLDEN, founder and CEO,
Holden Advisors

"A fascinating book with a much-needed, different point of view: One I have personally held for a very long time. This is big-picture marketing about companies whose entire orientation is 'to the market.' It's about people at vibrant and successful companies who orient themselves to the outside world of consumers, customers, and users. Everything Marketing Mavens think of and everything they do is in the context of the people who are actually buying the product and experiencing the brand. *The Marketing Mavens* is excellent. It's the right book at the right time."

—SHELLY LAZARUS, chairman and CEO,
Ogilvy & Mather Worldwide

"Think of this book as the Miracle-Gro for marketers. Put a little of Noel Capon's formula into your marketing root system and see your business flourish. It's time marketers dug much deeper into customer dynamics and drivers to make market understanding a real competitive advantage that can be both a differentiator and business value builder. Filled with valuable, relevant, and current brand marketing illustrations, Capon makes a compelling argument for advancing the need to architect and integrate your operations around the customer experience. Let's all make 'customer-focused action' a cultural imperative in our organizations!"

—DONOVAN NEALE-MAY, executive
director, Chief Marketing Officer (CMO)
Council

"Dr. Noel Capon's new book, *The Marketing Mavens*, is a much-needed book in the spirit of *Built to Last* by Collins, by digging deeply into the strategies, tools, and track records of leaders. Most books in this tradition treat marketing as one factor (often small) in the company's impressive track record. This book, *The Marketing Mavens*, as the title suggests, is all about great marketing. Any marketer, any manager who needs marketing to be at their best will glean useful stuff—ideas, cases, and tools—from this timely book. The in-depth look at integrated marketing is especially valuable in today's fragmented marketplace."

—JOE PLUMMER, chief research officer, The
ARF—*The Research Authority*

"While many talk about the necessity of being 'customer-centric,' in *The Marketing Mavens*, Noel Capon clearly identifies and illustrates the essential elements that enable companies to achieve and sustain leadership by continuously delivering value to their customers. I highly recommend this book to business leaders of all ranks regardless of whether they are looking to build a new business model, transform an existing organization, or better understand and strengthen an already thriving organization."

—SIDNEY TAUREL, chairman and CEO,
Eli Lilly and Company

"*The Marketing Mavens* unearths the shared characteristics of customer-centric companies that consistently outperform their rivals. It defines fundamental truths that apply from Toyota to IBM, from Amazon to Alcoa. This is a 'must read' for business leaders and marketing executives who are committed to leading and winning the battle for growth in today's competitive markets."

—GARY S. TUBRIDY, senior vice president,
The Alexander Group, Inc.

ALSO BY NOEL CAPON

Corporate Strategic Planning
with John U. Farley and James M. Hulbert

The Marketing of Financial Services:
A Book of Cases

Planning the Development of Builders, Leaders,
and Managers of 21st Century Business

Why Some Firms Perform Better than Others:
Toward a More Integrative Explanation
with John U. Farley and James M. Hulbert

The Asian Marketing Case Book
with Wilfried Van Honacker

Marketing Management in the 21st Century
with James M. Hulbert

Marketing Management in the 21st Century (Chinese edition)
with James M. Hulbert and Willem Burgers

Key Account Management and Planning
<www.keyaccountmanagement.com>

Total Integrated Marketing
with James M. Hulbert and Nigel E. Piercy

Managing Global Accounts
with Dave Potter and Fred Schindler

Managing Marketing in the 21st Century <www.mm21c.com>
with James M. Hulbert

The Virgin Marketer <www.mm21c.com>

THE MARKETING MAVENS

NOEL CAPON

CROWN
BUSINESS
NEW YORK

Library of Congress Cataloging-in-Publication Data

Capon, Noel.
The marketing mavens / Noel Capon.—1st ed.

1. Relationship marketing.   2. Customer relations.   3. Marketing—Management.
I. Title.
HF5415.55.C37 2007
658.8—dc22   2006101945

ISBN 978-0-307-35409-9

Printed in the United States of America

Design by Joseph Rutt

10 9 8 7 6 5 4 3 2

First Edition

To Deanna, Merna, Ellen, Paul, and Peter
From near and far, you are my global family

Contents

THE MARKETING MAVENS

Introduction

Why Marketing Mavens Spell Marketing with a Capital *M*

Over the past dozen or so years, globalization has turned business on its head. For almost a half century, from the late 1940s until the 1990s, the overriding factor that dominated the economic scene was scarcity of supply. Companies did not have to be all that good, much less great, and competitive innovations in another country or region presented little threat. If somebody, somewhere, found a better way to do something, there was plenty of leeway to ignore it or slowly acquiesce to change.

Companies no longer have the luxury of such behavior, and customers no longer dance to their tunes. Today, the overriding factor that dominates the economic scene is scarcity of demand. Notwithstanding dozens of bloody civil, local, and regional wars, a half century of peace in the world at large has combined with technological advances and other forces to foster substantial economic growth, not only in the United States and western Europe but also in Asia, Australasia, and South America. As a result, the next innovation, the next killer competitor may come from anywhere, anytime, to take your customers—and thus your business—away from you in the virtual blink of an eye. Today customers around the world have multiple choices for everything they want to buy. Hence, the most profitable customers in every business-to-business and consumer sector are increasingly scarce on the ground.

Mediocre companies remain mediocre, if they survive at all, because they still practice marketing with a small *m*, that is, they view marketing in its traditional roles of communications and sales.

Great companies become and remain great because they practice marketing with a capital *M*. They know that thriving despite demand scarcity means doing business differently because they understand that one of the central facts of business life today is that customers *don't* have to do business with you. Great companies are populated at every level of the organization with Marketing Mavens obsessed with the idea that everything a company does, from R&D to customer service, must be focused on anticipating and meeting customer needs.

Ensuring that scarce customers do business with you is front and center a marketing job. The chief marketing officer (CMO) usually has the responsibility for analyzing and articulating which customers you want and how you will secure and retain them. Some CMOs do this job better than others and the best of the lot are Marketing Mavens. But Marketing Mavens are not just found in marketing. In the most successful companies the Marketing Mavens include not only the CEO and all senior managers but everyone in the organization from product developers to people in the Research and Development (R&D), Sales, Finance, and Human Resources departments. Marketing Mavens in short change the ways that their companies think about and do marketing by making marketing everyone's business.

The mission of this book is to share the lessons from Marketing Mavens in a host of industries and change the way you think about and do marketing in your business.

Marketing Mavens know that everyone in a company, not just those in the Marketing Department, must help create and retain customers. Marketing cannot be a separate function—it must be the job of the business as a whole. Marketing (with a capital *M*) must be a philosophy for your entire organization. Let's face it: if you don't have customers, you don't have anything. So whether you're a marketer, a plant manager, a chief financial officer (CFO), or chief executive officer (CEO); whether you're in R&D, Information Services, or Human Resources; whether you're a senior executive, a middle manager, or have just been hired in an entry-level position; and whether you have a customer-facing role or do a job deep in the organization, you must understand how to put customers at the center of what you do on a day-by-day basis.

The late Peter Drucker sounded a prescient call for this perspective in his classic 1954 text, *The Practice of Management.*

> There is only one valid definition of business purpose: to create a customer. It is the customer who determines what a business is . . . What the business thinks it produces is not of first importance — especially not to the future of the business and to its success. What the customer thinks he is buying, what he considers "value" is decisive . . . [A business enterprise] has two — and only two — basic functions: marketing and innovation . . . Marketing is so basic that it cannot be considered a separate function . . . it is the whole business . . . seen from the customer's point of view. Concern and responsibility for marketing must, therefore, permeate all areas of the enterprise.[1]

Few companies heeded that call consistently while scarcity of supply still held sway. Now all the top companies have made marketing an organization-wide priority. For example, Michael Hines, senior vice president of Global Marketing and Communications for Prudential Financial, lately one of the more successful companies in consumer financial services, captured this dynamic in the very first interview I conducted as part of the research on which this book is based. "There is a lot of supply and a lack of demand," Hines said. "What we base our marketing on, is that people don't need to do business with us." The same is true in virtually every market and industry sector in today's economy. To put it bluntly, you need customers more than they need you. Hence, caveat emptor (buyer beware) has become caveat venditor (seller beware)!

Make no mistake, customers are your core assets — they must form the centerpiece of your activities. You will be successful with customers, you will survive and grow, and the market value of your business will increase if, and only if, your products and services deliver greater value to customers than your competitors deliver. If you fail in this task, and your competitors deliver greater value, ultimately you will go out of business. It's that simple. The problem, of course, is that competition is getting tougher. As someone working in today's business environment, you know only too well that competition comes from so many different places beyond your traditional rivals—from different industries with different technologies, from different countries, and even from your suppliers and distribution channels.

Finding the Marketing Mavens

To date there has been little in-depth study of how successful companies focus on customers throughout their operations and how they put this focus into action on a daily basis. To fill that gap and understand better how the best companies husband and grow their customer assets, I formed and led a research team at Columbia Business School in a multiyear study of top marketing companies.

To identify marketing leaders, we began our research by studying lists of top companies, such as *Fortune*'s Most Admired Companies, the *Forbes* Platinum 400, *BusinessWeek*/Interbrand's100 Most Valuable Global Brands, *Advertising Age*'s Global World's 100 Biggest Advertisers and annual Marketing 100 lists of America's best marketers, and *PROMO* magazine's 50 Best-Promoted Brands. We looked for consistent repeat appearances, especially on multiple lists, as well as dramatic recent entrants. We combined the short list that emerged with quantitative data from a rich database housed at the strategy-consulting firm DiamondCluster International, and customer satisfaction data from the University of Michigan's American Customer Satisfaction Index. (For a detailed discussion of the research methodology, see appendix 1.)

Using these data, we constructed company and brand rankings for three broadly based criteria that we developed: *market leadership*—focused on marketing and financial performance; *company/brand reputation*—focused on reputation in areas such as innovation, product quality, brand equity, and customer satisfaction; and *market power*—focused on influence among marketing professionals. We tallied the scores for each of the three criteria and then calculated a combined rank for each organization. Our final universe, spanning twenty-four industries, ranked the top 150 public companies, one hundred brands, and forty private companies.

We then interviewed fifty-seven executives from forty organizations in a broad array of businesses. Interviewees included CEOs; chief operating officers (COOs); CMOs; and other business professionals in public, private, and not-for-profit organizations spanning eighteen of twenty-four industry categories such as banking and investment; business services; industrial materials; media, entertainment, and information; health-care services; and transportation and logistics. Most organizations were based in the United States, but we also had significant representation from Asia and Europe. Many companies were global in scope, but some were purely domestic. Quite deliberately, we omitted some high-ranking enterprises so that we could show you data across a wide array of economic sectors.

This book would not exist in its present form if it were not for the participating executives' generosity with their time and insight. We did not want a snapshot of perceived excellence in a single year or a single business climate but proven excellence over time. Short-term winners may have seductive appeal—remember when Enron was, briefly, a most admired and envied company? But this book is about the lessons of long-term winners. We conducted our first interviews in 2002, usually in person, and our last follow-up interviews, more usually by telephone and e-mail, in 2006. Some of our original interviewees no longer have the same positions. Some have different jobs in their organizations; others have moved on to new challenges—after all, the market for high-quality marketing talent is increasingly vigorous. Some executives we interviewed once; others we interviewed on multiple occasions. (This book notes interviewees' titles at the time of the most recent interview.) To make sure that the views from the top accurately reflected the organization as a whole, we also conducted focus groups with marketers on the front lines, including more recent college and MBA graduates. Over the same time span, we also performed extensive secondary research on each organization that we interviewed.

In the chapters that follow, I present lessons drawn from the successes of Alcoa, Amazon, Bloomberg L. P., Dell, ESPN, ExxonMobil, L'Oréal, Mayo Clinic, Nestlé, Oracle, Pfizer, Progressive, Prudential Financial, Samsung Electronics, SAP, Starbucks, Target, The Home Depot, Toyota, UPS, and others. Despite being in disparate businesses, they share the common characteristic of a fierce company-wide focus on the customer.

For example, it will come as a surprise to many readers that Alcoa is not just an aluminum company, but manufactures and sells many composite products that do not even include aluminum. As Dick Melville, vice chairman of Alcoa Industrial Components' Aerospace Market Sector Lead Team told us, "[In general] our customer is not normally the person who actually puts the aluminum or other product to its final use. In many cases we go three, four and even five customer levels deeper to reach the end market and gauge trends, assess our positioning, and analyze how we can pull value through the chain."

Nestlé Prepared Foods has seen substantial organic growth with its Stouffer's and Lean Cuisine brands by digging deep into the different needs of key market segments. President Stephen Cunliffe said, "We recognize that product requirements are different at different life stages. What does a teenager want to eat? What do a young married couple, both working long hours, want to eat? What does a working mother want to feed her family? What do empty nesters want to eat?" By forming segments based on customers' needs and their attitudes toward food, and precisely positioning its products at target segments, Nestlé has come to dominate the prepared-foods business.

Mayo Clinic has been providing exemplary medical care for over a hundred years and is the most well-known and powerful health-care brand in the world. Mayo's excellence is based on two simple yet powerful operating principles: "The best interest of the patient is the only interest to be considered" and "Two heads are better than one, and three are even better." Operating with these principles overcomes the interfunctional and interdepartmental tensions that are present in so many organizations.

Starbucks' success is legendary; chairman Howard Schultz credits that success to a company-wide, customer-focused marketing culture. "[T]he culture of our company allows our people to feel so positively about Starbucks that, without being asked to, they want to convey the attributes, the characteristics, the aspirational qualities of what we do for the customer."

In the past few years, Sony has faced tough times from competitors but even so has managed to improve its position on the 2006 *Business-Week*/Interbrand rankings of the top one hundred global brands. Sony spends enormous effort on measurement, driven by the mantra "If you can't measure it, you can't manage it." Ron Boire, president of sales for consumer electronics, told us how Sony's metrics for its major accounts became customer focused, and in this regard abandoned small *m* marketing for Marketing with a capital *M*: "We used to do classic sales compensation: budget versus sell-in. If you had a budget target of a million dollars for a category and you sold at $1.1 million, you did a great job, you made a good bonus. Regardless of what was stuck in the barn at the end of the month or the end of the year. Regardless of whether or not they could pay for it. Regardless of whether you delivered it to them on time." Sony shifted to customer-focused metrics. Said Boire, "[We] ask each customer, 'What's important to you? What are your targets? What are your strategic concerns?' . . . and our salespeople are given bonus compensation twice a year based on their customer scorecards."

Just like Sony, some of the other companies highlighted in this book have stumbled. Even great companies must sometimes go through rough times. Their resilience in adversity goes hand in hand with their consistent pursuit of excellence and resistance to complacency in good times. One or more of these companies may be facing rough weather as you read this book, but I believe that their collective best practices will continue to stand the test of time.[2]

It was fascinating to hear these stories of marketing achievement directly from the Marketing Mavens themselves, and I have tried to preserve the immediacy of the interviews by quoting extensively from them. But vividness and entertainment value are not the main reason for sharing so much of what we learned from winning companies in their executives' own words. Paraphrase simply cannot always capture the internal dynamics, the thinking, and the actions that make great companies great. The qualitative research data we obtained from our interviews offer a window through the income statement, balance sheet, and stock price to the interactions between a company and its customers that ultimately produce the sales increases and declines, the profits and losses, and the rises and falls in shareholder value.

The evidence from the combined qualitative and quantitative data my research team amassed points again and again to a simple—and for many—a radical message. Marketing is not just about sales and communications, nor even about that old chestnut of the "4 Ps" marketing mix: product, price, placement, promotion. Marketing is about focusing all

of the firm's energy on meeting five linked challenges that place customers at the center of strategic and tactical decision making. Indeed,
these challenges form a new system of five linked imperatives that
companies and businesses must follow if they are to be successful
in the increasingly challenging environments of the twenty-first
century:

- Pick markets that matter

- Select segments to dominate

- Design the market offer to create customer value and secure
  differential advantage

- Integrate to serve the customer

- Measure what matters

Toyota is now the number two automobile firm in North America
with a market value ten times that of General Motors. It didn't achieve
its position overnight but has been on a long, steady climb. Toyota is
all about systems and has long drawn praise for its quality manufacturing system, which delivers high perceived value in reliability and performance to customers across the full Toyota, Lexus, and Scion ranges.
But Toyota's increasingly strong lead over the rest of the global car industry also depends on excellence in several other systems that allow it
to deliver superior design, dealer management, and customer service
and communications.

Toyota adheres closely to all five imperatives and its consistent excellence in fulfilling one customer-focused imperative leads to excellence in fulfilling the others in a virtuous iterative cycle. Designing
and making cars better suited to customers' needs enables Toyota to
promote the cars more efficiently. This in turn enables it to direct resources to *pick markets that matter* and segment them well, as it has
done better than any rival; integrate operations in a company-wide
marketing culture; and assiduously measure what matters, from defects
on the assembly line to customers' satisfaction with their ownership
experience.

The bottom line of business survival and growth is that next year's profits do not depend on this year's numbers—they depend on next year's customers. If you want to know how the world's leading companies identify future customers, figure out what they need, and then deliver greater customer value than their competitors, please read on. If these issues do not concern you, then pick up a novel instead!

ONE

The New Market Model

For decades, IBM was the world's leading computer manufacturer and widely considered the best-managed company in the world. It averaged over $6 billion in profits per year from 1981 to 1990. Earnings in 1990 were over $6 billion. In 1993 the profit number exceeded $8 billion. There was just one little problem: it was negative—a $14 billion profit swing in just a couple of years![1]

When Lou Gerstner became CEO in 1993 he was given plenty of advice on how to turn around this once all-powerful, but then floundering, computer giant. The prevailing view, inside and outside IBM was almost unanimous: break it up. The emerging new information technology (IT) industry was so fragmented by smaller specialized companies, the argument went, that a fully integrated product line was passé. IT customers wanted the freedom to pick and choose the best products and services for their needs from an ever-growing universe of suppliers—mainframes here, servers there, software somewhere else.

This model was based on what many people *imagined* were the needs of IT customers. Certainly, as Gerstner observed, a lot of customers wanted to "break IBM's grip on the economics of the industry," achieved through bundled prices. They also wanted the distributed computing that PCs offered but which IBM had been painfully slow to deliver. As IBM was preparing for a breakup, it was "rocketing down a path that would have made it a virtual mirror image of the rest of the industry."[2]

But this conventional wisdom was based on a superficial reading of the IT marketplace. Gerstner had a radically different view. As CEO of American Express, he had seen IBM from the *customer's* viewpoint. Restructuring the IT industry had indeed delivered more choices and lower prices. But Gerstner understood that the new model left customers struggling to integrate their diverse hardware and software choices. This task was hugely complicated by a lack of uniform standards.

Gerstner was convinced that companies did not want to be their own general contractors. "I knew firsthand that integration was becoming a gigantic problem," Gerstner wrote. "So when I arrived at IBM in 1993, I believed there was a very important role for some company to be able to integrate all of the pieces and deliver a working solution to the customer."

Gerstner also took exception to another prevalent myth—that the IT industry would continue to move toward totally distributed computing. "Even before I crossed the threshold at IBM, I knew that promise was empty. I'd spent too long on the other side. The idea that all this complicated, difficult-to-integrate, proprietary collection of technologies was going to be purchased by customers who would be willing to be their own general contractors made no sense."

Gerstner's view was right, and the conventional wisdom wrong. The decision to keep IBM together was the cornerstone of its historic turnaround and, said Gerstner, "the most important decision I ever made—not just at IBM, but in my entire business career." It formed the basis for IBM's corporate strategy for the next decade and ushered in IBM's highly successful migration from providing big boxes of equipment to delivering integrated value-added solutions in which services play an increasingly critical role.

On April 1, 1993, the day Gerstner became IBM's CEO, the company's market capitalization was just under $30 billion. On December 31, 2002, the day he left IBM, market capitalization was just over $130 billion. The numbers prove the soundness of IBM's customer-focused strategy and execution under Gerstner's leadership.

How could so many pundits—academics, securities analysts, business leaders, financial journalists—have been so wrong? The high-concept notion of distributed computing and a distributed IT industry captured the imagination of many observers. But those observers lacked one element that Gerstner possessed: *the vantage point of the customer.*

Bringing Strategy Down to Earth

The problems IBM faced in the early to mid-1990s have since become commonplace. The ground-level reality of competitive forces has made the rules for creating workable strategies tougher and more complex. Competitive intensity has never been greater. And it comes from everywhere, not just from within your industry. For the sea change in your competitive environment, you have to thank tectonic shifts in technology; demographics; customer preferences; economic and political realities, including transitions in government regulation and deregulation; and the financial markets—all in an increasingly globalized context. The cumulative result has been a shift from a commodity-based economy to an information economy, exemplified by the Internet. Increasingly, you acquire advantage over competitors not by controlling material resources but by doing a better job of amassing and deploying knowledge resources, especially strategic insights into changing customer needs.

In this new environment, formulating realistic strategies is an increasingly difficult task. And translating strategic thinking into marketplace actions requires a heightened willingness to take risks. But it also demands a much sharper focus on the real-world details of execution. Looking down from thirty thousand feet, planners see one kind of landscape. Leaders sighting customers at ground level, as Gerstner did at IBM, see a different reality. If you don't understand your marketplace options from the ground up, and if the people in your business don't systematically dedicate themselves to fulfilling customer wants and needs, you will lose out to competitors who do.

Technology alone has upended much of marketing's conventional thinking. Consider Metcalfe's law, aka the network effect, which postulates that the value of a product or service is directly related to the number of people it touches. Metcalfe's law raises the importance of achieving first-mover status. For example, the more buyers eBay has, the more valuable it is to sellers; vice versa, the more sellers eBay has, the more valuable it is to buyers. As the first mover in Internet auctioning, eBay won in the United States and many other (but not all) countries and has sustained a substantial lead that no competitor has yet come close to matching. Two other recent Internet successes that depend at least in part on network effects are PayPal, the payment system, and Skype, for making free telephone calls over the Internet. Interestingly, eBay acquired both PayPal and Skype to facilitate payment and communication on a customer-to-customer and customer-to-company basis.

Likewise, Netflix, the first nationally successful DVD lending library, secured first-mover advantage and benefited from the same kind of lead in 2005, when Wal-Mart and Blockbuster introduced competing services that copied the Netflix model: customers order DVDs online, then receive and return them in prepaid mailers for a monthly subscription fee. Wal-Mart quickly folded its tent and made a promotional deal with Netflix. Online Wal-Mart does not have the low-price advantage over competitors that it has in bricks and mortar, and it has struggled to build business in that arena. Blockbuster has been able to make some in-roads against Netflix by pairing DVDs by mail with in-store promotions and giving customers the convenience option of returning DVDs received in the mail at any Blockbuster store.

Netflix has maintained market leadership by its steady focus on customer needs. For example, the "Friends" feature on its website encourages subscribers to form groups of movie lovers who learn about each other's picks and pans through automated e-mails. And long before they are available on DVD, you can pick movies to put in your personal queue, to be sent when the release date arrives. But as the bursting of the dot-com bubble showed, first movers only waste money if they fail to deliver on customer needs with a sound business model. Etoys.com and Meals.com are just two examples of firms that failed for lack of a sound model (but later reemerged in different forms).

Another major trend is the growth of outsourcing. Spurred especially by the evolution of the information economy, major changes in organizational boundaries are being driven by reductions in transaction costs between one organization and another, and the identification of pools of skilled labor in low-wage economies.[3] What started as outsourcing of ancillary activities such as payroll, security, and food service has led managers running businesses to identify critical core competencies and to outsource other activities. Many now regularly outsource such previously fundamental functions as manufacturing and R&D. But outsourcing a problem cannot mean putting it out of mind.

For example, I am writing this book on an Apple computer that the packaging emphasizes was "designed by Apple in California," but it was manufactured in China, a fact that is buried in the small print. Whether Apple likes it or not, however, "manufactured in China" is now part of its brand identity. A globally connected information economy gives customers access to all sorts of information—and misinformation—about such "internal" matters as a company's environmental, labor, and outsourcing practices. In summer 2006 Apple was forced to respond to accusations of unsafe and exploitive labor conditions in Chinese factories producing iPods.[4] After investigation, Apple reported that the workplaces were in fact quite safe, but it had to admit that workers were coerced into working over sixty hours a week by the Chinese factory owners. Apple promised that it would no longer let this happen.

There is no single right answer to the outsourcing question. Indeed, the growth of outsourcing for everything from components to customer call centers challenges the leaders of every business to be ruthlessly honest about its capabilities versus those of outside vendors. What aspects of satisfying customer needs are best kept in-house? What aspects are best farmed out to others? For example, outsourcing your customer call center to an outside vendor halfway around the world may reduce your costs, but how sure are you that this supplier is treating your customers appropriately? Answering these questions is not a onetime decision, but another daily task of execution. Outsourcing a function may ease your headaches in the short term but may be devastating in the long term if it drains away competencies you may need later. On the other hand, a function that has historically been part of your operations and is a cherished part of your self-image may well need to be moved to an outside supplier to position your business for the future. And either way, your company will still retain the ultimate responsibility, in customers' minds, for everything the outsource provider does or does not do.

To make things more complex, what makes sense to outsource will likely change over time. For example, some top marketing companies prefer to in-source as much as possible, including bringing in-house traditional "outside functions" such as advertising production, as Prudential Financial has done. Oracle also produces its advertising copy in-house. "At the end of the day," Oracle's Mark Jarvis told us, "the people who work here have more skin in the game" and a better understanding of the customer.

Reengineering the supply chain and outsourcing a host of activities—two of the favorite recommendations of today's business consultants—can greatly help you create customer value, but they can also put your business at risk by creating new rivals. For outsourcing to work, you must build relationships and share information with suppliers and distributors. But one day these same organizations could change their strategic goals and become your competitors. Those managers who have rushed, lemminglike, to outsource key elements of their supply chains to low-cost, but increasingly sophisticated, firms in China, India, and Taiwan, take note!

The shift from a resource-based to a knowledge-based economy, which invites competition from both upstream vendors and downstream intermediaries, fast-moving technology, changing customer needs, and a complex regulatory and political landscape create an intense Darwinian struggle for survival. Some companies will die; others will thrive. The difference maker will be a customer focus that begins with internalizing the fact that whereas companies need customers to survive, customers do not need any particular supplier. In today's world, customers always have more options than suppliers, and companies must compete for customers in the midst of global oversupply in every market sector.

The Only Business Purpose

Marketing Mavens understand that no matter what else you do—how energetically you strategize, choose and motivate your people, create your products, and control your costs—you won't succeed unless at the end of the day these efforts provide a more persuasive value proposition and more positive customer experience than your competitors. Put simply and to reiterate, you *must* put the customer at the center of your business. To revise a slogan from the 1992 U.S. presidential campaign, "It's the customer, stupid."

When you consistently operate with a customer perspective, you view the monies spent to acquire and retain customers as *investments*, not as expenses. And like Intel, Wal-Mart, Starbucks, and other marketing leaders, you continue to invest in recessionary times. Good choices with your customer investments may secure financial returns for many years into the future. You must look beyond this year's sales and profits from customers large and small to their lifetime customer value. Indeed, once you create a new customer, just consistently deliver value and then hang on for the ride—the rewards can be enormous. Consider Boeing's 1971 decision to sell a couple of Boeing 737's to a start-up airline flying intra-Texas routes among Dallas, Houston, and San Antonio. Thirty-five years later, continuously profitable Southwest Airlines now flies seventy million passengers per annum to sixty U.S. destinations, over three thousand times per day, and is the largest domestic airline of the United States. And, for thirty-five years, Boeing has been Southwest's sole airplane supplier. How's that for a return on investment in customers?

Yet time and again market-leading companies have been dethroned by complacency. As Ed Zander, Motorola's CEO says, "I think we ought to get back to putting the customer first . . . [It's something that] every corporation around the world takes for granted."[5] Hungry competitors have done better jobs of seeing their businesses from the customer's point of view: Detroit gave way to Japan's automakers; the old IBM to makers of minicomputers and PCs; Sears to Wal-Mart; Xerox and the old Kodak to Japanese companies with digital copier technologies; and the old Motorola to Nokia, Samsung, and LG. And this is just the tip of the iceberg.

All these leaders (and many more) lost ground to competitors because they did not provide (or did not provide as well as competitors) what their customers wanted. They were the best placed to understand customer needs, yet in each case they were beaten to the punch by competitors who had a better understanding. Some have recovered from their mistakes; others have not. The new EasyShare Kodak, for example, has focused so well on customers' desire for digital convenience and capability that it has regained the market lead from Japanese manufacturers in four important categories, including digital cameras, although it still has a way to go to regain profitability and become as healthy a company as it once was. And the new Motorola is giving its cell-phone competitors a run for their money.

Consider what can happen when the business isn't customer focused and practices marketing with a small *m* rather than Marketing with a capital *M*. A major corporation I consulted with recently came very close to losing one of its best customers. The salespeople had promised delivery of a special order by a certain date. But when the plant had produced the product and was preparing to ship, the plant manager realized it would only fill half a railcar. To minimize costs, he waited for a couple of weeks until he was able to fill the whole railcar, and then he shipped. The customer was furious at being kept waiting. The plant manager argued that he was just doing what he was paid for—minimizing costs. Hadn't top management made cost containment a corporate priority?

Instead of understanding their customers' needs, such companies focus attention on their products, internal processes, and balance-sheet assets such as technology and plant and equipment. They ignore the fundamental truth that in the long run, customers are an organization's most valuable assets.

Failing to recognize the centrality of customers and marketing can trap your business in the past. Back when sellers were in the saddle, marketing essentially referred to the *marketing mix*, the set of implementation programs—product, service, promotion, distribution, and price—that a business developed to address a particular market or segment. Later came the era of *strategic marketing*, as companies realized they needed to choose markets and segments, and position offerings in those markets and segments, before they designed their marketing mixes. That's essentially where we are today.

Is the marketing mix important? Of course! Should the firm strategically choose markets and segments, and position offerings in those markets and segments? No question! The more salient issue today is who makes these decisions and what influences are brought to bear on them.

The responsibility for market strategy decisions has never been clear-cut. Depending on the organization, it typically floats between business managers and senior marketing executives. As a result, the responsibility for acquiring and retaining customers is most often relegated to a silo—a marketing department whose work is essentially tactical. It never fails to amaze me how in so many well-known corporations, marketing executives spend their time on the day-to-day trivia and rarely have time to even think about market strategy, let alone develop well-researched and well-reasoned market strategies. In so many of these organizations, marketing is charged only with communications and preparing sales aids—that's why so many people mistakenly equate marketing with advertising. In this view, marketing is "overhead," just one part of that line in the income statement that lists selling, general, and administrative expenses. Does that sound like the right place to account for the central purpose of the business?

Let's take the measurement issue one stage further. Ask yourself the following two questions. First, if you were to go to your accountants and ask them the profitability of several individual products and services, would they be able to provide a decent response? For most readers, I suspect the answer will be a resounding Yes! They've been doing this for years and it's built into the financial management system, in part to evaluate product manager performance. But now for the second question. Suppose you ask these same accountants the profitability of your individual customers or even market segments—will they be able to provide a decent response to this question? For most readers the answer will be No!

Let's think about that for a second. Customers are your core assets and are central to the health and welfare of your organization, right? Yet you don't know which ones are the most profitable? Right now, you are probably losing money on some of your customers and/or market segments. The fact of the matter is that although customers are your firm's core assets, not all customers are assets—some are liabilities. You probably operate with some version of the well-known 80:20 rule— 80 percent of your sales come from 20 percent of your customers. What is equally important, but less well understood, is the 20:80 rule—20 percent of your sales come from 80 percent of your customers. Question: what does it cost to serve those 80 percent of customers? Answer: a lot! That is really scary. But what is even scarier is not knowing which customers are profitable and which are not. Remember the tried-and-true maxim, "If you can't measure it, you can't manage it," and get with the program.

And just to turn things on their head a little more, consider your firm's balance sheet book value—assets less liabilities. Mostly the fixed assets are plant and equipment to make the products to sell to customers. But in today's fast-moving environment, customers' needs change and today they want different products than they wanted yesterday. What, then, about those fixed assets? For many firms they are not assets at all; rather, they are strategic liabilities. These "assets" act as an inertial force that stops or at least slows the firm from responding to customer needs. How else to explain newcomer Amazon's dominance in Internet bookselling over the previous market leader, Barnes & Noble, or IBM's conceding the personal computer space to Microsoft and Intel? Barnes & Noble and IBM had significant investments in bricks-and-mortar stores and mainframe computers, respectively. These investments operated as liabilities when it came to addressing challenges from the Internet and personal computers. Never forget that balance-sheet assets are only assets if they contribute to your goal of attracting and retaining customers—profitable ones.

Marketing Is Everybody's Job

Lately, the world's best firms have begun to put marketing at the center of their organizations. Just a few years ago, Stephan Haeckel, director of IBM's Advanced Business Institute, observed, "Marketing's future is not as *a* function of business, but as *the* function of business."[6]

A growing number of CEOs are breaking with the traditional functional view of marketing and doing their best to create cultures that do put marketing at (or near) the center of the business. Jeff Bezos at Amazon is fanatical about building a customer-focused organization. Larry Ellison, Oracle's CEO, is ultimately responsible for all the firm's key marketing decisions—he's the key contact for one of Oracle's major customers, GE, and even writes advertising copy and sets Oracle's creative policy. These CEOs are true Marketing Mavens!

In researching this book, I found increasing numbers of executives focused on "internal branding," that is, getting employees to really understand what their companies are about from the customer's point of view.

Born out of Bell Atlantic, NYNEX, and GTE, Verizon faced the challenge of establishing a new identity. It initiated a massive communications effort to brand Verizon internally. General managers in Verizon operating companies and employees in the ranks provided answers to a very simple, yet very powerful, question, "What is this company all about and what can you do about it?" The entire organization got the message—on the internal TV system, at its website, via e-mail and voice mail, and in face-to-face meetings. As senior vice president of brand management and marketing communications Jody Bilney put it, "People knew this was endorsed, and that they had permission literally and spiritually to embrace it and to really think about it. If we don't bring it to life internally—if it isn't sort of our mantra and if it isn't what we do every day—then we've missed the boat."

The evidence points to one conclusion: you can only put the customer at the center of the business if marketing is a guiding philosophy for the organization as a whole. Marketing has to be everybody's business. No matter where you sit in the organization, and no matter what your specific job responsibilities, developing satisfied and delighted customers, and getting them to return time and time again, is an integral part of your job, because customers are the *only* source of revenues, and *they pay your salary.*

Whatever their titles and job descriptions may be, from CEO and CMO on down, Marketing Mavens remember that fact and act on it every day, raising their companies to the top and keeping them there through good times and bad. Now let's see exactly how they do so and how you can become a Marketing Maven yourself and develop Marketing Mavens throughout your organization.

TWO

Execution in Marketing

Ford Motor's "Quality is Job 1" was a terrific slogan. There was just one problem: Ford's manufacturing organization couldn't consistently deliver on its promise. For example, its compact Focus, introduced worldwide in 1999, was designed as an entry-level car to stimulate future purchases of higher-end Ford vehicles. It won wide praise from car magazines and drivers for its combination of practicality and sportiness.

But the Focus was riddled with defects. During its first three years on the market, Ford recalled it eleven times for safety-related problems; U.S. regulators investigated it five times for defects. *Consumer Reports* rated it number one among small cars in 2002 for its features— then urged readers not to buy because of poor reliability. North American sales of the Focus, which reached 286,000 in 2000, its first full year, and best ever, had fallen 20 percent by 2003 and in 2005 were down to 185,000. Ford eventually solved the quality problems on the Focus. Indeed, the 2005 *Consumer Reports* recommended it—and Focus became the number one car in its category in Europe. But total sales significantly underperformed the company's hopes at launch, especially in the most important North American market.

There was a serious disconnect between the marketing organization and the rest of Ford. The impact on Ford's credibility from its Focus problems exacerbated the damage suffered from its role in the Firestone tire debacle. Quality was clearly *not* Job 1 with the Ford Focus. That slogan only rubbed salt in the wounds of disaffected buyers.

Webvan, launched in the Internet boom by Louis Borders (founder of Borders bookstores), seemed to have everything going for it. There was a compelling concept: people could order groceries online and Webvan would deliver the goods to their homes. It secured hundreds of millions of dollars in funding from such high-profile investors as CBS, Yahoo!, Softbank, and Benchmark Capital. It lured George Shaheen, former head of Andersen Consulting, to become CEO. It developed revolutionary technology for sorting and picking goods in its warehouses. And according to most customer accounts, Webvan provided friendly, on-time delivery and an easy-to-use website.

But none of these advantages could compensate for a poorly executed market strategy. Many customers complained about product selection and errors in order fulfillment. Also, Webvan overreached by building too many warehouses in too many markets before it had proven its business model and acquired a solid, loyal customer base.

In Great Britain, the supermarket chain Tesco has achieved success in online grocery sales by delivering orders to customers from its existing stores, piggybacking e-commerce on its existing bricks-and-mortar inventory. By contrast, U.S. online grocery sales have been more successful on a limited market basis. For example, New York City's FreshDirect has built a successful online grocery business by beginning with the most affluent Manhattan zip codes, then selectively extending its service area to more of the city, neighborhood by neighborhood.

It remains to be seen whether the online grocery business can work in the U.S. market on a larger scale. In July 2006, in another bold gamble, Amazon.com announced the opening of www.amazon.com/grocery. Amazon is now selling over fourteen thousand nonperishable grocery items, and all items are eligible for Free Super Saver Shipping.[1] If this initiative is successful, it will dramatically revalidate Amazon's business model and its distinctive way of relating to customers.

In any event, Amazon.com's approach is more like Tesco's than Webvan's, inasmuch as it is piggybacking grocery products onto its existing business rather than starting from scratch. And like FreshDirect, Amazon.com is being highly selective. For example, it is not trying to sell perishable fresh foods but only dry goods that pose no special problems in handling, packing, and shipping, areas where Amazon has highly developed competencies.

The Lethal Gap

The Ford Focus and Webvan.com launches had one thing in common: a lethal gap between the company's promise and its ability to deliver on that promise. This fundamental disconnect is the most common reason why businesses fail.

As Larry Bossidy and Ram Charan observe:

> When companies fail to deliver on their promises, the most frequent explanation is that the CEO's strategy was wrong. But the strategy by itself is not often the cause. Strategies most often fail because they aren't executed well. Things that are supposed to happen don't happen. Either the organizations aren't capable of making them happen or the strategic leaders of the business misjudge the challenges their companies face in the business environment, or both.[2]

Why don't companies execute better? Bossidy and Charan point out that most people make the mistake of regarding execution as the tactical side of business. To the contrary, they write:

> Execution is a systematic process of rigorously discussing hows and whats, questioning, tenaciously following-through and ensuring accountability. It includes making assumptions about the business environment, assessing the organization's capabilities, linking strategy to operations and the people who are going to implement the strategy, synchronizing those people and their various disciplines, and linking rewards to outcomes. It also includes mechanisms for changing assumptions as the environment changes and upgrading the company's capabilities to meet the challenges of an ambitious strategy.[3]

Good execution means the difference between success and failure. IBM was a failed organization in 1992. As Lou Gerstner observes, "Fixing IBM was all about execution."[4] And "[e]xecution is the tough difficult daily grind of making sure the machine moves forward, meter by meter, kilometer by kilometer, milestone by milestone."[5]

Failure to practice the discipline of execution makes an organization less than the sum of its parts. All organizations, other than sole proprietorships, have to practice internal differentiation—they must develop parts or specializations to get the work done. In the various functional parts such as accounting, finance, human resources, operations, marketing, sales, and R&D, people work on discrete agendas to achieve their individual goals. Unfortunately, many of these functions are organizationally distant from customers and, in any event, are typically rewarded for their success in reaching their individual goals—sales organizations for making sales, operations for reducing costs, R&D for developing new products, and so forth. There is nothing inherently wrong in achieving these goals, except when the functions operate independently as individual silos or stovepipes, with minimal if any concern for customers' needs, and when vital linkages among the functions are missing.

That's when you get the plant manager for a leading cell-phone supplier cutting costs by replacing a crucial part with a cheaper alternative, and having the cell phones fail; when salespeople for an office supply firm, striving to make quota, push unwanted products onto customers, then disappear when service problems erupt; when the Finance Department at a major medical device company, anxious to improve profits, insists on raising prices yet cuts back on service budgets, leading to customer dissatisfaction; and where engineers at a major camcorder manufacturer add technical gadgets to increase product virtuosity but significantly complicate the buyer's experience and see sales decline. Do any of these examples resemble your own experience?

Marketing is especially prone to being treated as a silo. Far too often, CEOs devote their energies to acquisitions, partnerships, divestitures, and the management theorists' fads du jour. Then marketing becomes just one of several functions competing for senior management's limited time. Rather than be treated as an individual silo, marketing must be the central thrust around which the firm's various parts are integrated. Indeed, if customers are truly the firm's core assets, shouldn't a committee of your board of directors focus on customers?

Two things have to happen for marketing to become the central purpose of your business:

1. Everybody in every function must put the customer at the center of the business; that is, marketing must be the guiding philosophy of the organization.

2. Leaders in both the marketing organization and the company as a whole must have a clear understanding of how to put the philosophy into practice.

Leaders at many companies strongly support these principles rhetorically. But what sets the top companies apart is their ability to make these marketing principles operational on a company-wide basis, not just talk about them. Long-run successful companies execute on the following five central imperatives that are the sequential building blocks of excellence, high profitability, and increasing shareholder value. They:

1. Pick markets that matter

2. Select segments to dominate

3. Design the market offer to create customer value and secure differential advantage

4. Integrate to serve the customer

5. Measure what matters

These are not onetime events. They are continuous processes that need constant iteration, and they may also be painful. To execute these imperatives effectively, you will have to help your line organization evolve, build and rebuild your structures and processes, match your human resources to the tasks at hand, and develop a customer-focused culture. As the key elements in developing and implementing a market strategy, the five imperatives are also integral to your corporate strategy. They must be linked tightly with corporate direction and with the operations of your entire organization.

Imperative 1: Pick Markets That Matter

Choosing the right markets is one of the most important strategic decisions you can make for your business. If you get this decision right, the
value you will earn for your shareholders can be enormous.[6] But if you
fail, you may really have a problem, and if you're not careful you'll end
up in commodity hell. I have my own favorites for making good market
choices, and I'm sure that you have yours. I like Cirque de Soleil's
combination of circus and theatrical performance, Google's Internet
advertising, Netflix's Internet DVD service by mail, and GlaxoSmith-
Kline's entry of Paxil into the Japanese depression market. You'll meet
some more good picks in later chapters of this book, since companies
cannot be marketing leaders without doing well on this imperative —
Amazon for online stores, Bloomberg in financial information, Nokia's
cell phones, Pfizer's Lipitor for LDL-cholesterol suppression, Starbucks' retail coffee stores, and Target in up-market discount retail, to
name just a few.

Making good market choices is not easy. Opportunities that may
look attractive at first glance — new products, acquisitions, product line
extensions — turn into quicksand if you don't understand what you're
getting into. Make no mistake about it, you are in the bet-making business. But you have an advantage over the gamblers in Atlantic City,
Las Vegas, and Monte Carlo — you can shift the odds in your favor by
accurately answering seven questions:

1. Is our current market at risk — should we hold, raise, or fold?

2. Can we differentiate ourselves and make money in a potential
   new market?

3. Can we really deliver something customers will want more than
   anything the competitors can offer?

4. Who will our competitors be?

5. How will they respond?

6. Will we be able to beat them?

7. Equally important, what markets should we *not* be in?

Getting the right answers to these questions grounds your strategy in reality. That's what execution in marketing is all about. You must secure deep insight about potential markets. The answers also require that you develop as much insight as you can about the customer. But—and this is all too often overlooked in companies that don't execute well—it also requires deep insight into both your competition and yourself.

The business landscape is littered with the remains of companies that failed to gain, or regain, insight into how they could best meet changing customer needs and secure competitive advantage. In the mid-1990s, Kodak launched Advantix, a breakthrough in chemical film technology developed in concert with other major players such as Canon and Fuji. Advantix was a significant advance over existing film. The problem: digital technology, which Kodak knew had the potential to make chemical film obsolete, developed more quickly than expected. Several established Japanese camera makers, along with newcomers such as HP and Sony, none of whom had a stake in the photographic film business, responded faster to customers' interest in digital products with their greater ease of use, and Kodak's once dominant position in capturing images was gone.

To Kodak's enormous credit, it has rebounded after several difficult years with its EasyShare digital cameras and PerfectTouch digital printing/imaging technology. Kodak now has the lead in the U.S. market in four key areas: digital cameras, snapshot photo printers, retail photo kiosks, and online picture sharing sites.

Returning to leadership is possible when you recognize and act on the five core marketing imperatives in time. Kodak could not have fought its way back to market leadership—in 2006 it still had a long way to go to regain its former profitability but was making some headway toward that goal—if it had failed to recognize that the digital arena had become the crucial one for customers sooner than expected or failed to concentrate its resources effectively on delivering value to customers in that market arena.

Once you have identified the *markets that matter*, you must have a realistic understanding of how your strengths and weaknesses apply to them. What are your true core competencies—and your core dysfunctions? Suppose you truly know what the customer in the most important market wants and needs, and believe you can beat competitors. You won't get far if parts of your business can't deliver to the right specifications, at the right time, place, and price. Ford failed to grasp (or ignored) weaknesses in its manufacturing organization when asserting "Quality is Job 1." Webvan's strategists failed to integrate the market response with operational challenges and financial realities. In chapter 7 we'll explore how Toyota has successfully linked world-class execution in three competencies: research and development, manufacturing, and marketing, the last with a special emphasis on dealer management and customer service.

Ford and its fellow Detroit automakers have been declining, market segment by market segment, since the energy crisis of the 1970s. At first they ceded leadership to the Japanese in the economy car market segment, then in midsize and full-size cars and pickups and SUVs, and now they have been left behind by the Japanese in the shift to hybrids. Think for one moment about customer needs and environmental challenges, and compare the signature vehicles in recent years from GM and Toyota—GM's gas-guzzling Hummer versus Toyota's energy-efficient Prius just about says it all. To be sure, GM makes some very fuel-efficient cars and Toyota makes some gas guzzlers, but there is also no doubt that Toyota has made itself eco-friendly in the public's mind, in a way that only Honda has come close to matching.

Focusing complacently on your core competencies can lead you astray. As the Detroit automakers have found again and again—without management's ever making the changes needed to prevent it happening again and again—your competencies can be copied and surpassed by others. In addition, a core competence for one market opportunity may be a weakness in another! For example, a low-cost inflexible manufacturing system may be terrific if customers require a basic product and product design is fixed for the long run. But this strength will be an incredible weakness if customers demand continuously evolving product variety.

Furthermore, you may identify significant market opportunity where you currently have little core competence. Should you therefore automatically walk away? Should Jeff Bezos of Amazon.com have given up his idea of an online bookstore in the early 1990s because at that time he had little competence in building one? Should Howard Schultz of Starbucks have given up his dream of a chain of coffee houses because he had not interned first at a retail restaurant company like Dunkin' Donuts?

The companies highlighted in this book demonstrate a courageous disregard for such thinking. Many have identified market opportunities and then fashioned the necessary competencies to exploit them, where none previously existed. In addition to Amazon.com and Starbucks, consider GOJO Industries, a supplier of industrial hand cleansing products. GOJO served only institutional customers and had previously failed in an attempt to enter the consumer market. Yet it had the guts, vision, and flexibility to make another consumer-market bet and establish its waterless hand cleanser, Purell, as a category-establishing consumer brand in the tradition of Kimberly-Clark's Kleenex and Johnson & Johnson's (J&J) Band-Aid.

To pick markets that matter requires a disciplined approach to investment. It demands that you embrace the principle of *selectivity and concentration*—select the best opportunities and concentrate your resources against them. The flip side is, arguably, even more important. You must deselect (or not enter), those markets where you can't compete profitably. Even retail giant Wal-Mart decided to exit the German and South Korean markets when it finally decided that it could not compete successfully. Running a business is not like managing a stock portfolio where diversification is the mantra for avoiding risk. In this hypercompetitive world, managers must make bets on markets. They must select markets and ruthlessly concentrate their resources against those market targets. That is the only way to beat increasingly tough competitors.

Texas Instruments (TI) was once a technology leader but lost out to Intel in microprocessors as the PC market burgeoned. In the 1980s TI diversified widely, but by the late 1990s it was withdrawing, by divestiture, from many markets that *didn't* matter. TI exited from chemicals, defense electronics, inspection equipment, memory chips, mold manufacturing, notebook computers, software, and others. Focusing on markets that *did* matter, TI became the market leader in chips for wireless phones and large-screen television processors. TI's products can be found in a host of new electronic devices like the Slingbox, which transfers television programs from the user's home to a PC anywhere in the world, as it focuses on the market for mobile TV service to cell phones and other devices. TI has outgrown the semiconductor market for the past several years—its focus on markets that matter has been re-warded in the stock market, where it trades in the high $20 range, a vast improvement from the 1980s and early 1990s.

Consider also the remarkable growth of Samsung into a top-level consumer brand. In chapter 9, you'll hear Eric Kim, Samsung Electronics' CMO, explain how in the late 1980s and early 1990s Samsung was making major sales to Wal-Mart and Kmart. Yet it walked away from these customers, preferring to go up-market with the likes of Circuit City and Best Buy. Combined with a product line focused resolutely on leading-edge design, Samsung's retailing selectivity and concentration have paid off hugely. (If you wonder how it could make sense for Samsung to turn its back on Wal-Mart, that is a fascinating question indeed, as we'll see in later chapters.)

Gone are the days when a superstar athlete could excel in more than one sport (or in more than one position in a single sport). Basketball star Michael Jordan couldn't make it in baseball. Englishmen of a certain vintage know that we shall never again see the likes of Dennis Compton, who played on English national teams in both cricket and soccer. The same holds true in business life; you will only survive and prosper by carefully selecting market targets and concentrating your resources against them. As we'll see in chapters 3 and 4, top marketing companies such as Alcoa, ExxonMobil, L'Oréal, Progressive, and Sir Richard Branson's Virgin Enterprises base their ongoing success on the rigor with which they pick markets that matter and then execute to serve those markets.

Imperative 2: Select Segments to Dominate

Grouping customers into market segments is standard business practice. The more a market suffers from oversupply and underdemand—the new status quo in a relentlessly globalizing economy for both high-tech and low-tech goods and services—the more vital it becomes to identify, and perhaps help create, attractive submarkets and provide tailored value propositions for them. This is what Apple has done with the iPod and iTunes under Steve Jobs's leadership. The iPod and iTunes have not only hugely boosted Apple's bottom line, and quite separately increased the sales of its Macintosh computers, but have also accelerated the growth of the MP3 player market as a whole.

Yet even business leaders who understand the importance of market segmentation in developing a market strategy often approach the process as ritual. Many use outdated segmentation methodologies ("That's how we've always done it"), or they rely on generic information (government or trade association data), which their competitors are also studying. Pharmaceutical companies are a prime example. They are awash in prescription drug data at the physician level and are able to pinpoint their prime physician customers. They have "what" and "who" data that firms in many other industries would die for—what was prescribed and who prescribed it. But these data tell them nothing about the "why?" of patient and physician decision making—what patient or physician need did the prescription satisfy. Pfizer, however, stands out in the pharmaceutical marketplace precisely because of its ability to track, and influence, those whys, and in chapter 6 you will hear, again directly from one of the senior executives involved, how Pfizer innovated by transforming its sales organization to achieve this, traveling a path different from all its rivals.

Most companies follow the herd. Rather than spending effort to identify sources of unserved or underserved customer needs and then leveraging distinctive competences or unique resources, marketers trot out "me too" products determined by early entrants. Do you have enough choices of bottled water in your supermarket, or would you prefer a few more? Perhaps this is a rational response if firms don't understand customer needs and can't figure out how to secure differential advantage. But it's generally not the route to making profits. Or they spread their resources around, chasing after customer needs that prove to be ephemeral.

Many firms have achieved leadership positions through effective segmentation and targeting. Marriott has done a great job with its family of hotels, each aimed at a different segment—Courtyard by Marriott, Fairfield Inn, Residence Inn, TownePlace Suites, Ritz-Carlton, and others. Another great example is automobile rental. Which firm do you think is the market leader? If you said Hertz, you'd answer like most executives, but you'd be wrong. Avis? Wrong again! These firms lead in the segment you know best—busy executives dashing off planes, headed to their appointments and paid for by your companies. And when you go on the family vacation and you're paying, chances are you switch to Alamo, Dollar, Budget, or other players in the leisure segment. The market leader is none of these established players—it is Enterprise Rent-A-Car, the largest car buyer in the world, at eight hundred thousand annually. Enterprise identified and targeted the market segment of people whose cars are in the garage. The business model is very different with regard to rental locations; key influencers on the rental decision—garage mechanics; and the selling effort. Regardless, Enterprise is the unparalled leader in this segment, and now is number one in car rental overall.

Segmentation is both science and art. It demands a high degree of insight about customers and competitors. You cannot do it well using only methods based on simple demographics. How, for example, would you segment the dog-food market? You might start off, as some have done, on the basis of type of dog—old dogs versus young dogs, big dogs versus little dogs. But think how much greater insight you might gain from examining the relationship between owner and dog, and the emotional relationship embodied in the owner's choice of dog food: dog as grandchild (indulgence), dog as child (love), dog as best friend (health and nutrition), and dog as dog (cheap/convenient fuel).

In the world's most successful companies, marketers use a variety of approaches for studying the wants and needs of existing and potential customers. They continually push the boundaries of marketing research techniques to gain fresh insights in their drive to identify and address the most attractive market segments. Some techniques are quantitative (extensive survey data, complex multivariate statistical techniques for analysis, and data mining of transactions), while others are highly qualitative (one-on-one discussions, focus groups, and increasingly popular anthropological methods such as "a day in the life of [the customer]," or DILO).

Chapter 6 looks closely at the problem of figuring out what customers value, but in the meantime let's recognize that defining segments is just the first part of the job. In the real world of finite resources, you cannot address all the segments you identify. Even the biggest businesses like ExxonMobil, for example, as we'll see in chapters 3 and 4, must rigorously practice the principle of selectivity and concentration if they are to stay, as ExxonMobil's Hal Cramer puts it, "that crucial one step ahead of competition." No matter how large your company, you just don't have the resources to win everywhere at once.

You must pick your battles well, attacking the most attractive segments within your reach and conceding the others. Choosing the right segments requires a solid understanding of the opportunity represented by each segment and a good recognition of your company's capabilities versus competition (current and potential).

Execution in segmentation is not just a challenge for the marketing department or using the right tools well. In a world of global oversupply and underdemand, that narrow approach invites failure. It widens the gap between the objectives you set back in January and the results you are achieving in October, and it complicates longer-term planning as well. The integration among market selection, firm capabilities, and segment strategies has to be closer than ever.

The best companies know what the organization can and cannot deliver. Senior leadership gives full attention to the relationships between selected markets, target market segments, and the type and amount of required firm resources. It focuses laserlike on the trade-offs between the firm's opportunities and its resources.

The all too frequent "sales versus marketing" caricature is long gone at the best companies. They inform their thinking with real-world, real-time judgments from the front lines, from the employees who meet and deal with customers on a day-by-day basis. What you *don't* hear is this conversation:

Sales: Marketing is just a bunch of ivory-tower idealists who have no idea about what really goes on in the world.
Marketing: Sales spend most of its time on expense-account lunches and playing golf.

Rather, intuitive judgments and creative insights from the field often provide the critical difference between success and failure. For example, Pfizer rigorously schools its field salespeople to ask questions and feed information back to the firm (see chapters 6 and 9). Target expects all employees who travel—whether on business or pleasure—to write reports on trends in other parts of the world (see chapter 8). This kind of information gathering can give your business an edge. It can pinpoint needs that customers *don't yet recognize*—needs that by definition won't show up in traditional data gathering. You should be striving to meet and exceed customer expectations not only by solving their current problems, but by anticipating future ones, and then proactively devising solutions in existing and emerging market segments.

One example of segmenting to find the sweet spot in a market is Nokia's success in the cell-phone market. We'll explore the Nokia story in more detail in chapter 5. For now, suffice it to say that Nokia's focus on the standard-setting, fashion- and lifestyle-oriented youth segment was the core decision that drove it to global market leadership. Likewise, Nokia's slippage a couple of years ago relative to Motorola, Samsung, and LG, and its subsequent gains against the same rivals, testify to the importance of identifying the sweet spot in the market and doing what is necessary to delight those customers.

Imperative 3: Design the Market Offer to Create Customer Value and Secure Differential Advantage

Differential advantage is a familiar concept: what can you offer that customers want, don't think they can get elsewhere, and are prepared to pay for? When you secure a differential advantage, that's when you earn price flexibility and your margins start to look really attractive. Gillette does a great job at creating differential advantage year after year as there seems to be no limit on its ability to innovate in the way people shave. In recent years, Gillette has added battery power to its traditional manual shaving systems, and it continually adds blades to its shavers—three for the Mach3 and five blades in its latest Fusion model. And its prices and margins just keep increasing.

But securing differential advantage over the long term has plainly become more difficult in an economy of global oversupply and underdemand. There are simply too many competitors out there, and they're constantly chipping away at your differential advantage, and getting better at copying your innovations. They market them with a twist of their own—lower price, better performance, a catchier promotion—and do it increasingly quickly. That makes marketing execution, delivering value for the customer, an urgent daily task for everyone in an organization.

You'll recall that Peter Drucker defined marketing as the most important function of any business and innovation as the second-most important. He went on to explain, "Innovation can no more be considered a separate function than marketing. It is not confined to engineering or research, but extends across all parts of the business."

We tend to think of innovation mainly in terms of technological and other breakthroughs. But innovation isn't just a new product or service per se; it's the steak, the sizzle, and everything else people throughout the organization can think of as they strive to seamlessly integrate the several elements of the marketing mix to create more value for their customers.

Let's be very clear, I'm not talking about being *different* from your competitors but about securing *differential advantage*. Creating customer value is what distinguishes the two, for customer value is the wellspring of differential advantage. When you think of innovation this way, the possibilities are endless. At Starbucks, the coffee may be the steak, but the sizzle includes everything from store design to the way employees treat customers. As Starbucks chairman Howard Schultz explained to us, "As a customer, I walk into the store and I'm swept away for a minute, even if I get a coffee to go, because I'm part of this experience that makes me feel better. A missing part of our lives as consumers is that we don't feel valued. So we really take notice when someone touches us and says, 'I appreciate you, I respect you, and I can help you.' "

Delivering customer value is not a onetime affair. Customer needs are a shifting target and you must monitor them continually or the world will pass you by. World-class marketers continuously invest in marketing research to probe deeply into customers' needs, priorities, expectations, and experiences and to feed these results into their product development processes. If you fail to take this challenge seriously, you will surely join the many once proud companies that gained the pinnacle by serving customers well, only to take their eyes off the ball and plunge downward. We already met the IBM that immediately preceded Lou Gerstner's arrival and, to pick a different industry, retailing, Sears and Kmart in the United States and Sainsbury's and Marks & Spencer in Britain also took this downward path. Think about your own industries: What firms can you identify that fall into this category? And what are you doing to ensure that the same fate does not befall you?

A business that executes well in designing offers that deliver customer value does not have "commodity" products. The potential number of marketing mix permutations for just a single market segment is infinite, differentiated by design novelty, purchasing convenience and/or related services. Unless you deliberately choose imitation, only lack of imagination and capability can be blamed for offers that are indistinguishable from those of your competitors. A good example of securing differential advantage is U.S. auto insurer Progressive (see chapters 3 and 4). Progressive has distinguished itself from competitors, and grown hugely, by offering insurance customers rival quotes, in addition to its own, and by vastly speeding up the claims-adjustment process.

You must meet or exceed customer expectations with respect both to their current stated needs, as well as new or unrecognized needs by looking through the attributes and benefits of the goods and services you offer to their value in customers' lives. The attributes of an electric drill include power, drill bit hardness, drill speeds, and portability. The benefit to a customer is that he can use the drill to make holes and drive screws easily. But the potential ultimate value of the drill to a customer who wants to use the drill in home-improvement projects, or to a tradesperson who wants to use the drill at work, will be much more than the sum of the drill's mechanical attributes and benefits. For the nonprofessional customer, the value of the drill lies in its ability to help transform his lifestyle. For the tradesperson, the drill has literal survival value in helping her to earn a living. Or as Charles Revson, cofounder and longtime head of Revlon, liked to say, "In the factories we make cosmetics; in the drugstores we sell hope."

Imperative 4: Integrate to Serve the Customer

The customer can't be the center of your business if you organize by silos. The curse of the functionally organized business is that each function has its own goals, metrics, mind-sets, and reward systems. How often have you seen poor advertising sabotage the prospects for a good product, poor product quality destroy the most carefully crafted value proposition, or a clumsy credit department drive customers away? Consider the experience my neighbor—let's call him Jack—had with a bank. Jack parked his car next to a FREE PARKING FOR BANK CUSTOMERS sign, cashed a check, and asked the teller to validate his parking ticket. The teller refused because Jack had not made a deposit.

Jack explained he had a longtime relationship at another branch of the same bank, including several million dollars in deposits. Neither teller nor bank manager would budge. Jack drove forty blocks to his regular branch and told the manager he would close all accounts unless he received a phoned apology by the end of the day. No phone call was made and Jack closed all his accounts.

In the larger scheme of things, companies get into the wrong markets and wrong segments because business leaders don't ask the right questions, and they fail to create differential advantage because interfunctional conflict and other organizational weaknesses stand in the way of delivering customer value. Consider a memo that one senior executive at a major multinational firm wrote to his incoming superior: "There have been too many years of business units versus corporate, too many years of control versus trust, too many years of operating in silos, too many years of manipulating facts to serve personal interests, and too many years of defending internal turf at the expense of market share and position."[7] Does any of this sound familiar, or do the senior executives in your company *get it*?

They get it at Valeo, a major French car-parts manufacturer where a senior executive opined, "Customers expect seamless delivery, and they don't care how we're organized. We have to work as a team and forget our internal battles."[8] Or as a highly placed 3M executive put it, "The fact that we are a multiproduct, multibusiness, multinational company, should not be the customer's problem." And Jack Welch famously made boundarylessness a core value in his tenure at GE.

Integrating the functions to serve customers is what makes good execution possible. It's the hardest imperative to achieve if it's not already designed into the firm and living in the culture. Integration demands organization-wide clarity about external and internal realities, along with clearly shared values and priorities, an appropriate organization design, supportive systems and processes, the *right* human resources, cross-functional teamwork, and common reward criteria. Collaboration must take place within and among the different functions—between marketing and finance, sales and operations. It also must take place up and down the line, from the CEO to the people at the bottom of the organization, who may well have the greatest customer facing responsibilities, especially in service companies like ExxonMobil's consumer gas sales operations (see chapters 3 and 4). The CEO must set the example by acting as the chief marketing person and salesperson, and everyone else must be motivated to follow suit.

IBM would never have recovered without a Lou Gerstner, whose insight and authority changed the behaviors of IBM's engineers, managers, and salespeople even though, initially at least, he knew little about computer technology. Likewise Toyota, UPS, Starbucks, Bloomberg, Target, Oracle, and SAP, among others, could not have achieved and maintained dominant positions in their markets without integrating all their operations and nurturing a company-wide marketing culture—beginning crucially with the CEO and senior management—to satisfy constantly evolving customer needs (see chapters 7 and 8).

Alcoa's integration of its operations, from aluminum smelting to the provision of highly engineered components and finished products, includes focused pricing responsibility to global customers like Airbus, as we'll see in chapter 3. At Verizon (see chapter 8), the integration of GTE, Bell Atlantic, and NYNEX into a single coherent company required an all-out campaign of internal branding to employees from the three merged entities. Internal branding may be a major component of integrating employees into a company-wide marketing culture in non-merger situations, as well. At both Dell and Target, for example, there is a clear recognition that if employees cannot articulate the identity of a brand in the time it takes to fill a coffee cup, customers will never be able to do so.

Imperative 5: Measure What Matters

The old saw says that you can't manage what you can't measure. Everyone knows it's true, and every company today is awash in a flood tide of computer-generated data. These data are mainly useless, because they don't measure what really matters to a specific company and its customers. Companies *appear* to be measuring the right things—for example, they have metrics for gauging customer satisfaction, and they have made rational-seeming choices about whether to pursue, say, profitability rather than revenue growth. But at the end of the year, the strong results they projected are nowhere to be found.

The problem starts when measurement and control systems aren't grounded in reality. The annual budgets are products of fantasy and gaming. They stipulate outcomes that people have negotiated, without regard to marketplace realities and without incisive questioning of how or even if those results can be achieved. No doubt you've all come across organizations where the basic message to operating managers from above was simply "Just get the number. I don't care how you do it!" As the examples of Enron, WorldCom, and Sunbeam show, that way madness lies.

Some firms do get it. Take Enterprise, the leading firm in car rental that we met a couple of pages back. A few years ago, founding entrepreneur Jack Taylor was so upset about service deterioration and the level of customer complaints that he developed the Enterprise Service Quality index (ESQi). The ESQi score is made from responses to just two questions: (1) On a scale ranging from "completely satisfied" to "completely unsatisfied," how would you rate your last Enterprise experience? (2) Would you rent from Enterprise again? Enterprise makes follow-up phone calls to one in fifteen customers, and every branch receives its ESQi score. To put real teeth into the measure, managers whose branches don't meet the company average don't get promoted. In early 2006, for the first time, Enterprise's overall ESQi score revealed that 80 percent of all respondents were "completely satisfied" with their rental experience.[9]

Don't try to achieve too many goals. Do you want increased market share? Sure! And higher profits? Of course! And greater cash flow to fund new opportunities? Why not! Can you have them all at the same time? Not usually. You must understand the trade-offs among the different types of goals and distinguish between the critical and the less important, or you will send mixed messages to the organization and sow confusion in the ranks.

I am all in favor of stretching the organization to achieve the height of its capacity, but you must be careful in setting your stretch goals. As a simple example, increasing profits doesn't take managerial genius. Just cut your advertising, trim R&D, and fire a few customer-service reps. Next quarter your profits will go up; I can almost guarantee it. But how long before your hollowed-out business collapses? How else to explain the results from one business unit I came across recently. This unit grew its bottom line at double-digit rates, while increasing top line at only 2 percent per annum. After a few years, this unit collapsed.

And then there are those customer satisfaction measures pegged to internal perceptions, not external realities. When Michael Walsh took over as CEO of Union Pacific Railroad, his operations people told him the railroad's on-time performance was 98 percent. Great performance, right? Wrong! Customers were furious because of slow deliveries. Operating managers were measuring performance based on the time it took for a train to leave one rail yard and arrive at the next. The measurement system excluded the days, even weeks, that customers' shipments languished in rail yards in the course of their journeys. And with market share and profitability dropping like a stone, incoming CEO Lou Gerstner found that IBM's customer satisfaction ratings couldn't have been better. The problem was that salespeople managed the customer satisfaction process and gave the survey only to their favorite customers.

One problem is not understanding the relationship between goals and behavior. In comes the new CEO with the rousing turnaround speech and new goals everyone can endorse, but two years later nothing much has changed. The fact of the matter is that people do not do what is *expected* of them; they do what is *inspected*. What you measure is among the most crucial actions your company takes.

The ultimate reality check is having clear, achievable goals and targets. Then there has to be follow-through, to make sure the right people are held accountable for the results they promised and to take remedial action if results are lagging. You must pick the right things to measure. The traditional measures like product revenues and product profitability are obviously important. But the centrality of customers demands that you develop systems for measuring customer revenues and customer profitability, across the various products and geographies where you do business. You must measure things the right way, from the point of view of meeting customer needs rather than company preferences, as in the example of Union Pacific. A brutal requirement to make the numbers for appearance's sake, like "Chainsaw" Al Dunlap imposed on Sunbeam, may pay off in an attractive stock price in the short term, but sooner or later the truth will come out and the stock price will plummet. In chapter 9 we'll look closely at how superb marketing companies such as The Home Depot, Samsung, ESPN, and Prudential measure what matters.

We'll also consider the need to expand the traditional practices for measuring company performance in terms of inputs, outputs, and intermediate variables. The world's top performing companies are determined to get as precise a handle as possible on the market and customer trends that underlie decisions about which markets and market segments to enter, and that inform efforts to craft market offers to deliver customer value and secure differential advantage (Imperatives 1–3). This complicates the measurement task, because it is often extremely difficult to quantify data in these areas. But the payoffs for factoring these data into a company's measure-what-matters equation can be large, as we will see.

•   •   •

Execution in marketing is a systematic focus on defining the results you want and doing the things that yield those results. It requires the disciplined practice of selectivity and concentration to pick markets and market segments, a clear understanding of differential advantage and the ability to create customer value, seamless integration of the five marketing imperatives into the firm's strategic goals and operations, and well-designed measurement and control systems.

Companies that excel in marketing address the five marketing imperatives head-on. But they don't do it wearing blindfolds. Their decisions are based on three critical building blocks: insight about markets, customers, and competitors. Fail to secure any of the three, or fail to probe sufficiently deeply, and you will not succeed.

Furthermore, the top marketing companies know the roots of where they can secure differential advantage. They identify opportunities, then select the markets and segments where they know, realistically, that they can create customer value. They concentrate their resources on those markets and segments. They design winning market offers because they understand customer wants and needs better than the competition, and they more finely hone their resources. And then they make it happen—in the research laboratories, in the factories, in the sales force, and in the service organization. In these companies, marketing is an essential part of the culture that helps define the results everyone is expected to achieve.

To see some of these imperatives in action, let's now take a comprehensive look at two of the top marketing companies that were part of our research.

Nestlé Prepared Foods: Building Megabrands

The number of people who don't have time for traditional cooking is growing—resulting in the prepared-foods category being a bright spot in the marketplace. In the mid- to late 1990s, Nestlé Prepared Foods (NPF) was deadlocked with ConAgra Foods for U.S. market leadership. Today NPF holds a commanding lead based on its two key brands in frozen meals, Stouffer's and Lean Cuisine, and its Hot Pockets brand of stuffed sandwiches, acquired in 2002. In addition to ConAgra (Marie Callender, Banquet, and Healthy Choice), major competitors include H. J. Heinz's (Smart Ones and Boston Market).

Stephen Cunliffe, NPF president, believes that, in some cases, it succeeded in this crowded and fiercely competitive market with strategies that were significantly different from the competition. In other cases, the strategies were similar, but NFP simply did a better job of execution.

Pick Markets That Matter

NPF concentrates its resources on a small number of *megabrands*. "We're in the business of leveraging the strength of the brands we've got, not building new ones," says Cunliffe. "For example, Stouffer's is a billion-dollar brand, Lean Cuisine a half-billion-dollar brand." Since we first met Mr. Cunliffe, NPF has almost doubled in size—Stouffer's is now worth well over $1 billion in annual sales, and Lean Cuisine is close to a $1 billion brand. "Our competitors have smaller businesses spread over more brands, so think of the power we can give to our brands." This resource concentration gives NPF leverage in many different forms, including consumer advertising and trade promotions, that its competitors do not enjoy. It also puts Nestlé's management talent to the best possible use.

Building megabrands requires meticulous execution, linked seamlessly to a sound strategy. For example, when NPF's people consider designing a new product or launching a marketing program, they ask themselves two questions. First, will this initiative enhance profitability? Second, will this initiative enhance the brand's value? Whether it's a small brand extension or a new product category, the starting point is consistency within the brand in the eyes of the consumer.

Because the cost of launching new consumer brands is so high, many companies put significant effort into leveraging their brands into new categories, hoping that their brand value will carry over from the existing product categories to the new category. NPF is skeptical about these strategies and makes an important distinction between brand stretching and brand strengthening.

Peter Brabeck, the Nestlé S.A. CEO, believes that when a brand is introduced into a new product category, it should strengthen the brand and not stretch it. If Nestlé came up with a Stouffer's ice cream because it's frozen, it would consider that stretching the brand. But new recipe dishes or new family meals for Lean Cuisine or Skillet Sensations would be considered strengthening the brand by building critical mass where the brand belongs. When we met again in 2006, Cunliffe told us, "This year we have introduced a range of Panini, under both the Stouffer's and Lean Cuisine brands. This is a great example of brand strengthening rather than stretching, as we move these two mega brands into new eating occasions."

Select Segments to Dominate

What do you do when competitors are filling up one of your target segments and the segment is getting stale? How about redefining it? Two decades ago, NPF created the healthy frozen-food segment with Lean Cuisine, but today it's a very crowded segment. However, Lean Cuisine continues to lead. One reason is NPF's continuous product line renovation and innovation. But perhaps more important was the decision to reposition Lean Cuisine. Instead of continuing to plug the weight control and fitness benefits, as every competitor seems to do, NPF promoted Lean Cuisine dishes as tasty, easy-to-prepare, and of course, healthy, alternatives to leftovers.

"In our advertising, we used a key consumer insight that we're not just competing with other healthy frozen foods like Healthy Choice and Weight Watchers," says Cunliffe. "We're competing with all the junk that people have in their fridge that they're likely to dig out and serve at the last minute." Nestlé has not neglected weight loss as a primary concern among customers and, in 2006, placed a major bet on the obesity segment by acquiring the Jenny Craig diet company and Australian healthy cereals and snacks maker Uncle Toby's, both of which it placed in a new weight-management division. But the "well-being" rather than "weight loss" positioning for Lean Cuisine has proven to be remarkably robust, which Nestlé sees as part of a significant shift in consumer perceptions of frozen prepared foods. As people came to realize they could feed their families with premium quality frozen-food products, rather than fast food, multiserve—frozen food packaged in a multiple serving size—has become a great axis of growth.

Acting on this insight, in 1998 NPF launched a multiserve product, Skillet Sensations, under the Stouffer's and Lean Cuisine brands. Stouffer's Skillet Sensations established NPF as the leader in multiserve and grossed over $120 million in sales in the first fifty-two weeks of broad distribution.

Design the Market Offer to Create Customer Value and Secure Differential Advantage

The better you understand the customer, the more likely you will be able to create customer value. Sounds obvious, yet how often have you seen launches fail because the people who designed the products had poor information or limited insight about customers?

NPF doesn't just guess what its customers want, or use generic studies, which as often as not leave a company guessing. It relies heavily on qualitative research and good judgment. "Intimate conversation with a few consumers is going to give you this sort of information more than the standard type of [research] approach," says Cunliffe. It was just such conversations that gave birth to Lean Cuisine's icebox insight and suggested how its frozen food could be repositioned as offering better quality and nutrition than leftovers or fast-food chain restaurants. The learning from intensive focus groups and one-on-one interviews also enabled NPF to fine-tune its segmentation approaches.

NFP generated consumer insights to understand the wide range of users and usage occasions, and ceased treating frozen food as a monolithic business. It recognized that product requirements changed by life stage. What a teenage kid wants to eat, what a young married couple wants to eat, and what a homemaker with kids wants to feed her family all differ.

NPF increasingly uses the Internet to deepen its relationship with customers. "Every offline promotion has an online component for that brand site," says Cunliffe. "For example, we have a Stouffer's recipe contest every year. We make the winning recipe affordable, manufacture it, and put it on the shelf." In 2001, the company bought the failing Meals.com website that hosted branded websites, including Nestlé's own VeryBestMeals.com. Today, Meals.com offers over fifteen thousand recipes that consumers can choose, review, and use to make shopping lists. Naturally, NPF uses these recipes to promote Nestlé products (along, to be fair, with recipes for those leftovers that compete with its prepared foods). But the site is at least as valuable for what the company finds out. "We can learn what these consumers are interested in, and what they're not interested in," says Cunliffe.

NPF's consumers have created well over a million shopping lists on Meals.com. From this aggregation of individual preferences NPF can glean additional information about customers' needs and wants to compare with its focus group and interview research.

Breakthrough product innovation is often seen as the key to creating new types of customer value. Innovation certainly plays a role in NPF's continued success and leadership, but growth is underpinned by a continuous process of product renovation. "Renovation is the sort of blocking and tackling in the market," says Cunliffe. "It's not glamorous, but it contributes enormously to the number of items you have on the shelf. This is one of the key drivers of sales and it keeps the consumer interested."

To translate customer understanding into products, NPF splits this execution task into two functions. Renovation is in the hands of the Product Development Group, separate from R&D and staffed by approximately fifty people. Product Development focuses on creating new recipes and enhancing existing product lines. R&D develops more radical technical, process, engineering, and packaging changes. A good example, said Cunliffe, "[is using] our understanding of dough technology to deliver 'grilled' panini right out of the microwave!"

Integrate to Serve the Customer

For any business that truly focuses on the customer, marketing should be the glue that binds the organization together. Marketing should be right in the middle and touch every other function. NPF lives this view of marketing by hiring as marketers people with strong skills in project management. They bring together such groups as Purchasing, Manufacturing, Product Development, R&D, and Suppliers to facilitate continuous improvement in processes.

Integration is not just a matter of everyone singing from the same songbook. Sometimes it requires high-level support for the marketing function with specific actions that are neither obvious nor clear-cut. For example, the increasing strength of channel partners is a growing headache for producers like Nestlé. Many of its competitors have seen their profits sucked dry by retail distribution titans such as Wal-Mart, Carrefour, Tesco, and Royal Ahold. Nestlé has avoided this fate, in part by putting its heavy-hitting, most senior executives into account-management roles. For example, the leader of its Wal-Mart team until recently was Joe Weller, the now retired president of Nestlé USA. Other executives were dedicated to the account, but a person of Weller's stature could get action at Wal-Mart, and some very good dialogue.

Nestlé USA has also gained leverage over retailers by consolidating sales forces. Unlike competitors that employ separate sales forces for different product lines, it presents one face to the customer. (The sole exception is the Pet Care Division. With the acquisition of pet-food giant Ralston Purina, Pet Care is large enough to warrant a separate sales force.) Using a consolidated sales force to sell megabrands provides NPF with capabilities to execute such programs as "For the Way You Live." Through this program, Nestlé bundles products for both consumer and trade promotions.

Measure What Matters

A common objective and metric, real internal growth, serves to emphasize the importance of marketing throughout NPF. Large banners with NPF's internal growth goals and past performance hang in the entryway of NPF's Solon, Ohio, headquarters. Cunliffe believes that NPF's clear focus on an internal growth metric fosters creativity and a customer-oriented philosophy across the entire business.

Amazon.com: The Ultimate Segmenter

Amazon is not just a dot-com survivor. It increasingly dominates the world of consumer e-commerce. Slowly but surely Amazon is seeing its business model validated in the stock price.[10] Amazon remains the leader in online book sales in the U.S. market, and third overall in total sales behind Barnes & Noble and Borders, with about 8 percent market share.[11] But the big growth is coming from elsewhere. Today Amazon's website is a virtual mall, comprising over thirty different stores selling everything from books to computers, housewares, apparel, industrial supplies, and nonperishable groceries. Amazon North America's Electronics, Tools, and Kitchen (ETK) products accounted for 15 percent of revenues in 2002, and its share of total company revenues has grown rapidly since then. During the Thanksgiving 2004 shopping weekend, consumer electronics surpassed books as the number one revenue sector for Amazon. International sales are also experiencing breakneck growth. Amazon has also launched a major foray into business-to-business product sales. Amazon's head of worldwide marketing, Lance Batchelor, wants it to be "the place you go online and buy anything."

How is Amazon succeeding where so many others have failed? Because of execution. From the outset, it emphasized marketing leadership within the company, learned all it could about its customers, designed its marketing offerings with well-defined visions of their wants and needs, and focused on the total customer experience. Throughout, it uses real-time techniques to measure its results against those it has aimed for.

Pick Markets That Matter and Select Segments to Dominate

It may seem that Amazon's ambitious goals violate the imperatives of choosing markets that matter and selecting segments you can dominate by concentrating your resources against them. But Amazon has built the foundation for moving to market after market by developing, honing, and leveraging its core competencies.

None of these competencies is more important than its ability to

serve microsegments. More than any other company, Amazon has succeeded in creating the ultimate in market segments, segments of one
for each individual purchaser. "Most marketers use proxies to try and
understand their customer base," said Batchelor. "So if I'm trying to
aim a product at, say, fashion-conscious women, I'm doing it because I
believe they will want to buy products like mine. At Amazon we've
been able to cut straight through that. We know what people actually
buy. We may not know their gender. We have no idea if they're young
or old. All we know is a name and a zip code. We've generally been
able to target 90 percent of our marketing directly in the most relevant
possible way, without knowing or caring if you're an eighty-year-old
woman or a twenty-year-old man."

The Internet provides an ideal environment for creating segments
of one and, more than any of its rivals, Amazon has perfected this art.
Many marketers spend enormous sums of money to acquire and analyze demographic data, but Amazon has realized the most relevant information it can obtain about its customers is who they are and what
they buy. These data are all it needs to create highly customized promotions and offers that are likely to be relevant to individual customers. Technology is the key to Amazon's success in using this
one-on-one marketing data. "We use a lot of predictive technology,"
says Batchelor. "We have a large number of people engaged in developing these technologies and algorithms that will guide you around
the site. The moment you go through that rotating door, you are identified, recognized, and offered a personalized selection of products.
And we can use our algorithms—something we're very, very good at
doing—to get you to visit the stores you haven't visited before. The
company gets better and better at marketing over time because each
interaction you have with Amazon improves its understanding of your
preferences."

Amazon uses one-on-one marketing to get you to buy more of what
you already buy, but its real value lies in cross-selling. Amazon's long-
term profitability depends on this capability. Amazon's proprietary
technology is expensive to develop. Its expansion into such new categories as kitchen accessories and apparel, and even dry goods as I mentioned earlier, has in part been driven by the objective of leveraging its
technology investments. It has also been driven by a decline in new

customer acquisition rates as the e-commerce space matures and consumers become more accustomed to shopping online. According to Batchelor, "The challenge for us is to get our customers to shop across all our stores so that we maximize the value of those customers."

Amazon concentrates its resources by effectively deploying people in the marketing organization. It divides marketing into two teams, each with a different challenge. "The job of the first team," said Batchelor, "is to drive customers to Amazon.com. If you like, the analogy there is, 'Drive them to the rotating door at the entrance.' Once you arrive, the second team, our internal marketing folks, take over."

Amazon separates marketing into two teams because each demands a very different skill set. External marketing people specialize in such areas as developing partnerships with Amazon's one-million-plus "Associates," or other websites that direct traffic to Amazon; creating compelling advertisements; and understanding competitors. Internal marketing staff must have a greater aptitude for technology to focus on the website's look and feel, and on cross-selling.

Originally, each store had a separate marketing team and budget. Batchelor created a unified marketing department focused on building the brand. "If you looked at the individual budgets of those marketing teams—$3 million or $5 million apiece—they were not going to get you anywhere," he noted. They were unable to break through the market clutter and get decent levels of regional frequency. According to Batchelor, there was also a risk of pushing out contradictory messaging to the Amazon customer base.

After a major internal debate, Amazon decided it was not made up of multiple brands like P&G. Rather, it was more like Target. As a retailer, it had one customer base, one brand and one brand equity. Amazon's recognition that only brand-focused marketing could support its strategic objectives has made a critical difference in improving its marketing execution capabilities.

Design the Market Offer to Create Customer Value and Secure Differential Advantage

Amazon focuses relentlessly on the total customer experience. For example, it brings in consumer groups to work with trial versions of new technologies. Based on what Amazon learns, it puts the beta version out to 10 percent of the customer base for a month to see how that affects purchases. It then goes back and talks to a cross section of a thousand consumers to see what they think about it. When we met with Batchelor, Amazon was testing beta versions of online stores for industrial supplies, art and hobby supplies, car parts and accessories, and pet supplies.

Customer offers are tested no less rigorously. Batchelor said that Amazon tries as much as possible to use online to lower costs and speed up turnaround times for gathering data. Amazon likes e-mail because it can be treated just like a website. It can measure the click-through rates, and run A/B tests on multiple legs of every message it sends out, almost in real time. Every 5, 10, or 20 percent of Amazon's customers are shown a different treatment of some kind. If it sends out twenty million e-mails over three days, within one to three hours Amazon starts to get a feel for which messages work better and can then start to tweak the remainder.

Amazon also targets a cross section of daily visitors on all its websites with pop-up surveys that asks them what influenced their visit; this helps Amazon get a snapshot of customers. "For example," says Batchelor, "if a new print campaign launches it would be nice to see some reflection of that, and you do. And you do tend to see a percentage of your customers say, 'Oh, I saw an ad today. It reminded me.' Likewise we go back to a cross section of pretty much every e-mail leg that we sent out. We talk to them online with e-mail usually about what they saw and send surveys out to them."

Sometimes rigor consists of knowing what *not* to do. For example, Amazon does not favor A/B price testing since it's hard to explain to customers later why they were being charged more or less than the others. Amazon sticks with everyday low pricing and focuses instead on different treatments of offers—their looks, feels, and layouts.

That kind of discipline pervades Amazon's entire approach to customer contact. Everyone who's spent time online knows how annoying unsolicited questions and pestiferous pop-ups can be. Then there are privacy concerns: just how much information do those people have about me, and what are they doing with it? Amazon takes pains to avoid being intrusive, both with the communications it sends and the information it collects.

"In the last four or five years, we've learned a lot about how to deploy e-mail as a tool effectively," Batchelor says. "Before then I think we were in the same place as everyone else—you send as much as you can and you get the returns. Now we're very, very disciplined about what we call in-box management. We don't want you to feel overwhelmed by irrelevant Amazon mail. We've learned exactly where the tipping point is in terms of how much to send—how much will be received warmly by a customer versus how much starts to feel like an invasion of your space. We've learned an enormous amount about effective use of that e-mail headline to get you to open it, and also about layouts, offers, how to click through for mails, and so on."

Another no-no is overreacting to short-term competitive challenges that can skew key elements of a market strategy. Amazon recognizes that frequent adjustments to prices, the look and feel of its website, and other brand components can easily confuse customers—not to mention making the jobs of its marketing team a living hell. Amazon does competitive analysis but doesn't spend a lot of time on it because most competitors are offline and change year to year. Instead, Amazon is much more focused on the customer. Batchelor's advice to other marketers is to pick an everyday low-price positioning. "[L]ock it, live with it, and review it monthly to see how you're doing. Don't overreact to individual competitors that mount short-term, probably unprofitable, challenges on you."

Amazon's focus on customer satisfaction started early. It realized that word of mouth was far more effective and relevant than promotion, advertising, and other traditional marketing techniques. Batchelor said, "If the pricing is low, the shopping experience is a pleasure, the product arrives quickly, and it's exactly what you ordered, the odds are extremely high that you're going to tell other people about it. Amazon didn't have big marketing budgets in the early days, yet it built a customer base of thirty-five-million-plus customers." In 2006 Amazon's customer base was around forty-five million and continues to grow as it finds creative ways to stimulate word of mouth such as its "Refer a Friend" program. Customers receive a discount if friends they refer to Amazon purchase similar items. This resulted in hundreds of thousands of referrals and incremental purchases.

It's easy for customers to communicate with each other online, and even a small number of disappointed customers could wreak havoc with Amazon's business. To stop trouble before it can start, Amazon employs several tactics to ensure delivery of a consistent customer experience:

- *It provides a consistent global experience.* The only noticeable differences across Amazon's international websites are language and currency. Amazon also uses similar marketing tools such as its Associates Network of websites that forward traffic to its own site, in international markets. Not only do customers benefit, but Amazon can more easily expand abroad. Indeed Amazon's UK (amazon.co.uk) and German (amazon.de) subsidiaries reached profitability in half the time it took the company in the United States.
- *It selectively chooses partners.* Partners—including suppliers— play a key role in influencing brand perceptions, and Amazon applies enforceable quality standards.
- *It develops common goals for customer service and marketing.* Amazon holds the service organization accountable for many of the same metrics as the marketing group. In addition, Batchelor's team has daily interactions with customer service to review customer contacts. These interactions provide an early warning to marketing of out-of-stock items, shipping errors, or other problems that could damage the customer experience.

Integrate to Serve the Customer

At Amazon, marketing is the culture and it starts at the top. Jeff Bezos served as his company's first chief marketer and, as Batchelor cheerfully acknowledged, still retains that role to some extent. Bezos remains intimately involved in such details as marketing initiatives and routinely meets with customers and responds to customer e-mail (he publishes his e-mail address and invites customers to write to him). Bezos is a consummate pitchman for the company. For example, when he appeared on a CNBC interview, he proudly announced that "every stitch of clothing" he was wearing, including his underwear, had been purchased from Amazon's new apparel and accessories store.[12] He plays a key role in fostering an internal marketing culture. Bezos holds every member of his senior management team accountable for the firm's revenues. He also continuously reiterates—both publicly and privately—that serving customers is the entire company's top priority.

That includes people in the Applications Group, the developers of new online tools. There's no hard financial incentive for those who develop the successful tools. Amazon has immense respect for their intellectual agility and technological prowess. Hence, a person working on an element of 'Search,' that drives half or more of all sales on Amazon's site, is very popular.

The customer-centric culture drives a high level of collaboration among Amazon's different functions. For example, working with partners like Fidelity, Target, Office Depot, and WeightWatchers is more of a business-to-businesss model, a kind of extended enterprise, requiring a customer-centered team approach. Salespeople in the Business Development Group set up and build Amazon's relationships with potential vendors. Then, when a contract is signed, the Account Management Group takes over. Each account has its own general manager with overall account responsibility. Account managers are very plugged into the Applications Group, which develops new technologies, and to the Marketing Group. They are drawn from other parts of Amazon, so they know how to get around the firm and get the tools built that they need for their accounts.

Vendors are part of the extended enterprise. Not only do the merchandising organizations have a tight, daily relationship with the supply chain, but also weekly meetings where Amazon goes through the marketing plan with them on a rolling basis for the next month so they can see what's happening. Batchelor gives them a feel for past experience of what lift Amazon gets when it sends out e-mail or advertisements appear in Sunday circulars.

Growth into new markets often wrecks successful companies: they get in over their heads, or lose sight of what made them successful in the first place. Amazon's focus on the customer carries it into all its new ventures by ensuring that it adheres to the imperatives of marketing execution. When we asked Batchelor to list Amazon's greatest recent successes, his answer was telling. "The first one I'd point to is— despite all the temptations—maintaining consistency in our messaging and in our philosophy. With all of these stores that we've launched, and the fact that we've gone into new countries, and the fact that we've tied up a host of partnerships, it would have been very, very easy to take our eye off the ball and start focusing on different messages every few months.

"Frankly, we flirted with that idea over and over again. It would have been very easy, for example, to focus on the selection that only comes with signing a Circuit City. It would have been very easy to focus more of our marketing effort on managing relationships with Wall Street as opposed to with customers. But we've been very single-minded. We want to be the place you go online to find, discover, and buy anything. And we've been very disciplined in saying, 'Carry on focusing on the customer or focus on the convenience and value above all.' We have cut all these deals with other companies not because our philosophy has changed, but because we believe it's a better way to serve that philosophy."

As may already be clear, Amazon.com is highly dependent on, and highly adept at, measuring what matters to customers. Tracking every click of every visit to its website, every response to its e-mails, and every follow-up interaction with customers, Amazon uses this information stream to make appropriate recommendations to individual customers, tailor e-mail promotions for maximum effectiveness, and streamline customer service.

•   •   •

I've given you an overview of how Nestlé and Amazon.com focus on the five core marketing imperatives. The remainder of the book investigates each imperative in depth. We'll start with how the Marketing Mavens of the world's leading companies pick markets that matter.

IMPERATIVE 1

Pick Markets
That Matter

THREE

Identifying Opportunities

Perhaps the most critical decision Marketing Mavens must make is "which game to play." Thirty to forty years ago, conglomeration was all the rage—be in lots of unrelated business to diversify your risk. Today, as competition has become so much fiercer, the most successful businesses tend to focus their energies on fewer markets where they have a better chance to win.

Deciding where to play through either organic growth or acquisition means you must also decide where not to play. Resources *spent* on picking the *wrong* markets, are resources *not spent* on pursuing the *right* markets.

It takes very bold leadership to pull out of markets where you may once have been dominant to shift direction to a new market. Intel, under CEO Andy Grove, did so when it withdrew from memory chips, the product on which it was founded; American Can, the number two U.S. can manufacturer exited the can market for financial services, as it morphed into Primerica (now part of Citigroup); Westinghouse shed its core electrical businesses as it transferred its attention to media with its purchase of CBS (now part of Viacom); and DuPont spun off its once world-leading textile fibers operation. We'll see the same sort of discipline clearly displayed by Nokia.

Finding new markets and expanding existing markets is key to long-term survival and profitability in good times and bad. The Marketing Mavens in the companies we focus on have a great variety of approaches to the strategic task of deciding in which markets to do business, yet they all agree that rigor in practicing the principle of selectivity and concentration is absolutely crucial.

Identifying Markets for the "Metal Without a Market"

Alcoa Inc., the world's leading aluminum and aluminum products firm, has been named one of the world's most sustainable corporations by both the Dow Jones Sustainability Index and the World Economic Forum in Davos, Switzerland. It has long excelled at picking markets that matter and concentrating its resources to exploit them profitably.

Alcoa was founded by young inventor Charles Martin Hall and six Pittsburgh businessmen in 1888 to exploit Hall's process for large-scale aluminum smelting. Around the same time, Frenchman Paul Heroult produced aluminum by an almost identical process, and two years later German scientist Karl Bayer developed a competing process. The theory behind these processes had been known for decades, but putting them into action depended on using large quantities of electric current, then becoming available for the first time.

No one knew how aluminum would stand up in actual use, however, and for some time it was the "metal without a market." With the support of his six financial backers, Hall went to work on two fronts. First, he improved the process, quickly lowering the cost per ton. Second, he campaigned to persuade manufacturers that aluminum was right for them by casting it in myriad forms and making demonstration products in Alcoa workshops. Today, the drive to create new markets and extend existing markets seems part of Alcoa's corporate DNA.

Alcoa has been active in the automobile and aviation industries since the 1930s, and it has nimbly remained the dominant enterprise in each sector of those markets. It has managed to continue building on its successes in spite of a 1945 U.S. government antitrust decision that forced it to divest its Canadian subsidiary, Alcan, which has since become its main rival. Alcoa holds well over a 10 percent share of the world aluminum market, roughly equivalent to Alcan, thanks to Alcan's 2003 acquisition of the French aluminum giant, Pechiney. But the financials give Alcoa a distinct edge. In 2006 Alcoa earned $2.16 billion income from continuing operations on its $30.4 billion revenues. By contrast, Alcan's income from continuing operations was $1.79 billion on $23.6 billion revenues.

Since World War II, Alcoa's focus on improving both process and product technology to satisfy changing customer needs and minimize its cost basis, in part by offering an increasing number of products containing no aluminum, has ensured that company preferences do not trump those of its customers. Dick Melville, vice chairman of Alcoa Industrial Components' Aerospace Market Sector Lead Team does not see it strictly as an aluminum company. While Alcoa is the largest of the integrated aluminum companies, it also fabricates aluminum into intermediate products, and in some cases makes the final product, where aluminum is but one of several components. But there are also some markets where the product life cycles have moved away from using aluminum at all.

If customers no longer want your products, one choice is to exit the market. But if you are focused on the customer, there has to be serious consideration to continuing to serve that customer with new and different products based on new technology. This is not always successful, as FedEx found when it tried to take advantage of fax technology with ZapMail. But Alcoa's customer focus and technological investment has enabled it to make the switch in a number of cases. It now manufactures and sells products in plastics, in vinyls, in metal-matrix composites, high-strength alloys, titanium, copper/nickel, and high-strength steels. As a result, none of Alcoa's competitors look like it in size or breadth. And many of Alcoa's competitors in finished products are its customers in primary metals and alloys.

Melville said that Alcoa is active and profitable in fifty-two industrial segments around the world. "Only a handful of companies in any of these areas make the return on cost of capital consistently. In the commodity metals business, only Alcoa does. In the aerospace market, which drives much of our basic research and development portfolio, Alcoa has about one-third of the revenue that is generated at the original equipment manufacturer level worldwide, and probably closer to 75 percent of the profits."

Sustaining such wide-ranging success requires that Alcoa continually extend its existing competencies and acquire appropriate new competencies. Its enviable earnings record demonstrates it has managed this balancing act with remarkable consistency over the years. For example, in 1991, Alcoa's top management, under then chairman and CEO Paul H. O'Neill, President George W. Bush's first secretary of the treasury, decided that to continue its success in innovating for customers and exploiting new opportunities, Alcoa should accelerate its transition from a business model of "make for inventory" to one of "make for use."

In the old, resource-dominated economy, many firms followed a make-for-inventory model, effectively telling the customer, "You can buy from the range of products and services we choose to offer. Take it or leave it." In the new information-dominated economy of global oversupply, global competition, and technological evolution, Alcoa's make-for-use approach now effectively says to customers, "We are not restricted to aluminum or our existing product lines; tell us what you need and want, so we can make it for you or help you to make it."

Alcoa calls its company-wide initiative for executing the make-for-use strategy the Alcoa Business System. "Make for use" implies a readiness to adapt company competencies to changing customer needs in existing and new markets. For example, much of the bottle-cap business has migrated from aluminum bottle caps to plastics. Rather than let its bottling expertise atrophy and its market share decline, Alcoa migrated along with the market. As a result, in 2006 Alcoa Closure Systems was a significant Alcoa business, the global leader in beverage closure design, production, and application in both aluminum *and* plastics.

Wall Street, once enamored of widely diversified conglomerates such as ITT, under Harold Geneen, and Gulf & Western, under Charles Bludhorn, now generally prefers companies with a narrower mission identity. Financial analysts even speak of widely diversified companies, with the exception of a few still favored ones such as General Electric and Berkshire Hathaway, as trading at a "conglomerate discount." That might have argued for Alcoa's spinning off its packaging business. But with the rest of its businesses united around aluminum and high-tech alloys, Alcoa could retain and grow its packaging assets and expertise without excessive concern that it was blurring its focus. Indeed, Wall Street should understand that technological diversification in the pursuit of serving the needs of its customers is no vice.

Moreover, there is a long-term strategic benefit to Alcoa in having competency in plastics packaging. Alcoa's leaders realize that the composite materials of the future may well include non-metals. In that regard, retaining the packaging business after the shift from metal to plastic represents a savvy hedge investment for Alcoa. It demonstrates that Alcoa truly understands that marketing is the central purpose of business and accordingly accepts the necessity of being a customer-focused company. It shows that Alcoa ultimately picks markets based not on its existing asset base and current competencies but on insights into current and future customer needs. As a general rule, it is typically more effective to serve the needs of current customers that you already know well, than to search for new customers. Bottling and packaging expertise contributed significantly to 2006 packaging and consumer goods revenues of $3.2 billion, over 10 percent of total 2006 Alcoa revenues.

Alcoa has scarcely neglected aluminum, especially in aviation and automobiles. The Aerospace Market Sector Lead Team works hand in hand with Boeing, Airbus, and defense aviation to ensure that tomorrow's planes fly better and safer with Alcoa aluminum and aluminum alloys. Likewise, the Automotive Market Sector Lead Team partners with automobile manufacturers to create aluminum space frames that make cars lighter—to increase fuel efficiency—and more rigid—to make them safer in crashes.

Alcoa has a low-cost base, rigorously developed and maintained over decades by constant refinement of core product and process technologies. Similarly, Alcoa matches intensive R&D efforts to emerging market trends, striving to be the low-cost/high-value-added supplier in each of the fifty-two industrial market segments in which it competes worldwide. Describing the unifying principle that drives Alcoa's success, Melville said, "We tend to focus on end products, and we look through our first level of customer. We recognize clearly that, with the exception of our own consumer brands like Reynolds Wrap for kitchen use, our customer is not normally the person who actually puts the aluminum or other product to its final use. In many cases we go three, four, and even five customer levels deeper to reach the end market and gauge trends, assess our positioning, and analyze how we can pull value through the chain."

Perhaps nothing better illustrates Alcoa's ability to find new markets that matter than the aluminum baseball bat. "In organized baseball and softball from Little League to the NCAA championships," Dick Melville told us with perhaps some overstatement, "every bat used in the United States today is an Alcoa product. It came from the research we did with the U.S. Navy in 1975 to develop high-strength extrusions and plate for the F-18 fighter jet. Same alloy, high-fracture toughness, formable, and it is safe."

Aluminum bats cannot crack and splinter like wooden ones sometimes do, spewing sharp pieces like shrapnel from an explosion. Aluminum bats are also lighter and easier to swing, but they have their own safety issues. The increased speed at which the ball comes off an aluminum bat contributes to higher batting averages and home run numbers, which makes it popular with players and fans. But some believe it also contributes to an increase in serious injuries. Although this controversy is ongoing, the aluminum bat is not only the clear market favorite, Melville said, it has also "cut down the number of lawsuits for our customers by orders of magnitude."

Alcoa has since launched alloys for mountain bikes and other sporting goods equipment. And it has collaborated with DuPont in combining an aluminum composite with fabric made from DuPont's ultrastrong Kevlar fiber to produce an architectural panel that can withstand wind-borne debris and wind speeds common in category 3 hurricanes, which continued global warming promises to make more common. Later in the book, we'll consider other examples of Alcoa's culture of innovation and its repeated ability to identify profitable markets and concentrate resources against them effectively. What is important to recognize here is how Alcoa picks markets based on insight into present and future customer needs, something it has in common with all the top marketing companies.

From Servicing Cars to Serving Drivers

Another longtime giant—its premerger parent companies each have over one hundred years of history—ExxonMobil often ranks as the world's largest company by annual revenues.[1] As a petroleum, petrochemicals, and plastics company, ExxonMobil does an enormous amount of industrial business. But consumer gasoline sales continue to define it and the entire energy sector.

ExxonMobil seems to be doing what it has always done; run an efficient and cost-conscious energy business. This observation, however, misses a profound market change that has challenged all the oil companies to adjust. Quite simply, automobiles have become much more reliable and the required levels of maintenance have dropped dramatically. Hal Cramer, president of Fuels Marketing, sums up that change, and ExxonMobil's actions to keep pace, in one customer service credo: "Keep your face to the customer, and your back to the company . . . not the other way around."

To understand the aptness of the credo, we need to appreciate the oil companies' need to find competitive advantage somewhere besides their products, which are virtually indistinguishable from one another. If ExxonMobil, BP, or Shell achieves a marginal performance advantage for its products, the other two will quickly duplicate it. From the customer's perspective, "gas is gas" (or, outside North America, "petrol is petrol"). The only way to deliver higher perceived value to customers and achieve a differential advantage over competitors is service. And that's where the story has changed in recent decades.

For most of the twentieth century, customers drove their automobiles to the Esso (later Exxon in the United States while continuing as Esso elsewhere), Texaco, Sunoco, or Shell station not only to have their tanks filled but also for routine maintenance and occasional repairs. Offering lube and oil changes, filter, belt, hose, and brake pad replacements, and so on, as well as rebuilding or replacing mechanical parts like clutch assemblies, bolstered margins for the gas station operator and fostered customer loyalty. Broadly speaking, that kind of service could make the difference between a customer's consistently buying gas at the local Esso or Mobil station, or patronizing nearby Sunoco or Texaco.

Customers in those decades wanted to see the station staffs' backsides as they bent over cars to fix and service them—even if that just meant cleaning a dirty windshield. Some of you will recall the oil companies' advertising images and slogans from the 1950s to the 1970s. A smiling service station man in a spotless military style cap and uniform salutes as you drive to the pump. Your windshield, still clean from your last stop here for gas, is cleaned again. Your oil is checked, again. Your tire pressure too. And the tank is filled. "You can trust your car to the man who wears the star, the big, bright Texaco star." Esso, for its part, was "the sign of extra service."

To be sure, the oil companies added sizzle to their marketing with distinctive image campaigns, such as Esso/Exxon's "Put a tiger in your tank," whose longevity currently includes an environmentally conscious "Save the Tigers" component. But these multimillion-dollar campaigns represented table stakes in the battle for customer aware-ness. Loyalty had to be won with the promise and delivery of good ser-vice for customers' cars.

Nowadays gas stations have self-service pumps and full-service pumps (although fewer and fewer of these), but no one cleans your dirty windshield. And if your car needs repair, the station may not be equipped to fix it. Even the smallest, least expensive cars today are as dependent on computerized black boxes as the newest commercial air-craft. If the proprietary iDrive software module in your $70,000 BMW Series 7 goes haywire, locking you in the car, as happened to more than one early buyer, the local gas station attendant can't get you out and, even though a GPS locator is built in, they can't come and find you either. But it's not a class thing: the gas station can't fix the mini-van's keyless entry system if it jams either.

Fortunately for all of us, cars today are far better, environmentally cleaner, safer, and more reliable than they ever used to be. The only reason manufacturers can afford to offer roadside assistance on new cars—standard even on many economy models—is that they know they've built the cars so solidly, that drivers will need very little of this expensive service.

Competition-driven changes in the automobile business have in turn changed the market equation for Exxon, Mobil, BP, Shell, Chevron, and other energy brands that have survived the past two decades of mergers and consolidations. Since cars don't need servicing like they used to, the oil companies can't use that as a differentiator. The flip side is that drivers have a whole new set of desires, created by long commutes and drive times brought on by suburban sprawl and other society-wide demographic changes. ExxonMobil has captured the essence of these new driver needs with the slogan "Life on the Move."

In a nutshell what this slogan captures is that today's drivers don't need help keeping the car running. Today's drivers need help keeping themselves and the rest of their lives running! The slogan marks the end of the service station and the beginning of the convenience station—a combination of gas station and convenience store. In terms of creating customer value and seizing differential advantage over competition, the market that matters, once servicing cars, is now ser-vicing drivers.

Recognition of this fact brought about the first convenience stores on gas station lots, a phenomenon that all the oil companies participated in to some extent. But ExxonMobil made a concerted push in this direction sooner and more effectively than its rivals. In the 1990s Mobil/ExxonMobil initiated its On the Run convenience-store business and put itself, in Hal Cramer's words, "at the front of the competitive landscape." By early 2006 ExxonMobil had opened more than fifteen hundred On the Run convenience stores in more than forty countries.

ExxonMobil's ability to get to the competitive forefront in this way is fully consistent with its recent emphasis on "keeping your face to the customer and your back to the company." The added value in transactions at the gas station no longer comes from the car service bay but at the convenience-store counter. This follows on the heels of the customer advantage ExxonMobil has derived from Speedpass, the credit card–or debit card–linked keychain wand that ExxonMobil customers can use to pay instantly for gas at the pump and for other items at the convenience store counter. Speedpass has proved to be enormously popular with customers. Likewise, following the ExxonMobil merger, the two original companies' credit cards and Speedpass quickly became usable at both Exxon and Mobil stations in the United States. ExxonMobil's competitors have not been nearly as quick to integrate their operations after their own mergers and acquisitions.

In later chapters we'll see some of the difficult work that went into executing these strategic market decisions. For now, it is important to recognize that Alcoa's and ExxonMobil's successes in picking markets that matter included staying out of markets that don't matter, those with insufficient long-term growth and profit potential.

As I noted above, the markets a company *deselects* are as important as the markets it *selects*. After all, company resources targeted at the *wrong* markets are company resources not targeted at the *right* markets. Of course, in general, you want to expand your customer base. But you want to pull off that expansion in the most profitable way possible, with as many of the most profitable customers as possible. It was one thing for Alcoa's Aerospace Market Lead Team to want to find nonaviation uses for its aluminum, titanium, and other alloys. It was quite another to identify a market in baseball bats and other sports equipment that was big enough to matter to a company the size of Alcoa. Dick Melville told us, "The sin in marketing that you don't want to commit at Alcoa is to be successful and be small. That would be bad." Alcoa is clear that small markets are ones it wants to deselect.

At ExxonMobil the decision to focus on servicing drivers' lives on the move, rather than on servicing cars, meant deselecting an outmoded relationship with drivers in favor of a new one. That decision also triggered many more choices in market selection. In what locations would the convenience-station concept work best? Where should there also be a streamlined service component such as a car wash or quick-lube bays? How should ExxonMobil approach competition with the hypermarkets, such as Wal-Mart in the United States and Carrefour in France, many of which now sell gas so cheaply it is sometimes a loss leader to bring traffic into the store?

"We used to look at our business years ago and think that we were just in the business of selling gasoline," Hal Cramer told us. "Now we look at ourselves as full-scale retailers, selling motor fuels, convenience products, car washes, and so forth, to optimize the full value of our business and real estate investments."

Worth It to More Women

During the course of a thirty-five-year battle with its chief rival, Clairol (now part of Procter & Gamble, or P&G), to be number one in hair color, L'Oréal Paris has also excelled at selecting the right markets in which to position its brands.

In the first instance, this has meant restricting L'Oréal's portfolio of hair-color brands only to premium-priced brands such as Preference, Excellence Cream, and Féria. By contrast, Clairol's brand portfolio has always covered every price point in the market. Indeed, many Clairol brands have competed directly with each other at the same price point. For years this shotgun approach gave Clairol the number one market share.

L'Oréal's belief in sticking to only a few brands at the premium end of the mass consumer hair color market is summed up in its famous marketing slogan, "Because you're worth it," the tagline for its Preference hair colors. The company began using this slogan in 1973, and it has since regularly been cited in shortlists of the most memorable and effective marketing messages.

"Because you're worth it," L'Oréal USA president Carol Hamilton

told my colleagues and me, "expresses the company's vision of bringing prestige codes to mass markets." *Codes* is the word L'Oréal favors in
many internal contexts, from R&D to advertising, distribution, and
even category management for large retailers such as Wal-Mart. *Codes*
implies an ongoing reliance on rigorous operational measurement that
originated in 1907 with L'Oréal's founder, Eugène Schueller, a
chemist who experimented with hair-color formulations in his bathtub.
Precise measurement is essential in the beauty business, which has a
heavy industrial and technological component in the acquisition and
processing of raw materials, and an intensive scientific component in
laboratory development of products for the body that are safe and convenient, as well as aesthetically appealing.

It takes a large market to justify the enormous capital and other investments that firms must make to be in the beauty business. And hair
color has been a big market for decades. In the late 1970s Clairol had
a 62 percent market share and L'Oréal only 18 percent. Although
L'Oréal progressively gained market share from Clairol during the next
fifteen years, the hair-color market as a whole experienced only marginal growth, despite apparently favorable, aging baby-boomer demographics.

The barrier to growth turned out to be underplaying the natural
fashion aspect of hair color.

This way of thinking was turned on its ear, at least for Carol Hamilton and L'Oréal, one morning in 1996, when she saw a young woman
at her gym whose flamboyantly colored hair matched the bright color
of her workout wear. This was a eureka moment for Carol Hamilton:
"That woman showed me that we'd been missing something. Hair
color wasn't just about covering gray, it was also about enjoying and
celebrating color—celebrating the unique combinations of hair color,
skin color, eye color, and fashion color."

This recognition freed Hamilton and her colleagues to reimagine
the hair-color market as teenage girls and women, ages twelve to sixty,
who wanted to have fun and be fashionable with hair color. Because
younger women don't have gray hair, this wider customer demographic in turn freed L'Oréal's research and development labs to formulate hair colors in a new way. Instead of focusing only on substances
that covered gray well, they could now formulate desired product attributes for their new customers—rich color and sheen.

Armed with its new insight into customer needs and new hair-color formulations to meet those needs, in 1998 L'Oréal introduced its Féria brand of hair colors, targeted at multicultural women under age thirty-five. In doing so, L'Oréal also pushed the premium price point in the market, offering the first $10 at-home hair color. As the firm had projected, Féria appealed to new customer age groups, and its success meant that L'Oréal could now offer an appropriate brand for each stage of its customers' life cycles, from youthful experimentations with color to covering gray fashionably later on.

In just four months after the Feria launch, Carol Hamilton's epiphany in the gym led L'Oréal to eclipse Clairol to become number one in hair color. It has stayed there ever since.

Later we'll explore the operational details of the L'Oréal story to learn how its steadfast commitment to "bringing prestige codes to mass markets" has made it the only beauty company that is a global leader in four product categories: hair color, hair care, skin care, and cosmetics. As we shall see in chapter 8, it is customer-focused marketing throughout L'Oréal's operations, including R&D, that keeps its "high-class mass," in one industry analyst's words, in the sweet spot of markets that matter.

We'll revisit both Alcoa and L'Oréal in chapter 6 in the context of creating customer value. There we'll have a chance to see how the other top marketing companies also practice what Dick Melville called "look[ing] . . . three, four, and even five customer levels deeper to reach the end market and gauge trends, assess our positioning, and analyze how we can pull value through the chain." This interconnectedness of the marketplace, enhanced by the growth in outsourcing that we discussed earlier, is the flip side of global oversupply and underdemand. One of the characteristic ways that top marketing companies multiply their profit potential is by taking advantage of that interconnectedness to deliver value to both trade and end use, or to both direct and indirect customers, as do both Alcoa and L'Oréal. Likewise Exxon-Mobil grows its "On the Run" brand through both company-owned and franchised outlets, and through well-managed relationships with suppliers and vendors.

One key insight from Alcoa, Exxon, and L'Oréal is that they take advantage of the interconnectedness of the market to create as many win-win relationships as possible. Delivering value to every level of customer is the only way that Alcoa can sustain a situation in which, as Dick Melville told us, "in many cases, our competitors in finished products are our customers in primary metals and alloys."

Listening to (the Right) Customers

When L'Oréal expanded its market opportunities by formulating hair colors to match the needs of a new customer population, it did so in a market environment where it had long been active and profitable, and where it had every necessary competency. By contrast, GOJO Industries, a maker of hand cleansers and skin-care products for use in away-from-home markets like industry, health care, food service, and education, entered the unfamiliar market of consumers and retail partners when it launched its waterless instant hand sanitizer, Purell—the first product of its kind in the retail consumer market. To grow Purell as a consumer brand, GOJO would need to acquire a new set of marketing, sales, packaging, and distribution competencies.

In launching Purell as a consumer brand, GOJO was responding to a growing volume of direct customer requests. GOJO had been selling an early form of Purell in bottles and portion-control dispensers for use in hospitals and food service. The dispensing systems were modeled after one of GOJO's first products, a hand cleanser for workshop and factory use. Jerome Lippman, GOJO's founder and the developer of its first products, only persuaded customers to try his hand cleanser after he devised and furnished convenient, durable, easy-to-maintain dispensers that delivered the product to users in single doses.

The early form of Purell, whose active ingredient is germ-killing ethyl alcohol, was more fluid and less aesthetically pleasing to use than the version now being marketed to retail consumers in plastic bottles with flip tops and pump dispensers. But it was a breakthrough product for conveniently killing germs throughout a busy day, when soap and water were unavailable or inconvenient, and it helped reduce the annual infection death rate in hospitals, currently estimated at eighty-eight thousand annually. Doctors and nurses, the biggest hospital consumers, began to call and write the company about Purell for their personal use. As Sandy Katz, vice president and leader of the Young Consumer Group at GOJO Industries, told us, "Through the early 1990s, the company began hearing an increasing volume of people saying, 'I love this stuff, I use it at work all the time. How can I get some for my family? How can I buy some for home?' "

The prospect of a retail consumer market for Purell was tantalizing. But GOJO had been down this path once before, in the early 1980s, and been burned. GOJO's body-wash product, Shower Up, was also the first of its kind in the consumer marketplace. But Shower Up was not a success, although the body-wash products that followed from larger competitors such as P&G and Colgate built a relatively substantial product category. GOJO didn't want to lead the way only to get burned again.

The crucial issue facing GOJO, or any company in relation to a potential new market, was to understand four things: its existing competencies, the competencies it would need to acquire to be successful in the market, the likely fit among them, and the usefulness of any new competencies it needed to develop for other markets. Only then could it shape a sensible decision, informed by an in-depth assessment of the costs and potential benefits of the new enterprise. In 1995 GOJO's managers decided to go forward with consumer marketing of Purell. What made Purell different from Shower Up, they felt, were four factors:

- Purell was a hand cleaner. Hand cleaners had been GOJO's core product since it was founded in 1946.
- Purell already had a solid, growing institutional market in bulk hand cleaners. Some of the competencies needed for consumer marketing, such as making the product more pleasing to use, would also enhance its value in the institutional market.
- In both institutional and consumer settings, the market potential was as great as the social need. In clamoring for a home-use product, doctors and nurses were expressing a concern about their families' health. That concern was likely to be a harbinger of concern in the general public, as awareness of the importance of more frequent hand washing throughout the day spread. Over 80 percent of all infectious diseases, from the common cold to the Ebola virus, are transmitted by manual contact. In society as a whole, too little hand washing leads to an enormous number of lost work and school days.

- Shower Up was a substitute for using soap and shampoo, and therefore it had to battle uphill against that universal normal practice. Purell was not a substitute for soap and water; it was for cleaning your hands on the go, when soap and water weren't available. This fact had two main implications. On the one hand, GOJO would have to establish more than just its own brand—it would have to establish a whole new product category in the hand and skin-care market. But on the other hand, it would not be competing with an established social practice. The challenge and the potential for GOJO in launching Purell as a consumer brand was to cultivate, and profit from, a developing social awareness that a new behavior, cleaning hands more frequently through the day when soap and water aren't available, was highly desirable.

In chapter 4 we'll look closely at how GOJO concentrated its resources to acquire and apply the needed competencies to compete effectively in the retail arena. GOJO's payoff so far has been substantial, fully justifying the company's hopes when it launched Purell. GOJO has passed a number of milestones in marketing Purell to consumers, from getting Purell stocked at Walgreens to securing placement and promotions at five different in-store locations within Wal-Mart. It has also seen the growth of public awareness of the need for products like Purell, including the emergence of the Committee to Reduce Infectious Death, including Nobel Laureate Joshua Lederberg and several of the country's leading physicians and hospital administrators, which makes more frequent hand washing its number one priority for both health-care providers and the public.

GOJO reached a double-edged milestone when established consumer soap makers like Dial and Lysol entered the market with copycat products. In focus groups, GOJO began hearing people say, "Oh, yeah, Purell, I use that, I've got it in my coat pocket," only to have the product turn out to be the one from Dial or Lysol. The kicker was that, when questioned further, these consumers repeatedly said, "See, here it is. This is Dial's Purell!" Sandy Katz said, "Right there we realized that we were succeeding in establishing a category defining brand, like Kleenex or Band-Aid."

This success was validated in a different way in October 2004, when the pharmaceuticals and health-care products giant Pfizer—another company that we studied—acquired the Purell brand from GOJO. The deal provided for GOJO's affiliate, QualPak, to manufacture Purell for both GOJO, which continues to sell it to business customers, and Pfizer. In announcing the deal Pfizer said, "The Purell brand is a very good strategic fit for Pfizer" and its major consumer health-care brands, such as Benadryl, Sudafed, and the germ-killing products Listerine and Neosporin. In mid-2006, Pfizer announced that it would sell its thriving consumer health-care business, including Purell, to Johnson & Johnson for $16.6 billion in cash, a four-to-one multiple of the business's $3.9 billion sales revenues in 2005.

The Unconglomerate

The cases we've looked at in this chapter show that in addition to picking markets that matter, one of the things all top marketing companies share is a knack for deselecting the wrong markets, and/or not picking the wrong markets in the first place. For GOJO, this meant resisting the temptation, after its first consumer successes with Purell, of blurring the brand's identity with a Purell shampoo or similar product that lacked the compelling market rationale of an instant hand sanitizer. After all, although people should wash their hands on the go, they don't need to wash their hair on the go!

GOJO's Sandy Katz told us that after Purell achieved substantial success as a consumer brand, "We discussed the possibility of quickly expanding the Purell name into other related categories. How far to extend the brand has been an ongoing debate. We have had some very passionate battles over the years, but in the end we believed it would have confused the customer." This goes to Purell's underlying brand rationale. It is not intended to displace any existing product; remember, it is a new product for the new and increasing behavior of cleaning hands throughout the day when soap and water are not available.

Few companies have practiced the art of deselection as well in recent decades as Nokia, the Finnish mobile telephone and telephone exchange equipment maker. In 1998 Nokia reached the number one position worldwide in mobile-phone sales, with revenues that year of $9.4 billion. The attention the last few generations of Nokia leadership have given to deselecting markets may owe something to the fact that, for much of its long history, the company was not completely free to pick its markets.

During the twentieth century, Finnish companies had to operate in a business environment that would stretch even the most able executives—civil war between communist and anticommunist factions, direct involvement in both World War I and World War II, and decades of uneasy, sometimes violent relations with czarist Russia and later with the Soviet Union. For Nokia, in particular, during some periods the Soviet Union was closed to its products; in others it was the company's biggest customer. Nokia's relationship with this huge market was especially difficult between 1945 and 1952 when Finland was forced to pay heavy war reparations for briefly allying with Nazi Germany in an attempt to reclaim territory the Soviet Union had annexed in previous conflicts. In short, the vagaries of twentieth-century global politics sometimes restricted Nokia to domestic markets and sometimes enforced reliance on a few international markets.

Finnish law had its vagaries too, especially in legislation focused on protecting the independence of Finnish timber and wood products companies. Nokia's history as a modern company begins with the 1966–67 merger of Nokia, a forest products company, with the Finnish Rubber Works and Finnish Cable Works, three companies that had been acting as a loose group since the 1920s. The Finnish Rubber Works was the largest and most profitable, followed by the Finnish Cable Works, with Nokia a distant third. But because Finnish law did not allow wood products companies to be merged into firms from other industries, the Finnish Rubber Works and Finnish Cable Works merged into Nokia.

Throughout the 1970s and 1980s, Nokia's market selection decisions were hobbled by internal battles over whether to retain the wood products businesses. But the firm as a whole grew in two main directions. First was power generation, begun with hydroelectric plants on Finland's many rivers and then extended into nuclear power. Second was electronics, including cables; wiring; landline phones, mobile phones, and telephone-exchange equipment; computers; televisions; and other products.

In the 1980s, Nokia focused its mission and decided that its future lay in electronics. Nokia then began completely divesting both its paper and wood products companies and its power generation business. This was a difficult process, not only because of Nokia's origins in wood products, but because Nokia was involved in many coventures with the Finnish government in both power generation and electronics. The state sold its final holdings in these coventures to Nokia in 1988, and in 1991 the company sold the last of its paper and wood products operations.

Nokia was now free to concentrate on electronics. But precisely what part of electronics was a puzzle yet to be solved. A solution became all the more urgent as the Finnish economy, and much of central and eastern Europe, entered a deep recession in 1991, triggered by the collapse of the Soviet Union and the fall of communist governments throughout the Warsaw Pact nations.

At the time, Nokia's biggest and most profitable business was its cable and wire operations. From many perspectives, the 1990s promised to be a growth decade for cable and wire makers. And so they were. "Fiber optics" was a mantra of the technology stock boom, and a lament of the technology stock bust!

Although Nokia's leaders couldn't guess how high the boom would reach, or how deep the bust would go, they thought they saw a better path in mobile phones. For one thing, the biggest customer for Nokia's cable and wire products had been the Soviet Union. Although cable and wire growth prospects in the rest of the world were high, Nokia faced formidable competition from U.S. and western European companies.

By contrast, Nokia had many assets and competencies for pursuing a strategy focused on mobile phones. Nokia had been building mobile phones and mobile-phone exchanges, analog and digital, since the 1970s. Although European firms Philips and Ericsson were far more substantial players than Nokia, top management believed Nokia could fare better against them than against the West's big cable and wire manufacturers.

In 1993, under CEO Jorma Ollila, Nokia adopted the motto "Connecting people" and committed itself wholeheartedly to the mobile-phone business. In a culmination of its deselection strategy, Nokia sold its profitable cable and wire business in 1996, while the market was still rising. After becoming the world leader in mobile phones in 1998,

Nokia nimbly adjusted its mobile-phone strategy to include convergence with the wireless Internet.

Compared with American rivals like Motorola, Nokia had good fortune in being a European company. The 1980s and 1990s was a deregulating period in U.S. politics and the U.S. government was unwilling to set a single national mobile-phone transmission standard. By contrast the European Commission, a forerunner of the European Union, set a single standard for Europe that in turn was adopted by most of Asia.

The perhaps counterintuitive benefit of regulatory action is that sometimes it can focus competition in ways that grow a market as a whole. As we'll have a chance to see in chapter 5, Dell has based its growth as a computer company on doing business only in areas where there are accepted industry standards for product platforms. Much current activity in consumer electronics is focused on battles to win acceptance for competing new DVD and CD standards, and it remains to be seen whether the industry will avoid a market-slowing episode like the home-video battle between Sony's Beta format and VHS videocassettes and VCRs.

A single mobile-phone standard for Europe and Asia greatly accelerated mobile-phone adoption in these markets. It also encouraged European phone makers to develop feature-rich phones in an ongoing search for differential advantage. The U.S. mobile-phone market has grown despite the lack of a single national digital phone transmission standard, but it grew more slowly and in the mid-2000s still remained smaller than the European market.

Rich Geruson, senior vice president for Nokia Mobile Phones USA at the turn of the century, told us, "There was a much earlier adoption of digital technology in Europe and Pacific Asia, and still to this day a quicker market maturity, higher penetration of mobile phones and usage of more features beyond voice than in the United States."

For example, short text messaging on mobile phones already far outstrips e-mail use in Europe. It has only recently become a significant factor in the United States, driven here as there by the staying-in-constant-touch habits of teenagers and other youthful mobile-phone users.

Nokia capitalized on the competencies and assets it developed in the European market to become as big a success in the United States as in the rest of the world, making life very difficult for Motorola. But Nokia also got way ahead of European rivals like Philips and Ericsson, later Sony Ericsson, by a relentless focus on the customer, especially the youthful customer. It was Nokia's ability to develop this focus that ultimately justified jettisoning its other businesses, no matter how profitable, and betting its future on mobile phones.

As Rich Geruson put it, "Nokia was the first to recognize the role of fashion and lifestyle in the phone business, and the first to execute on that as well. Early on, Nokia stuck a team of engineers and designers in Calabasas, Southern California, sent them to Venice Beach, and challenged them to develop phones that surfers, skateboarders, and Rollerblade users would want to have. Nokia has consistently been better than anyone else in the mobile-phone business at learning from the fashion industry, cars, movies, pop music, and other lifestyle indicators, and translating that learning into phones that are as cool and desirable and fun to use as they are reliable."

This strategy of making design and fashion the first and most important link to customers was undoubtedly the key factor in Nokia's becoming number one in the mobile-phone category. But between 2000 and 2005, Nokia forgot its own lessons, was caught flat-footed by a change in consumer tastes, and left the door open to a resurgent Motorola and two unexpected rivals, South Korea's LG and Samsung, the latter of which was then completing its transformation from a downscale electronics firm to a premier global consumer brand in its own right.

In chapter 9, we'll hear from Samsung's CMO how the company's transformation came about and the important role that innovative product design has played in it. Here let's just note that Nokia kept producing relatively bulky, single-piece mobile phones, while steadily losing market share to Samsung's and Motorola's clamshell-style phones, which flip open like *Star Trek* communicators. Not only are these phones more compact, allowing customers to incorporate them into their lifestyles more easily, but customers clearly deemed them inherently more modern and high tech than Nokia's one-piece units.

Technologically, all the manufacturers' phones at respective price points have more or less the same capabilities and cannot be distinguished in terms of features. That's why Nokia's initial design focus was such a market breakthrough. As in many other product categories, design is critical in mobile phones, because differential advantages in features are soon copied.

Although Nokia remains the leading mobile-phone manufacturer worldwide, with well over 30 percent market share, in early 2005 it had fallen back to second place in the North American market, behind Samsung, but ahead of Motorola. Its advertising around that time told a revealing story. Instead of emphasizing the design of its phones, Nokia's advertising played up their features, such as digital video capabilities, which again are indistinguishable from the features of competitors' phones.

It is a cautionary tale for any marketer that thinks it has things figured out once and for all. As I noted in the introduction and chapter 1, the new market reality is that no differential advantage can be sustained if a company loses focus on customer needs and instead makes decisions to suit company preferences. Nokia could have changed its production lines when Samsung first began taking market share. The change would have cost Nokia a lot of money, but surely less than it lost in seeing Samsung usurp its place as the design leader in consumers' eyes.

In summer 2005 Nokia finally marketed its first flip phone in North America, the Nokia 6255i. It launched this product with great fanfare not foremost in terms of its features but rather in terms of what Nokia clearly hopes will be perceived as an iconic, must-have design. And because of its size and flexible manufacturing system, Nokia can now cover the market with multiple cell-phone designs at multiple price points.

Measuring Markets and Playing Hunches

Identifying markets that matter may be based in rigorous quantitative measurements or in expert hunches. But as at auto insurer Progressive and Sony BMG Records, a hallmark of top marketing companies' ability to pick the right markets is their steady focus on understanding the customer. Whenever possible, the most effective companies measure profitability not just by brand, product line, industry, or region but customer by customer. They take each customer's market measurements as carefully as a bespoke tailor making a suit for a single client. When such precise measurement is not possible, they carefully examine all the available customer data and then extrapolate a future course based on the most relevant past experience of the market in question.

For U.S. auto insurer Progressive, as my colleagues and I learned from Dave Pratt, the company's general manager for Direct Marketing, getting a better sense of customers' varying risk profiles laid the foundation for a new business strategy. This strategy helped raise Progressive from thirteenth position to third place in market share. In the process, Progressive transformed the entire industry's pricing structure.

At number thirteen in market share, Progressive mainly served a population of relatively high-risk drivers who paid high premiums. And that's about as much as the company knew about its customers, and as much as it thought it needed to know. Then in 1989 California voters passed Proposition 103 in a referendum, mandating a 20 percent across the board cut in insurance rates.

This rate cut forced Progressive to withdraw from the California market, where it no longer had the margins necessary to serve its customer base of high-risk drivers profitably. But the huge size of the California market and the fact that it is often a bellwether for other states on automobile-related regulations and legislation meant that Progressive could not simply exit without another thought. Despite the steep cut in the rates it was allowed to charge, somehow it would have to find a way to make money in California and then reenter the market. To do that, the company felt it needed greater insight into its current and potential customers.

When Progressive analyzed its customers closely, it found that although they were all relatively high risk, they were by no means all the same size, shape, and cost to serve. In particular, Progressive discovered that although all high-risk drivers tended to get into accidents, high-risk customers with good credit ratings had fewer accidents than high-risk customers with poor credit ratings.

Securing insight into this strong relationship between customers' credit ratings and the prospective costs of servicing had two implications. First, if Progressive charged lower prices for high-risk customers with better credit ratings, the company could attract more of the lower-cost-to-serve customers. This pricing strategy could produce significant growth without reducing profit margins. Second, and more important, if this relationship held for moderate- and low-risk customers, it could be used to implement a dynamic growth strategy based on differential discount pricing.

Progressive found the credit rating/cost-to-serve relationship did hold among customers with all levels of accident risk. Progressive accordingly charged lower rates to the 70 percent of people with good credit ratings and higher rates to the 30 percent with lower credit ratings. "The year we rolled out that product design," Dave Pratt said, "we grew by a billion dollars. The hardest part of the whole thing was persuading regulators in the different states that this was a reasonable way to price auto insurance." As I noted in the introduction and chapter 1, a successful marketing initiative depends both on getting the strategy right and executing the strategy effectively.

To sustain its new growth and handle challenges from copycat competitors, including the industry's biggest players, Progressive had to acquire and execute some important new competencies, as we'll see in the next chapter. But top management knew it had a strong foundation for that effort in its new understanding of customers. It knew it wasn't just playing an idle hunch. As Dave Pratt puts it, "You've got to do the research. You can't let your intuition drive your understanding of what people want."

Car insurance has always been a number-crunching, data-based business. But in some industries, and particularly in entertainment, hard numbers can be scarce, and intuition—not idle guesswork but logical speculation and insight based on experience—may be the only guide. That is usually the case in the entertainment industries, including book publishing, motion pictures, and recorded music, where it's almost impossible to do effective numbers-based marketing, because every book, movie, and CD is a separate brand whose reception by the paying public depends on a host of difficult- and impossible-to-gauge factors. In the recorded music business, one success for nine failures is an extremely good average.

No wonder that the heroic business figures in entertainment tend to be impresarios like Clive Davis, who periodically win big and lose big. Head of BMG's Arista label during the years when Whitney Houston and other artists under contract were huge hits, Davis was replaced at Arista when BMG believed the major artists he had signed were past their sales peaks and not justifying their expensive contracts. But BMG soon found it advisable to bring Davis back into the fold with a new start-up label, J-Records, which he stocked with fresh young hit makers like Alicia Keyes, winner of nine Grammy Awards and seller of millions of CDs including *Songs in A Minor* (2001; eleven million) and *The Diary of Alicia Keys* (2003; eight million).

The rewards for guessing right can be sweet, as we learned from Stuart Rubin, Sony BMG's senior vice president for worldwide marketing. (Sony and BMG merged their record music divisions in 2004.) A New Zealand native with long music-industry experience in New Zealand, Australia, and Asia, Rubin knew the potential for this part of the world to be a market that mattered to his firm in its record business. He then battled with his U.K. counterparts to play a hunch with an Irish band that they controlled.

"I saw these five kids called Westlife perform at an awards show in Ireland before they'd even made an album. I heard their sound, I saw how good looking they were, and I just had an instinct that they would click with Asian audiences. I said to the general manager in the United Kingdom, 'Let me take this act to Asia before they go anywhere else in the world, and I think we can create a superstar.' Outside the United States, where they haven't done anything, Westlife's albums have been very successful. That's in the face of rampant piracy in all the markets—China, Japan, Thailand—where they're most popular." By 2006 Westlife had sold over forty million albums worldwide, seven of which are multiplatinum albums, and has had thirteen number one singles in Britain.

Guessing how people will respond to a particular CD, movie, or book is an inherently fuzzy game. There are as yet no surefire approaches that can help test-market the work of artists and extrapolate to the public at large. All an entertainment company can hope for, in the end, is that it picks the right markets and that its people have better hunches than the competition.

But if companies in the entertainment industries must often act in the absence of data, sometimes companies must also play hunches in the face of apparent evidence to the contrary. Sony CEO Akio Morita's insistence on launching the Walkman in the face of stiff internal resistance is legendary. And Starbucks chair Howard Schultz may also be said to have bet on a hunch when he first dreamed of a new kind of coffee shop for the United States. Both Morita's and Schultz's hunches were based on a deep appreciation of where modern lifestyles were tending. Akio Morita saw that a young population of intensive pop-music consumers would welcome the ability to listen to music anywhere and everywhere. The validity of that insight has since been confirmed by another company, Apple, with its iPod. For his part, Howard Schultz saw that modern lifestyles were leaving gaps in people's satisfaction that a new kind of coffee shop could fill with a sense of community as well as caffeine.

Starbucks' phenomenal growth has produced great reams of customer data that the company mines assiduously. But as Howard Schultz told us, "You can't always wait to see what the tea leaves say when you want to make a decision. When our domestic growth took off, we began to think about international markets and I was particularly interested in Japan. None of us had any international experience, so we hired a very expensive, blue-chip consulting firm to help us figure out what to do. They put a team to work, and eventually they came back and told us, 'We don't think Japan is a win for Starbucks. But if you insist on trying, change these five things,' which were things like our no-smoking policy that they claimed would never work in Japan because of the idiosyncracies of Japanese culture. They claimed that Japanese people would never carry a Starbucks coffee cup to sip as they walked along the street, like Americans do, and so on.

"I told them, 'I'm going to pay your bill, but I think this is the worst piece of work I've seen. You did a lot of research and you gave us a lot of facts, but you didn't give us any information.'

"We went ahead and entered the Japanese market without changing a single thing. We broke every rule the consultants warned us against breaking, and the result is that Japan is our best-performing market in the world. The reason we succeeded is that when we went to Japan we saw, correctly, that at a deeper level Japanese consumers wanted the same things from a coffee shop that American consumers wanted."

A Brand for All Seasons

At first glance the market picking of Virgin Enterprises and its well-known founder and CEO, Sir Richard Branson, seems to violate every principle of selectivity exemplified by Alcoa, ExxonMobil, and the other top marketing companies we have identified. Virgin Enterprises comprises almost fifty companies, large and small, international and local, from Virgin Atlantic, the transatlantic airline, to Virgin Brides, a Manchester-based bridal shop, and Virgin Limos, a San Francisco car service. The industries Virgin businesses inhabit include travel, air cargo, online and bricks-and-mortar retailing, financial services, mobile-telephone service, soft drinks, health clubs, gray market auto and motorcycle sales, and most recently, space travel.

For most people, this dizzying array of geographic and economic sectors, with no apparent rhyme or reason connecting them, would surely be enough to make integrated, coherent brand marketing difficult. In addition, there is an unusual ownership structure. Virgin Enterprises is not a traditional holding company with subsidiaries; rather, each Virgin company is an entirely separate business in which Virgin Enterprises may own only a small stake. Indeed, the most famous and profitable Virgin business, Virgin Records, was bought lock, stock, and barrel in 1992 for $960 million by EMI, which has complete control of its operations.

Will Whitehorn, brand development and corporate affairs director for Virgin Enterprises, told us, "You have to understand that Virgin is a brand name, not a company, and we act as owners of that brand name and invest in developing businesses which are basically branded venture capital exercises in which we have equity, relatively major or minor as the case may be, and sit on the board."

Does this mean that the businesses of Virgin Enterprises lack all coherence? Do they reflect nothing more than the whims of billionaire Branson and his management team? Not in customers' minds.

"The phenomenal thing about the Virgin brand," Will Whitehorn asserted, "is that it is one of the most focused brands and most intrinsically understood brands by the general public. It is a reputational brand, based on the reputation of Richard Branson and the companies he has been associated with, especially Virgin Records and Virgin Airways. People connect the brand with value, quality, innovation, adventure, fun, challenge, David beating Goliath, and a whole set of similar ideas." Virgin is above all "a brand of customer service and customer experience," and this "enables us to enter business segments where you wouldn't think the brand would work at all."

If we look closer at the Virgin companies to see what ties them together, it is indeed customer service and experience. As we'll explore in some detail in chapter 4, Virgin has evolved not haphazardly, but as a set of carefully chosen businesses. For Virgin, the markets that matter are those in which there is a high premium on customer service and an opportunity to leverage call center and related competencies across them.

In this regard it is interesting to note that although travel businesses, from air and train lines to vacation/holiday packages, form the most important segment of its portfolio of companies, Virgin has stayed out of the hotel business with the exception of three trophy properties, a private island in the Caribbean, a private game reserve in South Africa, and a medieval casbah in the Atlas Mountains—Kasbah Tamadot, which are rented out when Branson is not using them himself. As Will Whitehorn explained, Virgin-branded hotels would require a new set of competencies in physical plant management and the like that do not really fit with Virgin's core competencies in customer service and experience.

The Virgin brand works effectively as the organizer of the events that lead people to use the hotel, for example, Virgin Holidays selling travel/hotel/car rental packages to Disney World in Florida. Virgin buys the bed nights from the hotel owners and uses its brand to bring the various travel products together to create the experience for the customer. Virgin Mobile uses a similar model in securing access from Sprint, and then marketing the cell phones and service.

● ● ●

Alcoa, ExxonMobil, L'Oréal, GOJO, Nokia, Progressive, Sony BMG, Starbucks, and Virgin cover a broad swath of the business landscape. Yet these leading firms share a common characteristic. Each has carefully chosen markets that matter. Of course, these choices do not guarantee successful performance, but an inability to choose markets that matter almost certainly makes it very difficult to secure good performance. But choosing markets that matter is only one element in the principle of selectivity and concentration, concentrating resources against them is the other. In the next chapter we look at how leading firms concentrate resources—in particular, we focus on the necessary competencies that they develop to be successful.

FOUR

Matching Markets
with Competencies

If picking markets that matter is one side of the coin, then making sure that you have the right assets and competencies to serve customers in those markets is certainly the other. To pick markets that matter, you must ultimately develop and deliver on a value proposition that serves customers well—a value proposition that satisfies their needs, provides them with the experience and relationship that they desire with their provider, and beats competitors.

You will only be successful if you have the appropriate set of assets and competencies to execute on your value proposition. And since customers' needs and desires—and competitors' offerings—continually evolve, not only must your value proposition evolve, so also must your set of assets and competencies.

This does not mean that identifying a market that matters and realizing the needed competencies necessarily occur simultaneously. If you identify a market that matters and find that you have the required competencies, that's terrific—go for it! More likely, there will be a mismatch—the market looks great but you don't have the competencies, or you have the competencies but the market doesn't look so great.

There are obvious problems here. If the market looks great but you don't have the competencies, you have to believe that you can develop, build, or otherwise secure the necessary assets and competencies—by acquisition, joint venture, or some other method—within the required time frame and financial parameters. But beware the markets that fit well with your assets and competencies but do not look so great. The mantra of core competencies had a great run in the 1990s, but many's the firm that got into real trouble by focusing on what it did well rather than being concerned with what customers actually wanted—think mass production, the Model T, and Ford's rise and fall in the U.S. auto business in the 1920s and 1930s as General Motors, under Alfred P. Sloan, offered a variety of products like Cadillac, Buick, Oldsmobile, Pontiac, and Chevrolet to emerging market segments of car buyers. We looked at the struggles of such inward-oriented companies in chapter 1.

The additional benefit of an enlarged portfolio of competencies is that you can broaden your search for markets that look attractive. This is the way of organic growth exemplified by ServiceMaster whose long-run 20 percent compound annual growth rate over many years has been driven by careful selection of markets that matter and a continual expansion of core competencies, as it added carpet cleaning, general household and commercial cleaning, and grounds management to its original moth-proofing business.

In this chapter, we'll follow the stories of how Alcoa, ExxonMobil, L'Oréal, GOJO, and Progressive developed their competencies to keep ahead of evolving markets.

Honing Traditional Core Competencies

Alcoa's Market Sector Lead Teams put engineers and designers to work in customers' plants to keep pace with the needs of these customers. For example, when Airbus decided to build the A380, a jumbo jet bigger than Boeing's 747, Alcoa knew that composite alloys of aluminum, titanium, and other metals would be very important, particularly in areas like the wing and center wing box. The Aerospace Market Sector Lead Team worked with Airbus design engineers on Airbus's Initial Product and Technology (IPT) teams. Two and a half years ahead of the initial design requirements, Alcoa had prepared a series of alloys and finished products in the widths, lengths, gauges, and performance specs that the plane would require so that the Airbus A380 will fly with about two-thirds of its empty weight in proprietary Alcoa alloys.

Normally a company like Airbus would not want to link its IPT teams to a single supplier. They made an exception for Alcoa, according to Dick Melville, "because of our expertise in the design of specific aircraft components." An important benefit Alcoa derives from the opportunity to serve Airbus in such an intimate way is that it keeps its

core competences fresh, and enhances Alcoa's value for other customers, as well. Alcoa has successfully replicated this model in five
other market sectors besides aerospace. For example, the Automotive
Market Sector Lead Team helped innovate safer and lighter, and thus
more fuel-efficient, aluminum space frames for car bodies. Similar
teams in commercial transport, packaging, building products, and industrial products have also been successful.

These teams may put a group of Alcoa employees to work with a
customer, including a sales manager to handle day-to-day issues, an engineering applications expert, a quality-control expert, a delivery expert, and a safety expert, among others. Safety is particularly important
to Alcoa, and its "make to use" philosophy, discussed in chapter 3, emphasizes safety both for basic human reasons but also because it enhances efficiency and quality in any manufacturing process. A safe
plant or process tends to be laid out much, much more intelligently
than a non-safe one.

While Alcoa sometimes charges for safety services, more often it
helps a customer install and implement the Alcoa systems for safety
and production as part of its engagement strategy with customers that
have to change their systems in order to take full advantage of Alcoa's
capabilities.

Alcoa is not the only company to find that competencies it acquires
for operational reasons can become profitable on their own account.
Disney sells other companies the distinctive customer-service training
it gives its own employees at Disneyland and Disney World. UPS, as
we'll see in chapter 9, has grown its supply-chain expertise into a thriving consulting business. Companies like Alcoa use their competencies
to create win-win situations for themselves and customers, by closely
integrating with customers' operations. Alcoa noticed that it was taking
three weeks for the railcars carrying extrusions or sheet and plate to
Boeing in Seattle to return to its plants in the Midwest. Alcoa put a
team in to develop a new system including purpose-built, Alcoa-owned
railcars and new contracts with the railroads, resulting in a time-saving
of about 80 percent. It was taking three days and a large crew to unload
a railcar, and they were hurting people while they were doing it. It can
now be done safely in two hours with one man.

Where Alcoa competes in finished products with firms that are also
its raw materials customers, as it does in several market sectors, it works

hard to balance relationships with current customers against its own long-term prospects. Alcoa seeks to navigate these difficult waters through dialogue with customers and the creation of "Chinese walls" between those Alcoa people serving specific customers and those who are competing against them. Often the deciding factor in whether or not to compete with a customer is whether it will significantly enhance core competencies or add valuable new competencies.

"In the baseball bat business, for example," Dick Melville said, "we have been selling bat blanks to all five manufacturers—J. D. Worth, Easton, Louisville Slugger, Mizuno, and Nike. Recently we contracted to supply one of them with the finished trumpet, as it is called, putting us in competition with the finish processing of the other four companies. They cried foul when we told them what we were going to do. But I went ahead with it because it allowed us to gain additional expertise in forming the new alloys used in the bats. It also allowed us to learn what finishing costs the other four manufacturers were putting into the bat blanks we sold them, which allowed us to put the proper value on the blanks and secure an increase in price for them.

"Ultimately, the way we approach our actions in a market is that at the end of the day we want to contribute to new best practices that can help all the companies in an industry to maximize customer value in their part of the manufacturing and sales chain. That's a core marketing value for every part of our business, from mining raw materials to computer controlled alloy casting for aviation."

As we observed in chapter 3, Alcoa's decision to keep its bottling and packaging division after customers had migrated away from aluminum closures to plastic ones made sense on two counts. First its packaging expertise was valuable in its own right, contributing 15 percent to Alcoa's total revenues in 2004. Second, this competence holds potential value for Alcoa's core competence in composite materials, because an increasing number of high-tech materials include plastics as well as pure metals and metal alloys.

Learning New Tricks

ExxonMobil also continually hones its traditional core competencies and looks for new end uses for its petroleum and petrochemical products. But when it began executing its "Life on the Move" market strategy in 2000, accelerating an early move away from the old-model service station to the new-model hybrid convenience store/gas station, it took on a whole new set of competitors and had to acquire a large set of new competencies. Its success in doing so brought to life the worst nightmare of one of its new rivals, the Southland Corporation, operators of the 7-Eleven convenience-store chain.

"Early in my career in the mid-1970s," ExxonMobil's Hal Cramer recalled, "I had a meeting with some folks from 7-Eleven, and they were very forthcoming. They said, 'You know, we "own" the convenience-store business. But what keeps us awake at night is wondering if you guys in the oil companies will ever figure this business out. We have a lot of midblock locations, but you've had the best corner locations in the top metropolitan markets for years. If you ever start putting convenience stores behind your pumps, you'll give us tremendous headaches.' Well, that's stayed with me all these years because that's exactly what has happened recently. Our 'On the Run' convenience store/gas stations have been major competitors to Southland's 7-Eleven stores, and others such as Sheetz, Wawa, QuikTrip, and RaceTrac, in areas across the United States from almost the day we opened them. We're giving them all a lot of headaches."

To shift from the gas-station business to the convenience-station business and successfully battle these competitors was not an overnight affair. To implement its new concept, ExxonMobil had to add a new mix of retail personnel, systems, processes, and support structures to fully leverage its rich base of real estate assets. On the process and supply side, it strove to secure efficient third-party providers to put the right inventory on the shelves. But it didn't do so passively. ExxonMobil has been keen to learn as much as possible about category management in convenience-store retailing so it can get the best deals and promotional support from its vendors.

In Hal Cramer's words, "Sometimes we learn more from our mistakes than from our successes. People are reluctant to expose their shortcomings or failures. So the folks who run our Center of Retail Excellence, and who also work with franchisees in the field, have to find creative, nonthreatening ways of illustrating solutions to common mistakes that convenience stores and gas stations make, such as inefficient scheduling of attendants and sales personnel, or just gruff interactions with customers. We're committed to taking that extra step to make sure that the people who touch the customer reflect the brand positively. We know from the focus groups we conduct around the world that if we treat customers well, and give them fast, friendly, quality service, we can really distinguish ourselves. It's important that we take care of the people who take care of our customers."

ExxonMobil backs up its training programs for franchise operators and their senior associates with reward incentives for workers and franchisees who excel at providing good customer service. The company has also worked hard to transfer its information technology competence in supply-chain and inventory management to the convenience-store environment. "Our success depends on helping the local operators of the On the Run stores and gas stations run their business," Hal Cramer said. "That runs the gamut from coaching and counseling about staff challenges to efficient inventory control.

"The gas-station and convenience-store businesses are so transparent that ExxonMobil can never acquire a lasting edge through product differentiation alone. Technology has helped us achieve a leadership position, but eventually that can be duplicated. The focus must be on the sustainability of being the best in every aspect of the business. Being first certainly can offer an advantage—being the best in everything we do is far more important. Easy words to say; very tough to do. It takes intense, disciplined focus every single day."

The reward for staying this difficult course is in the bottom line: convenience-store sales return double-digit margins, compared with traditional margins from retail gasoline that are in the low single digits. Of course, in the past couple of years, gasoline margins have skyrocketed, because of supply disruptions, a growing world economy overall, and China's economic boom in particular, but history shows that they are likely to cycle back to a lower point. Marshaling existing competencies and developing totally new competencies for its On the Run stores will thus play an ongoing role in ExxonMobil's efforts to remain at the forefront of the energy business.

Matching Current Competencies to a New Brand Vision

Carol Hamilton's 1996 customer epiphany about the hair-color market (see pp. 69 to 70) opened the door for L'Oréal to enter a rich new market with long-term growth potential. But it took many steps before L'Oréal was ready to walk through that door and serve the customers on the other side. As Carol Hamilton said, "The insight about the market potential of younger women was great, but then you have to marry it with the technology that your chemists have or can develop, so that you can deliver colors that are prettier, gentler, and easier to use than anything that has ever been available to the consumer before. How do you do that in keeping with your total brand agenda, which always has to be bigger than any single product line, no matter how promising or profitable? That was the challenge."

To meet it, L'Oréal drew on the company's long history of R&D investment and its technological expertise in developing safe and appealing products for the body. It also drew on a wealth of market research competencies that it had used earlier in the 1990s to successfully launch the Excellence Cream hair-color line, now the number two selling hair color in the market after L'Oréal's signature hair-color brand, Preference.

In developing and launching the Féria line of hair colors for women under age thirty-five, L'Oréal cast a global research and development net. The world market in beauty products comprises, in fact, three overlapping but distinct markets: Europe/Asia, North America, and South America. Consumers in these markets have traditionally had different preferences for such product attributes as the intensity and character of scents. Accordingly, L'Oréal products on the shelf in Singapore, say, differ ever so slightly, but crucially, from identical products on the shelf in Los Angeles. Product contents, labeling, and distribution can be sensitive to continental variation, yet advertising and packaging can be integrated into a single, cost-effective global campaign.

L'Oréal was careful to make sure the Féria campaign could be integrated sensibly into the company's selective brand portfolio. Féria formed a strong triad with Preference and Excellence Cream to cover the spectrum of women's hair-color needs through their life cycles, all positioned at the premium end of the mass market. For Carol Hamilton and her colleagues, this concentration of resources is ultimately what enabled L'Oréal to take Clairol's place as the number one hair-color brand as Clairol slid from its previously lofty perch in the 1970s.

Now owned by P&G, the number of Clairol brands has decreased somewhat, but there are still over a dozen, compared with three from L'Oréal.

The lesson is not that fewer is necessarily better, but that focus is essential in the firm's chosen market and that concentration on a smaller number of brands can help. It is probably less important whether the brands and their related products and services are developed internally as part of the firm's organic growth or whether they are acquired, so long as they match the firm's chosen markets and its competencies. For example, we can track Purell's path from organic entrepreneurial development to valued acquisition in terms of the competencies necessary to create and develop the brand at several stages in its growth.

Building Competence for a New Category and a New Brand

GOJO's launching of Purell as a first-in-its-category consumer product put it on unfamiliar ground. Unlike L'Oréal, which launched Féria on a history of consumer-marketing excellence in the beauty business, GOJO could not readily transfer its industrial and institutional marketing competencies in the health-care and food-service markets to the consumer arena, and that justifiably concerned GOJO's leadership. One alternative would have been to outsource the work to market Purell, but GOJO decided to go it alone. CEO Joe Kanfer charged his team with the task of creating a Purell consumer group in-house.

GOJO had to make the case not just for its product but for an entirely new product category—waterless hand cleansers—and in effect for an entirely new activity, cleaning hands using waterless hand cleansers. The need for a waterless hand cleanser was medically compelling, but the general public did not know that. Moreover, studies showed that most people didn't practice good daily hand washing. The competencies that GOJO needed to make Purell a success included not only consumer packaging and distribution, but dealing with mass-market media, consumer advertising, and consumer public relations. GOJO would have to make itself known and trusted by retailers and retail chain distributors and suppliers, members of the media, and the end-use consumer. Another key constituency for any health re-

lated product is the medical community, but this population's knowledge of Purell and positive attitude to it were fortunately already well
established.

GOJO faced the problem that all firms face—knowing in detail
who the various influencers and decision makers are in the purchasing
situation and then addressing them appropriately. To finally make a
sale, all of the "customer ducks" have to be in line. If the Purell business was going to work, the public would have to become more frequent hand washers, and this required the interaction of many
elements. But remember that GOJO had not decided to go forward
with the product in a vacuum. The requests for a home version of the
product that GOJO received from end-use consumers in the health-
care market gave the company the first indication of a shift in public
attitude and behavior, as knowledge spread of the negative consequences of not washing hands regularly.

The process of building awareness and understanding of the new
category in general, and the Purell brand in particular, was one of trial
and error. But this process was in such clear alignment with GOJO's
strategic agenda for healthy hands and skin, and Purell was such a
clear fit with customer needs, that it never strayed too far off track.

From the beginning of the Purell campaign, GOJO sought out and
nurtured alliances with thought leaders in the medical and public
health communities, government, and industry who wanted to educate
people on the need for more frequent hand washing, to reduce the
spread of colds, flu, and other infectious diseases and the number of
sick days. The first consumer advertising for Purell concentrated on
alerting consumers to the risk of transmitting bacteria through hand
contact. The advertisements included television commercials that
built awareness that germs can be found on many things we touch like
an ATM keypad and video rentals, and that using Purell can get rid of
germs that may cause illness.

Consumer research showed that the advertising and public relations
campaigns were increasingly successful in building an enhanced
brand image. Sales also increased so GOJO increased spending. Public relations efforts featured medical and public health experts speaking about controlled outcome studies that demonstrated significant
reductions in the spread of disease in many settings: schools, colleges,

workplaces, and hospitals. GOJO even won, and publicized, an admission by a chief scientific opponent of antibacterial cleansers that Purell and its ethyl alcohol active ingredient were completely safe and healthy to use.

GOJO also successfully focused its Purell advertising on reaching moms through a radio campaign at the beginning of the school year, combined with in-store back-to-school promotions. "Research shows that the appeal of Purell is really psychographic," Sandy Katz, who headed the Purell Consumer Group, said. "It cuts across all demographic lines. We targeted moms because that's where most of the volume potential existed. Plus, moms and teachers are hand-hygiene advocates. In fact, some of our radio commercials featured the germy situations kids get into during the school day, and let mothers know that here's a really convenient way for their kids to clean their hands before they eat lunch at school or after recess, and so on.

"We followed that up with a variation for winter cold and flu season, again targeted to moms who want to keep their families healthy and cut down on sick days home from work and school. Every parent we played that to in focus groups could relate to it. Once Lisa gets sick, a few days later Johnny gets sick, then Dad gets sick and has to stay home, and then finally Mom gets sick and everything falls apart."

In addition to learning how to talk to consumers about good hygiene and Purell simultaneously through effective advertising and public relations, GOJO had to learn how to do business with a new set of players—consumer wholesalers and retailers—and a new set of rules to go with them. GOJO found that in the retail environment, manufacturers and vendors are often expected to support their products with hefty co-op advertising and promotional allowances.

"We initially paid dearly for orders and shelf space and displays," Katz recalls. "We knew we had to pay a lot of promotional allowances, slotting fees, and so on, and we did. Over time, we were able to factually demonstrate the profitability of Purell and thus reduce or eliminate the retailers' request for marketing fees."

GOJO also had to build new in-house capabilities. For fulfillment, its manufacturing people had to learn to build very complicated "pack-outs of product," or packaging assortments, for retailers all across the country, and to deliver them on time, every time. Retailers are not forgiving. If you miss one delivery date, you have a major black eye. If you miss two, you might be off the shelf. As a fledgling brand, Purell was very vulnerable. Over time and through hard work, Purell learned to satisfy its customers and get a seat at the table with the retailers.

GOJO never lost sight of the fact that the ultimate customer for Purell was not the chain-store buyer who ordered so many product stock-keeping units per month, but the consumer who actually bought and/or used the product. Ultimately, GOJO believed, Purell was an experiential product, whose long-term success depended on nothing more or less than getting enough people to try it, and believe in it.

Purell's first opportunity in the retail marketplace was when the Mustard Seed chain of health-food stores in Ohio, GOJO's home state, agreed to put up product displays. Sandy Katz recalls, "These were early displays; they contained tester bottles—open pump bottles of Purell, with hand-drawn signs saying, 'No Water, No Towels, No Germs.' From time to time someone would stand at the display and encourage shoppers to try the product.

"Once people tried it, they couldn't get over what a cool concept it was. Purell just flew off the shelves. So then we took it to Walgreens, and we did the same thing though with a more finished approach, with proper signage and so on. And again, Purell flew off the shelves. People loved it. Kids called it 'magic soap.' Not only is it effective at killing germs, it is just a very pleasant product to use, it leaves your hands and skin feeling good, as well as being good for you.

"Once Purell gained traction at Walgreens, we started going to larger trade shows. Wal-Mart came in then and began expressing interest in taking us on. Initially, Wal-Mart refused to display tester bottles. It would put Purell on its shelves but not with any testers.

"The decision makers here at GOJO had the guts to trust their instincts and say politely, 'We want Purell in Wal-Mart, but if you don't put testers up, it won't sell like it can and should. So thanks, but no thanks. We hope you'll reconsider one of these days.' Later on, Wal-Mart did reconsider, and it took Purell with tester bottles, and sales have been great ever since."

GOJO continued to hone its new consumer market competencies for Purell into the mid-2000s with such success that it attracted the attention of the pharmaceutical giant Pfizer's consumer health-care division. As noted in chapter 3, in October 2004 the two companies announced that Pfizer had bought the Purell brand, leaving GOJO the exclusive rights in perpetuity to sell it in away-from-home markets. This brought Purell together with such Pfizer over-the-counter brands as Listerine and Neosporin and positioned it well for future growth in the consumer market.

In early 2005 Pfizer began to advertise Purell on television. The upbeat commercials assured mothers that their children can have safe contacts with others at school if they use Purell. The tagline: "You can touch. Then Purell." Johnson & Johnson (J&J) has since acquired Pfizer's consumer health products, including its arrangement with GOJO, and it will be interesting to see how large a consumer brand J&J can make Purell. In fall 2006 J&J ramped up Purell's consumer advertising with prime-time TV commercials featuring the slogan, "Imagine a touchable world." In the commercials, thanks to Purell, a quintessential soccer mom magically wipes away the grit and grime of daily tasks like gassing up the minivan, seamlessly extending the brand promise and potential that GOJO first saw in the product. The 2006 U.S. congressional election season brought another indication of Purell's growth into a Kleenex-like, category-defining brand, as Purell became the germ defense of choice for politicians pressing the flesh on the campaign trail.[1] Regardless of how much bigger J&J can grow Purell, there is no question that GOJO has seen its hard-won consumer marketing competence ratified where it counts the most: in bottom-line profits both for itself and for the companies that subsequently acquired the consumer rights to Purell.

Matching and Exceeding Competitors' Competencies

When Progressive rolled out a new discount-pricing model based on its analysis of the relationship between customer credit ratings and the losses accrued, it set the stage for selling policies to customers in all risk categories. This shift in strategy drove Progressive's growth from the thirteenth- to the third-largest in the U.S. car insurance market, with 2006 revenues of $14.8 billion and a stock price that increased from around $2 in the late 1980s (allowing for stock splits) to the $20s today.

The innovative new pricing model was not enough to fuel and sustain this growth, however. Progressive knew from the start that it was vulnerable to copycat pricing by rivals, especially the market share leaders, State Farm, Allstate, and Geico.

State Farm and Allstate appealed to customers on the basis of their service offerings, rather than discount pricing. But if enough customers migrated to Progressive, these firms could draw on their vastly greater economies of scale to match or beat Progressive at its own game.

If Progressive wanted to acquire, retain, and grow a new population of medium- and low-risk customers, it would have to beat, or at least match, the top two players at their game—customer service. Unlike high-risk customers, who had limited options for securing coverage elsewhere, medium- and low-risk customers would, sooner or later, have plenty of options available from companies practicing copycat pricing. Dave Pratt, Progressive's general manager for Direct Marketing, told us, "When we sold policies primarily to high-risk drivers, we weren't necessarily the friendliest company around. We knew we had to offer lower-risk customers better service as well as a better price, and that led to our rate comparison feature and a commitment to immediate response claims service, 24/7. We knew people hated shopping for car insurance because it was such a hassle figuring out whether or not they were getting a good deal. And we knew people hated waiting for insurance companies to process their claims and thought the companies didn't pay enough when they finally finished settling them. So we tried to make all that easier."

For its part, Geico, long the discount car insurance leader, had the resources to duplicate Progressive's pricing model and, if it wished, to beef up its service offering as well.

Providing customers not only with its own rates but also with those of three competitors, often the three largest ones, might have seemed counterintuitive because in some cases a competitor's rate was lower than Progressive's. But as Dave Pratt explained, Progressive's rate comparison service built tremendous awareness and goodwill among customers.

"The rate comparison service had an inherent side benefit for us," Pratt elaborated. "Remember, we were number thirteen in the market when we introduced this service, so most customers didn't know who we were and whether they could trust us to insure them properly. When we offered to give people our rates and the rates of three other leading insurance companies, we labeled ourselves as a leading company in customers' minds."

Progressive backed up its promise that it was a good company and would do a good job through fast, friendly claims adjustment around the clock. It spent a lot of money on fleets of white SUVs with big blue Progressive logos for its claims adjusters to meet customers at their homes, offices, or the scene of an accident. It featured quality service along with its rate comparison service in advertising. Both things built awareness for the brand, and Progressive is now the fourth- best known, and third-largest, car insurance company.

"That was an expensive strategy for us at first, but it has turned out to be the most efficient, economical, and profitable way for us to sell car insurance," Katz said. Building up the claims adjustment capability was expensive for Progressive, and it did it in a tough business climate when the competition was cutting back on its customer service costs to save money. But Progressive believed it would get better accuracy for claim settlements and attract more customers with superior service. And that's what happened. As Katz said, "Basically, if you provide good service and don't piss customers off, you can quickly settle for a fair amount instead of [their] feeling mistreated and trying to gouge you because you're slow and hard to deal with. Settling claims quickly is actually less expensive, because we spend less time and effort on each claim."

Progressive has not sat on its laurels. To sustain its momentum, it has addressed one of the toughest areas—total loss coverage. As Dave Pratt told me in 2006, "Total loss claim customers have historically been our least satisfied. We pay what their car is worth, but they don't need a check—they need another car. The traditional process is particularly frustrating for people who owe more than their car is worth. Before the accident they're making monthly payments on the vehicle they need to get to work. After the accident they have no car, they still owe money to the bank, and [they] can't get to work. Rather than simply paying the claim, we're trying to solve the customer's problem. Total Loss Concierge offers to help the customer buy another car. We're building relationships with lenders and car dealers to provide preferred service for our customers. Our people act as the customer's advocate. We locate the car our customer wants, negotiate the price, and then arrange for a test drive or delivery to the customer's house."

This new service innovation is squarely in line with the philosophy enunciated by Progressive's founder and CEO, Peter Lewis. When Progressive initially withdrew from the California market, as Dave Pratt told me, "Peter insisted that we evaluate everything we do from the customer's point of view. This 'do what's best for the customer' is driving Total Loss Concierge, just as it has driven all of our other innovations."

• • •

Concentrating resources is one thing; making sure those resources are the appropriate ones for the markets that matter to a firm is quite another. We are not just talking about competencies in general, we are talking about the specific competencies that lead to satisfied and delighted customers. Essential competencies may lie in product and process technology, business or consumer sales, distribution, advertising, packaging, design, human resources, or elsewhere—based on a very focused customer view.

Progressive grew exponentially in market share, including becoming a leading insurer in California on its eventual return to that bellwether market, by linking several key competencies, some of which we'll explore further in later chapters: mathematics-based R&D to innovate new pricing schemes, customer-friendly claims service, industry-leading ease of purchase and support on the Internet, and communications (including advertising) that furthered a new brand identity as the company that gave its competitor's quotes, even if they were lower, and that sent its claims agents to customers in distinctive white SUVs.

Likewise, Alcoa, ExxonMobil, L'Oréal, and other top companies have grown and prospered by matching an evolving set of competencies to profitable markets. Their successes indicate two mistakes that you must avoid. The first mistake is picking markets that matter that require competencies you do not have or cannot acquire. The second mistake is investing in competencies that do not match with a market that matters. As you look back at your own company in recent years, you can easily develop three columns:

1. Markets that matter that your firm *matched* with good competencies;

2. Markets that matter that your firm *did not match* with competencies;

3. Competencies that your firm possesses but that it *did not match* with markets that matter.

See where you have invested over the past few years. I hope you have many entries in column 1. But look at columns 2 and 3 and ask yourself how these came about, and what you can do in the future to avoid wasting resources.

You must achieve clarity in these matters by being customer focused, and by making decisions about what markets to do business in, and what competencies to retain or acquire, based on customer needs rather than company preferences. In the next two chapters, we'll see how to identify market segments in which you can secure the greatest differential advantages against competitors.

Select Segments to Dominate

FIVE

Segmenting to Find the Sweet Spots in a Market that Matters

In one sense, segmenting markets and targeting specific segments is rather like picking markets that matter but with greater analysis and insight into the market, customers, and competitors. What specifically joins these two imperatives is that in both cases you must practice the principle of selectivity and concentration—place your bets and concentrate your efforts. However, selecting segments you can dominate requires a deeper understanding of who the customers are, their specific needs, and how they can be served profitably, than picking markets does.

Marketing Mavens know that you must do a thorough job of segmenting markets that matter. You must decompose each market into several segments. In each segment, customers have roughly similar need profiles, but these need profiles differ from segment to segment. Then you must select the best segments for you, the sweet spots in the market where you can deliver superior customer value and secure differential advantage. Of course, you may identify more than one sweet spot, and your sweet spots may be quite different from your competitors' sweet spots. After all, Toyota does a great job with both the Camry and the Lexus, but these products address two very different segments each with very different need profiles. BMW is the leading player in yet another segment of the automobile market. By insightful segmenting and targeting, you can set the stage both for serving customers well and minimizing the impact of competition.

Segmentation must be ongoing, since markets, technologies, competitors, and customer needs never stop evolving. The top marketing companies pay constant attention to the evolution and emergence of market segments.

Where Customers Are, Where They Are Going

In 1993 Mobil looked at its core retail gasoline business and saw a very challenging future, a prescient vision given the ups and downs of the energy industry since then. Slowly but surely, the power of the great oil brands—Amoco, Arco, BP, Chevron, Conoco, Elf, Exxon, Mobil, Phillips, Shell, Texaco, and Total—was beginning to fade. Many factors were driving this trend. But in a nutshell the oil business was fiercely competitive, with global oversupply and low-entry barriers at the retail gasoline level. These market conditions led to increasing price pressure, brutal gasoline "price wars," and declining profitability.[1] In addition to traditional rivals, Mobil also faced a host of new competitors in the early 1990s. Among the most alarming were big-box retail stores and hypermarkets that were using low-priced gasoline to drive increased traffic to their retail backcourts. Competing on price is nothing new and some firms, such as Dell in personal computers and Southwest Airlines, JetBlue, Ryanair, and easyJet in airlines, have thrived with a low-price strategy. But success with low prices only occurs if one critical condition is fulfilled: you must be the low-cost producer. Mobil was not the low-cost gasoline producer, and senior management believed that a future of decreasing profit margins could spell long-run decline for the company.

Hoping to find a profitable way to meet these market challenges, Mobil conducted a groundbreaking segmentation study, researching the perceptions, behavior, and demographics of more than fourteen hundred U.S. consumers. The study revealed that consumers did not perceive any of the oil companies as being truly customer focused, targeting distinct customer segments, or offering unique positioning.

Equally important, Mobil's study identified five distinct customer segments:

- Road Warriors (generally higher-income, middle-aged men, heavy drivers) accounted for 16 percent of the population.

- True Blues (moderate- to high-income drivers, brand loyal, and sometimes gas station loyal) accounted for 16 percent of the population.

- Generation F3 (Fast, Food, Fuel) (upwardly mobile young men and women, constantly on the go) accounted for 27 percent of the population—historically Mobil's target customers.

- The Price Driven accounted for 20 percent of the population.

- Homebodies (usually housewives shuttling children around during the day) accounted for the remaining 21 percent of the population.

Analyzing its data closely, Mobil saw that the first three segments in effect formed a megagroup of customers with shared priorities and behaviors. Road Warriors, True Blues, and Generation F3 represented 59 percent of the population but 86 percent of Mobil's potential profitability.

Whereas the Price Driven and Homebodies both rated low price as a top need, Road Warriors, True Blues, and Generation F3 all rated their top needs in the areas of speed and convenience. If these needs were met and they got their money's worth, they would happily pay another penny or two per gallon of gas. As the retail gasoline business comprises many competitors all chasing very few cents per gallon of profit, this provided a clear incentive. With the billions of gallons pumped into consumers' cars each year, it promised significant additional profitability. Overall revenue is high but so are the costs of doing business. It was clear that Mobil would need to do everything very well for these customers to get a very small profit per customer. Every extra gallon pumped and every extra penny per gallon received would be key to its success. Mobil decided to target these three segments.

Most important, the Road Warriors and Generation F3 segments clearly represented the future of the retail gasoline market in North America, as urban sprawl and related social and lifestyle trends continued to increase time pressure in drivers' lives.

After conferring with its franchisees, Mobil launched the "Friendly Serve" program to offer customers in the three targeted market segments increased friendliness, cleanliness, safety, and speed. Central to "Friendly Serve" was Speedpass, which, as we saw in chapter 3, allows customers to pay at the pump and the convenience store simply by waving a small key chain wand linked to a credit card. In the two-year period following the "Friendly Serve" launch, Mobil's retail gasoline and convenience store sales increased significantly in focus markets, and Copernicus, the research firm that conducted the segmentation study, found that positive consumer perceptions of Mobil also rose markedly. Eventually, Mobil surpassed Shell as the preferred gas station for the most profitable consumers.

The market forces that triggered Mobil's 1993 segmentation study gathered momentum throughout the 1990s, putting pressure on even the largest oil companies to pursue even greater economies of scale. As we saw in chapters 3 and 4, ExxonMobil extended Mobil's 1993 segmentation scheme to encompass the profound shift in customer needs from car service to driver service. By adapting quickly to this change with its On the Run convenience stores, ExxonMobil seized and has sustained a differential advantage, keeping it, as Hal Cramer, Exxon-Mobil's president of fuels marketing, likes to say, "at the forefront of competition."

In 2006, nine years after Speedpass's introduction at Mobil stations and ten years after Mobil's launch of On the Run, its two largest rivals, BP and Shell, were still playing catch up in the race to win customers with convenience stores. BP is only just beginning to gain traction with an emphasis on redesigned gas stations with convenience stores behind the pumps.

Shell lagged even farther behind: in 2006 it still lacked a convenience–store brand focus and backcourt brand like On the Run. Shell was devoting major resources to redesigning its existing base of nine thousand Shell stations in the United States, and rebranding thirteen thousand Texaco stations as Shell stations. (Shell bought the stations from Texaco when ChevronTexaco sold them to gain regulatory approval for their merger.) Over the same period, Shell muddled through an embarrassing episode of having to restate its oil reserves, and the financials based on them, after it was discovered that company management was routinely inflating those reserves to bolster the company's stock.

Meanwhile, ExxonMobil has made On the Run and Speedpass a more central part of its advertising. In fall 2006 it reaffirmed its commitment to the strategy of serving drivers rather than servicing cars, and freshened its presentation to the public, in a new television commercial campaign. The commercials gave more time to customers using Speedpass when shopping in On the Run stores than filling up at the pump. And in emphasizing, "We're drivers too," they seamlessly built on the findings of Mobil's pioneering market segmentation.

From 1993 to 2006 ExxonMobil saw three segmentation principles validated in the marketplace. First, in most cases, the simpler the segmentation scheme the better. Simpler segmentation tends to be more robust, flexible, and cost effective over the long term. "With the low margins in the gasoline business," Hal Cramer says, "differentiating ten or twenty different segments of customers is a losing proposition. It's not that you can't define that many distinct customer segments, but you can't afford to keep differentiating ten or twenty different levels of service for them. So what we do is segment into a few simple categories that capture most of the customers' desires, and that helps us to better focus our offer and drive cost out of the business."

Second, segmentation should always reveal both where customers are now, and where they are going. In this regard, ExxonMobil is betting that its "Life on the Move" philosophy will not only epitomize more and more customer needs in the United States every year, but in the rest of the world as well. ExxonMobil is looking to On the Run to become a global brand and destination of its own, so it can put the same face before the customer in Cairo, Illinois, U.S.A., and Cairo, Egypt.

Third, segmentation analysis and strategy must be updated regularly. ExxonMobil ensures that its On the Run strategy remains relevant through an ongoing, worldwide program of customer focus groups. It has found that the customers it wants to reach around the world really want the same things in convenience, service, and value.

• • •

Just as ExxonMobil learned where the majority of gasoline customers were going, and bypassed the competition by focusing on three key customer segments, Nokia diligently segmented its markets to identify and serve customers who were pointing the way toward the future of the global cell-phone market. This brought the company enormous success. But along the way it has had to learn—and relearn—that segmentation must be an ongoing process. A great success can be threatened if a company takes its eye off the ball, and forgets to keep segmenting its markets, targeting the profitable market segments, and delivering value to the customers in those segments.

As we saw in chapter 3, Nokia and other European digital phone manufacturers had an advantage over U.S. manufacturers in the 1990s because Europe's early adoption of a single digital telephony standard accelerated market growth. But even in comparison to European rivals like Ericsson, Nokia seized an early lead that it progressively widened by targeting the youth segment with fashion and lifestyle-relevant features. Nokia recognized that young people's need to stay in constant contact with their friends would make them the most enthusiastic adopters of mobile phones, and that they would care more than other early users about how the phones looked and the neat things they could do. The company anticipated that as the digital phone market matured, other customer segments would adopt the habits and preferences of the youth segment. And so they did, with European business users quick to discover the usefulness of short text messaging.

One of Nokia's early steps in executing its youth-first strategy was to establish a design studio in Southern California to track the trendsetting lifestyles and gadget use in its multicultural population of skateboarders and in-line skaters.

Nokia not only led competition in serving the youth segment, it also demonstrated a keener sense of how other customer segments do, and do not, resemble the youth segment, matching heterogeneous products to heterogeneous market segments. It was not a strictly linear, price-value/good-better-best issue but one of different segments— youth, the Hispanic segment, one that wants security, another that wants convenience, the corporate-workhorse/power-user segment, and so on. The youth segment helps set patterns for the others, but they remain distinct segments in many ways.

When Nokia was ready to make a big push in the North American market, its subtler sense of customer needs enabled it to produce more targeted advertising and promotion than the competition, selling features and performance of Nokia digital phones to separate customer segments, not just trying to convince consumers to go digital.

To a far greater degree than in Europe, mobile-phone marketing in the United States has been complicated by the fact that end users in the different market segments generally do not buy their phones at full price directly from Nokia or rival manufacturers. Rather, they secure them at hefty discounts through calling plans offered by Nokia's trade customers, such as at&t (until 2005, when it sold its mobile-phone business to Verizon), Cingular (eventually to be rebranded as part of the new at&t), T-Mobile, Verizon, and Virgin. Indeed, Nokia's five largest trade customers represented 80 percent of its business in the United States in the early 2000s.

Rich Geruson, formerly senior vice president for Nokia USA, told us, "That's one reason why we have to understand the full customer life cycle, rather than just the average three-year working life of one of our phones. As the market has matured, sales of bundled phones and calling plans have increasingly been not to first-time buyers, but to second-, third-, and fourth-time buyers. That puts a tremendous emphasis on customer retention and customer loyalty.

"We have extensive segmentation models to track consumer habits and preferences, and the mobile-phone service providers have their models. We share selected data."

But there is an inevitable tension between wanting customers to do their talking and messaging and Web surfing on your airtime, no matter whose phone they buy, and wanting customers to do these things on your phones, no matter whose airtime they buy. For that reason, Geruson said, "I segmented my marketing operation in two: the partnering side and the pure branding side. The job of the partnering side was to help build Nokia's business through the trade customers' thousands of sales outlets. The job of the pure branding side was to reduce the power of the trade customer over the end user and increase our power. We wanted to create an end-user brand identity and end-user demand pull that increased our influence over end users and our bargaining power with trade customers.

"With successes like positioning a red, white, and blue Nokia phone at the center of at&t's 'One Touch' campaign, we became gurus, to the trade customers, on how to market digital phones to end users. At the same time, we leveraged the trade customers' advertising and promotion campaigns, putting Nokia at the center of end-users' perceptions."

Nokia's fashion- and feature-forward youth focus, and its adroit handling of the different needs of trade customers and end users, paid off handsomely. From 1991 to 2001 Nokia's global market share went from 13 percent to 37 percent. To retain its leadership position, Nokia knew it would continue to need sophisticated segmentation analysis and execution. It established a website, Club Nokia, designed to keep the company in step with customers, especially the youth segment that is the testing ground for other important market segments. It continuously updated the capabilities of its phones, offering wireless Internet-ready products with digital photo, video, and music features. And it plied its trade-customer marketing to keep Nokia phones part of the calling-plan/mobile-phone bundles that consumers bought from the wireless phone companies.

Unfortunately for Nokia, it could not maintain its leadership position unchallenged. Having outdesigned the competition, Nokia seemed to think that it no longer needed to hone its fashion edge. It missed, or badly underestimated, customers' preference for so-called clamshell-style phones that flip open to use. While Nokia was keeping its production lines churning out bulkier single-piece phones, Samsung was completing a transformation it had initiated in the late 1980s. We'll explore the Samsung story in greater detail in chapter 9. For now, suffice it to say that by the late 1990s, although Nokia and much of the business community at large missed it, Samsung had transformed itself into a first-rank, increasingly upscale global consumer brand of its own.

There are four important selectivity and concentration issues to this transformation. First, Samsung made an early decision to focus not only on consumer electronics as the key market that mattered to its future but instead on the digital products area in particular. Second, it emphasized design, making heavy investments in lifestyle-relevant research and development and initiating an all-out, increasingly successful effort to win the most prestigious design awards. Third, it focused significant resources on the mobile-phone market, seeing it as one of the key arenas for building consumer awareness of the new Samsung and its new digital, hiply designed products. Fourth, in the United States, it had the courage to end its profitable relationships with Wal-Mart and Kmart, so that it could take the new products upmarket at Best Buy and Circuit City. To readers outside of retail, turning one's back on Wal-Mart may seem self-defeating, and the distinction between Wal-Mart and Kmart, on the one hand, and Best Buy and Circuit City, on the other, may appear to be slight. In fact, customer populations in the two sets of stores are quite different, and placing its products in front of those customers it most desired was a key part of Samsung's successful transformation of its brand identity. Chapter 9 explores this issue in detail, in the perhaps surprising context of performance measurement.

In the mobile-phone market, Samsung's line of clamshell, flip-open phones, backed up by global advertising that emphasized the overall Samsung brand more than individual products, as well as by targeted marketing to the mobile-phone service providers, soon began eroding Nokia's market share. In early 2005, as I noted in chapter 4, Nokia was in second place in the North American market, behind Samsung but ahead of Motorola.

Over the same time frame, the mobile phone market as a whole grew enormously to 244 million units in 2005—and Nokia remained a powerful force with 84 million sold for a global market share of well over 30 percent. But its profits had thinned, and it faced the major challenge of recommitting itself to the disciplined, insightful segmentation—the keen selection of market-segment targets and the rigorous concentration of resources on customer needs—that had guided its transformation from a forest products, rubber, and cable company into the leading mobile phone manufacturer.

•   •   •

Whereas Nokia and Samsung decided to focus on the young customer segment as the bellwether of mass-market trends as a whole, Charles Schwab became a major player in the consumer financial-services industry by marching firmly in step with one demographic cohort of customers, the baby boomers, as they moved from young adulthood through middle age and on toward retirement.

From its founding in 1975, Schwab has concentrated its resources on delivering life-stage appropriate financial services to baby boomers. As Schwab executive vice president Jack Calhoun put it, "If you want to know where the next profitable client base is going to be, you just watch that pig moving through the python."

Schwab had its origins in a 1974 ruling by the U.S. Securities and Exchange Commission, which mandated a thirteen-month trial period for deregulation of certain brokerage transactions. Many established brokerage companies took that as a license to increase their fees. But Charles R. "Chuck" Schwab, formerly the publisher of a successful investment newsletter, seized the opportunity to create the first dis-count brokerage. Chuck Schwab bet that twenty- to thirty-something-year-old baby boomers would embrace the chance to get into investing without the high fees their parents paid to Merrill Lynch and the other long-established brokerage houses. He won that bet and took his grow-ing company on a long winning streak.

Taking good care of baby boomers proved to be a winning strategy for Schwab through three customer revolutions in the financial ser-vices business. "Revolution 1," Jack Calhoun told us, "was the cus-tomers' revolt against high brokers' fees and the beginning of a mass market of middle-class investors. Chuck Schwab helped trigger that revolution when he founded Schwab expressly as a discount brokerage. That brought more middle-class people into investing, and it brought in copycat discounters, which in turn enlarged the customer pool. By backing discount pricing up with great service, we won the battle for self-directed, price-conscious investors. Then we improved our posi-tion even more through Revolution 2, the explosive growth of mutual fund investing from the 1980s on, and Revolution 3, the arrival of on-line brokerages in the 1990s."

When we spoke to Jack Calhoun in New York, Schwab was in the thick of a battle to win Revolution 4 on a consumer landscape trans-formed on the one hand by discounting and online trading, and on the other by the collapse of the dot-com bubble and an era of corporate scandal that began with Enron and by 2005 had tainted both the mu-tual fund and insurance industries.

Schwab has been untouched by these scandals—it does not have an investment-banking arm, many of its mutual funds are indexed, and its actively managed funds are driven by Schwab's numbers-driven Schwab Equity Ratings. Schwab's advertising sensibly offered cus-tomers "advice not driven by commission" and branded "Schwab Equity Ratings: Get a clear perspective."

This was undoubtedly thinking of customers' needs in an appropri-ate way. But Schwab could not gain traction with its "advice not driven by commission" and "Schwab Equity Ratings" campaign, now aban-doned like several others of the early to mid-2000s, because it seemed to bungle the task of customer segmentation. Crucially, Schwab did not deselect the wrong market segments—the ones that it could not really serve profitably. The result was that Schwab dissipated its equity in its core discount market segment and squandered resources in market segments that were not a good fit for the brand.

Schwab's strategy seemed to be a good one. Quite a few of Schwab's baby-boomer customers had become high-net-worth individuals who needed, and were willing to pay, for more than discount service. Figuring that it could migrate with these customers, in 2000 Schwab bought U.S. Trust for its pedigree of profitable wealth management. Seeing that a number of discount customers were attracted by the ease, and even lower discounts, of online trading, Schwab also spent heavily to acquire Cybertrader. But it did not intend to be the low-cost provider. Instead Schwab was positioning itself between the lowest-cost discounters and Merrill Lynch. Based on the demographics, as we learned from Jack Calhoun, Schwab expected that as more and more of its middle-class baby-boomer customers approached retirement, they would be affluent enough to need, and willing to pay for, more than discount service.

"That's where the growth of the business is coming over the next ten years," Jack Calhoun said. "You can't keep squeezing healthy margins out of discounting once the increase in your customer volume begins to level off. The next big opportunity is providing advice to more affluent baby boomers. But it's got to be a different kind of advice. We've got to show customers that we're not just about do-it-yourself investing now. But we've also got to show that we don't do it for you, or to you, like the full commission brokers with their conflicts of interest have been doing."

To align its expanded offerings with customer need, Schwab grouped customers into three behavioral segments: Do It Yourselfers, who want to make all their decisions entirely on their own; Do It Yourselfers/Validators, who want to check their decisions against expert advice; and Delegators, who want to hand investment and management work off to someone they can trust to do things properly. Although each group comprises investors of varied asset levels, Delegators tend to be much more affluent than Do It Yourselfers. Schwab looked at the numbers of aging baby boomers and their substantial assets, even allowing for the dot-com bubble's bursting, and dreamed of acquiring more and more Delegators as customers.

Schwab accordingly also grouped its most profitable customers into three segments by wealth: Schwab Private Clients, customers who have assets from $500,000 to $1 million; Investment Adviser Clients, customers who work with independent financial planners and have assets of $1 million to $5 million, representing "30 to 40 percent of [Schwab's] business"; and U.S. Trust Clients, customers who have assets of $5 million to $50 million.

Schwab views itself as the most trusted discount and online broker, and its goal is to become the most trusted firm in all financial services. It sought to get there by offering "full brokerage," while continuing to charge less than full commission. As Schwab saw it, it would earn its spurs with baby boomers, and when Generations X, Y, and Z needed more choice and service, it would be ready for them also.

In hindsight we can appreciate why this apparently brilliant, logical strategy failed. In trying to serve additional market segments beyond its discounting core, Schwab opened itself up to countermarketing from more aggressive discounters, especially T. D. Waterhouse and Ameritrade, which later merged, and E*Trade. T. D. Waterhouse advertised itself as "the alternative to Schwab and higher-priced brokers like Merrill Lynch," effectively realigning Schwab as a high price, rather than discount, broker. And whereas Schwab charged online traders fees according to how active they were or how big their accounts were, Ameritrade, E*Trade, and T. D. Waterhouse offered one low price per trade to everyone. Meanwhile, Schwab was struggling to attract high-net-worth individuals and grow its asset management business in a way that justified the expensive acquisition of U.S. Trust.

At the height of the bull market that ended with the bursting of the dot-com bubble, Schwab briefly edged higher in market value than Merrill Lynch, $25.5 billion to $25.4 billion. In July 2004 Merrill Lynch's market capitalization was $47 billion, and Schwab's had shrunk to $12 billion. That month, Schwab CEO David Pottruck left, and Chuck Schwab, then serving only as chairman, again became CEO at the company he founded. Schwab continued to "bleed customers," losing forty-four thousand accounts in the second quarter of 2004, and saw online trading volume drop from 215,000 a day in January to 127,000 a day in June. Within the financial-services world, tongues wagged about Schwab's failed effort to leave "the average Joe" behind for "Joe millionaire."[2]

In the following months, Schwab moved to reassert its identity as a discount brokerage house. Chuck Schwab became the company's chief spokesman and the centerpiece of its advertising, as he had been in some of its best growth periods. "Since I founded this company, it has been my goal to lower the cost of investing. Great service at a great price," as a glossy image on the Schwab website put it. Schwab followed up this effort with a broadscale "Talk to Chuck" campaign that emphasized investment advice and a fair price for transactions

In the past couple of years, Schwab's stock price has inched upward from the single digits, and with over $1 trillion in assets under management, Schwab has the resources to renew itself. The irony is that Schwab's starting point for its segmentation was correct. If it had truly kept its efforts focused on the most affluent baby boomers, following "the pig moving through the python," and resisted the temptation to buy U.S. Trust and compete for high-net-worth customers with assets over $5 million, it might not have stumbled so badly. There are indeed a great many increasingly affluent baby boomers who need more than bare-bones discount service as they approach retirement. Remember that Schwab's segmentation included Investment Adviser Clients, those customers with assets of $1 million to $5 million who represented a significant 30–40 percent portion of Schwab's business.

In terms of the segmentation process, Schwab segmented accurately but failed to target selectively and could not deliver sufficient value to customers in the many segments it tried to serve. In trying to serve too many segments, Schwab seemed to get stuck in the middle between its discount brokerage and full-commission competitors. As we saw with Nokia, segmenting markets, targeting the most profitable segments, and delivering value to the customers in those segments is an iterative process. A company has to keep doing it right to stay at the top.

Strengthening Position in the Core Segment and Adding Additional Segments

The recent experiences of Nokia and Schwab show how critical it is for companies to maintain a rigorous clarity in segmenting markets, targeting appropriate segments, and delivering value to customers. Few enterprises have dominated their core market segments so completely as the *Wall Street Journal*, flagship publication of Dow Jones & Company, has since its founding in 1889. The business world's premier

newspaper of record, the *Wall Street Journal* is corporate America's
most trusted news source and favorite advertising medium. When we
spoke to Celia Currin, the *Wall Street Journal's* director of marketing
communications, the *Journal* boasted an enviable track record in jour-
nalism and customer satisfaction, commanding top prices for its ad
space, with "an 80 percent renewal rate among the readers that corporate America most wants to reach." Though the *Journal* was expensive, the perception among advertisers was that it delivered a lot for
the money.

In the 1990s, however, Currin told us, "We began to see signs that
we were becoming 'my father's Oldsmobile' to younger generations of
businesspeople." The problem, the *Journal's* editorial and publishing
leadership concluded, was not the paper's dense content. In many
ways, content was an inescapable part of its mission as Wall Street's
newspaper of record. And the *Journal* was justifiably proud of its read-
ability and relevance. For example, from 1991 to 2004 the *Journal* won
sixteen Pulitzer Prizes for investigative reporting, general news reporting, and feature writing.

The problem, focus groups and other customer research showed,
was primarily one of style. "Our awareness levels were off the chart,"
Celia Currin said. "Everybody knew who we were. To be more precise,
everybody thought they knew who we were. A good many people pi-
geonholed us and wouldn't give us a second look. Younger businesspeople, especially, had grown up seeing the *Journal* on dad's desk at
home or on the newsstand or in the boss's office, and because they'd
never seen the look of the paper change, they assumed it was still only
for people older and stodgier than they were.

"For so many people the sticking point was simply the front page,
which they found intimidating. Maybe that shouldn't have surprised
us, because the *Journal's* front-page layout and typography hadn't been
changed since 1941. So we looked in the mirror, and we decided to
spruce ourselves up."

Another motivating factor for an overhaul was that the *Financial
Times* (*FT*), long as dominant in Great Britain as the *Journal* was in the
United States, was making inroads in the U.S. market thanks to an ag-
gressive push from its owner, Pearson. The *FT's* distinctive pink pages
were showing up on many more U.S. newsstands and in many more
U.S. offices.

On April 9, 2002, the *Wall Street Journal* was delivered to most subscribers' homes and offices around the country by 6 a.m., as usual. What wasn't usual was the paper's friendlier-looking, less-crowded front page, the addition of color, and other features designed to help readers move through the paper more quickly and easily.

"We think our major competitor is time, not *Time!*" Currin said. "Our readers are busy people, and there are a lot more places where they can get information now. The quicker we can get you through the paper, the more likely you are to keep reading and subscribing. When you're looking at a subscription renewal form, there is nothing quite as disconcerting as ten unread issues piled up in a corner."

The design changes gave new prominence to the *Wall Street Journal*'s culture and lifestyles coverage. "It wasn't a question of changing the content, but of saying to readers, 'This part of the paper is worth your time. It's up to the minute, it's relevant to you. We're proud of it, and we're not going to be so shy about calling your attention to it.'

"There is an old expression in marketing, 'Will your customers give you permission to do that?' We didn't know if our credibility in business news was going to carry over to the lifestyle and culture piece. But it very fortunately did."

As its redesign gained traction among younger businesspeople, and avoided alienating older readers, the *Journal* also added new content. "For example, it became obvious that our readers could use more personal finance coverage," Celia Currin said. To help readers keep pace with the ongoing consumer product revolution in computers, cameras, electronics, mobile phones, PDAs [personal digital assistants], and the like, a column on "personal technology" also found a regular place in the *Journal.* Finally, the paper introduced successful new weekend-, leisure-, and real estate–focused sections.

In line with these changes, the *Wall Street Journal* reframed its mission as reporting not just business, but "business and the business of life." The paper has taken a number of steps to ensure that its enhanced content reaches business news readers of different ages and localities in appropriate ways. For example, an online version of the paper is available at WSJ.com by additional paid subscription, whereas almost every other newspaper's website can be visited for free.

Currin sees the subscription fee for WSJ.com as creating a sense of value for readers or advertisers. It does, however, provide free access to several specialized sites to attract advertisers: CareerJournal.com for job advertisers and job seekers who are past the Monster.com level; CollegeJournal.com for entry-level jobs and freshly minted BAs and MBAs; OpinionJournal.com, which contains the *Journal's* editorial and opinion pages; RealEstateJournal.com, which contains real estate information and property for sale listings; StartupJournal.com, which offers tools for entrepreneurs plus businesses for sale; and Market Watch.com, which provides real-time financial and market indicators with brief news capsules.

Unlike the other five sites, OpinionJournal.com lacks a natural advertising constituency to make it a profitable concern. But it serves as very cost-effective public relations for the *Journal's* editorials and columnists.

As most news media brands continued to maintain that free, advertiser-supported websites were a better model than subscription-based websites, some in the media business questioned the profitability of the *Wall Street Journal's* main website. But the *New York Times* eventually followed suit, at least in part, by creating a subscription-access tier of columns it calls Times Select. With over seven hundred thousand subscribers, WSJ.com remains by far the largest paid subscription news website.

Not content with its dominant position in the United States, the *Journal* has moved abroad to address a variety of international market segments. The *Wall Street Journal Asia* is the dominant financial newspaper in Asia, especially along the Pacific Rim of Singapore, China, Japan, and Korea. And the *Journal* produces a successful Spanish-language insert, the *Wall Street Journal Americas,* for eighteen leading newspapers in Central and South America on a shared advertising revenue basis. Following the same model, the *Journal* produces an insert for distribution in the United States, the *Wall Street Journal Sunday,* for over eighty small- to medium-size Sunday newspapers around the United States. "The inserts not only generate a substantial stream of additional advertising revenue," Celia Currin said. "They also seed our future subscription base. They get us in front of people who are not familiar with us, or who think we're not relevant to them, and they get them comfortable reading us."

In making these design and content changes, the *Wall Street Journal* benefited enormously from advertising by technology companies, but its ability to deliver value to the most profitable customers in its target market segments was seriously challenged by the bursting of the technology stock bubble. The many technology companies that went out of business used to advertise heavily in the *Journal* to get themselves in front of investors' eyeballs. In their absence the *Journal*'s advertising revenues suffered a precipitous decline.[3] To reverse the decline, the *Journal* is trusting to its segmentation strategy of offering news on "business and the business of life" to corporate America. In June 2005 it announced that starting in September subscribers would receive the *Wall Street Journal Weekend Edition* on Saturdays for no extra charge.

Naysayers opined that the *Journal* would not be relevant on weekends. But in August 2006, *Advertising Age* reported that *Weekend Edition* produced over $20 million in advertising revenue for the first half of the company's fiscal year and was on track to be profitable in two more years.[4] It remains to be seen how successfully the *Journal* can extend its brand to the nonbusiness day, but it has already attracted important advertisers, such as The Home Depot that had little presence in its weekday editions. Regardless, the *Wall Street Journal*'s efforts will continue to depend on doing a good job of segmenting its markets, targeting the most profitable segments, and delivering value to customers in those segments.

• • •

The *Wall Street Journal*'s ups and downs show how winning formulas must regularly be adapted to the changing circumstances of evolving market conditions, customer needs, and competitor actions, so as to solidify and maintain the position of your business in its core target segment. Nestlé Prepared Foods (NPF) makes this adaptation one of its critical recipes for success by continually tracking the evolution of customer needs in its target segments as well as investing in new segmentation studies to gain even deeper customer insight. These insights lead to revised positioning and product offerings, such as Lean Cuisine's evolution in step with the public's understanding that good food equals good health. Underneath that are two big trends that have an inverse relationship to each other. As the prevalence of culinary skills in the population decreases, the desire for high-quality prepared food increases. The less able people are to prepare good food for themselves, the more they need NPF to do it for them.

"There is no escaping the fact that more and more households are being formed now by people who grew up in homes where there was little cooking" says NPF's Stephen Cunliffe. Today, in a great many dual-income households, cooking is something people only have time to do vicariously by watching the Food Channel.

When Nestlé launched Lean Cuisine in the 1980s, product positioning was centered around calorie control. In the 1990s, the focus shifted slightly to low fat and low sodium. "In the 2000s we are overlaying great [taste] onto low fat and low sodium, giving Lean Cuisine a more general well-being positioning of 'tastes good and good for you.' The competition has different positioning. Weight Watchers' products remain positioned around weight control, and Healthy Choice has adopted a sports/fitness positioning."

A significant new segment that Nestlé has recently identified comprises the increasing number of consumers who are willing to serve frozen foods to the entire family. The greater acceptability to consumers of high-quality frozen foods has made "multiserve products that hold enough to feed more than one person a great axis of growth." For Cunliffe and his colleagues at NFP, there is no question but that "our understanding of customer segments has enabled us to be by far the major player in multiserve."

• • •

Despite some mid-2000s mishaps, computer maker Dell is a force to be reckoned with in eight major market segments of the computer business: consumer, small business, medium-size business, large business, global business, government, education, and health care. Its revenues of $55.9 billion in 2005 made it number one in both the United States and in global computer markets as a whole.

Such broad market dominance makes it easy to forget how young a company Dell is and to gloss over the fact that it has built its success step by step, market segment by market segment.

When Michael Dell founded his company as a college student in 1984, he had $1,000 and a conviction that the computer industry was ready for a direct marketing and manufacturing operation that would drive out cost by custom configuring every machine and eliminating retailers from the sales chain. To win big on this low-cost basis, as he intended to do right from the start, Dell knew his company needed two things:

1. Important product sectors developing around universally accepted industry standards, rather than product areas tangled in conflicts between rival proprietary platforms. Without such standards, it would be impossible to build high-value products at low cost.

2. Groups of customers who were not first-time buyers, but potential second- and third-time buyers. Without computer-savvy customers who could be sold and served efficiently on a direct basis, Dell would suffocate with sales and customer service expenses and/or have to share gross margin with retailers. To grow quickly, Dell needed customers who knew what they wanted and could quickly recognize that its products offered superior value.

In 1984, when personal computers were still in their infancy, these conditions did not hold in the consumer market. But they could be found in the business world. As a young start-up, Dell could not hope to go head-to-head with IBM and Hewlett-Packard (HP) for the biggest customers, so to begin Michael Dell decided to serve the small- and medium-size business segments.

It was no more than a few years before Dell's direct marketing and manufacturing model had secured it a significant position in these two segments. From there the company moved up the food chain to the large-business segment, and government, education, and health care, steadily broadening its product array from desktop and notebook computers to servers, workstations, data storage, and network switches.

In 1988 Dell went public at $8.50 a share. By 1992, Dell was a Fortune 500 company with annual revenues of $900 million. In 1993 it was one of the top five computer system makers worldwide. In 1995 an original $8.50 share was worth $100 on a presplit basis; in 1997 it was worth $1,000. In 2000 Dell became number one in worldwide workstation shipments with revenues in excess of $25 billion, and in 2001 it reached number one in global market share for all computer systems with revenues of $31.9 billion.

Only within the past few years have sales to the consumer segment begun to contribute significantly to Dell's growth. But from 1999 to

2002, Dell rocketed from a distant sixth place in the consumer segment to a commanding first place, which only lately has Hewlett-Packard been able to challenge.

Within each segment, Dell constantly looks for opportunities to sell customers a broader array of products. "One of the things we find," says Mike George, Dell's CMO, "is that two years after we acquire a large corporate customer, the revenue that we get from that customer will increase by a factor of five to eight times relative to the first year. We might start by selling them a thousand desktops, and then once they experience the validity of the direct model and realize that we have delivered just what we promised, the best products at the best possible price, customized to them, we can go back and sell them notebooks, workstations, servers, storage, software peripheral items, and services."

Trying to duplicate the same pattern in consumer electronics has proven difficult for Dell. There is increasing product oversupply in flat-screen televisions, with resultant pressure on pricing and margins for all manufacturers. And despite an announced emphasis on design, Dell has struggled to create products that appeal to consumers in the way of design leaders like Apple, Samsung, and Nokia. In August 2006 Dell announced that it was ending production of the DJ Ditty, the MP3 player it had launched little more than a year earlier to compete with Apple's iPod.

Dell faced some other serious challenges in the mid-2000s, as we'll see in later chapters. But with over 80 percent of Dell's sales remaining business to business via its direct model, the firm continued to be impressively profitable, its financials looking disappointing only in comparison to its own extraordinary record. Segment by segment, Dell has kept marching to its declared goal of winning 40 percent of the worldwide computer market and reaching $70 billion in sales. Any competitor that hopes to supplant Dell will clearly have to match its razor-sharp focus on segmentation and targeting, offering design, and execution.

The Right Offering for Each Market Segment

Until September 7, 1979, U.S. television sports was defined by programming in the sports departments at the big broadcast networks CBS, NBC, and ABC. With the exception of weekly sports variety shows, like ABC's seminal *Wide World of Sports,* sports programming consisted almost exclusively of coverage of major American college and professional team sports—baseball, football, basketball, and ice hockey—and professional golf. Back then, all sports programming together represented only a fraction of a typical week's offerings, mostly on weekend afternoons when dads were home with a beer and a bag of chips, watching games with commercial time-outs for beer, snack food, cars, razors, and other products targeted at male consumers.

A revolution started that day in September, more than a quarter century ago, when the Entertainment Sports Programming Network, or ESPN, began operating as the first all-sports cable television network with the premiere of its signature show, *SportsCenter.* In fact, following the approach of single-category retailers, ESPN was the first important single-category cable channel of any kind. It led the way for CNN's debut in 1980, the Weather Channel's in 1982, and ultimately for a proliferation of niche cable channels devoted to food, home improvement, travel, history, popular science, golf, tennis, motor racing, and so on.

"The ESPN viewer really is an ESPN fan," George Bodenheimer, ESPN's president since 1998, told us. "I don't think NBC kidded itself that a *Friends* fan was really an NBC fan; otherwise, it would never have paid so much money to keep the show on for so many years.

"The growth of cable turned the tide. It made vertical programming possible, where you don't really need to know what's on ESPN or CNN or the Weather Channel at that moment to be interested in tuning in for a while. Now, as a viewer, I may not care about this or that sport on ESPN, or a specific report or feature on CNN or the Weather Channel, but I'm going to give them a try because I know and like their brand approach. And I know that the odds are that before long ESPN will put on a sport I am passionate about, or CNN will cover my special interest, or the Weather Channel will give the forecast for my area or the places I'm traveling. And in the meantime whatever I'm watching is related to sports or news or weather, and I may get exposed to something new that I like and that will make me an even bigger fan of ESPN or CNN or the Weather Channel. It's a very different relationship from being a fan of a show, whether it's *Friends* or *The Sopranos.*

"What makes sports on ESPN different from sports on a multicategory broadcast or cable network, is that whatever we put on is part of the same strategy of serving sports fans and prospective sports fans. That's why ninety-nine times out of one hundred, we go commercial free from one program or event to another. Because if you're watching a football, basketball, baseball, or hockey game on ESPN, and you're enjoying the way we cover that, you might like our presentation of what's on next, whether it's lumberjack competitions at the Outdoor Games or billiards. We don't want you to turn us off just because the game ends."

For ESPN, sports is the market that matters, and the myriad sporting activities of the world represent so many targetable market segments.

"Last count, we televised over sixty-five different sports in a given year. From the start ESPN was happy to televise sports that didn't have large followings." By serving an increasing number of sports, ESPN was able to build its brand equity in a major way. Said Bodenheimer, "It stamped our identity as the people who care about sports, your sport, the same way you do. The X Games are the signature example of that. We saw all these so-called extreme sports like skateboarding, snowboarding, surfing, and mountain biking, each with a rabidly loyal fan base that sports television was ignoring, and we paid attention to them and we created an event to showcase them. When everyone else was disrespecting these sports and their fans, we respected them. We showed them that we cared about them. And there's nothing more powerful than showing sports fans you care, because sports are very emotional. Some of our critics smirk at some of the sports we cover. We'll serve the fans of those sports any day, because we know they'll be among ESPN's most loyal fans."

Speaking to the profits that can be gained from targeting the right segment and delivering value to the customers in them, Bodenheimer added, "And then you can find that these so-called marginal sports will appeal to an awful lot of people if you present them well. The X Games have become a global enterprise. Cities everywhere are clamoring for us to come to town. And there's no question that the popularity of the X Games helped convince the Olympics to adopt extreme sports."

ESPN's continual identification of different sport segments to serve has driven its growth as a global sports programming brand reaching geographic-segment audiences through multiple channels. In North America its outlets include ESPN, ESPN 2, ESPNNEWS, ESPN Classic, ESPNU (devoted solely to college sports), ESPN Deportes (all

Spanish language programming) and the ESPN Radio Network. Outside North America, ESPN sells its programming piecemeal to cable TV providers in many geographic market segments, and it has established several of its own foreign cable channels: ESPN Latin America, ESPN + (in Argentina, Chile, Paraguay, and Uruguay), ESPN Dos (in Mexico, Central America, and South America), ESPN Pac Rim (in the Pacific Rim countries), ESPN Atlantic (in Africa and the Middle East), and ESPN Classic Sport (in 39 European countries). And ESPN.com is its sports website in the United States.

"Wherever and whenever the sports fan needs and wants information or entertainment," says Ed Erhardt, president of ESPN ABC Sports Customer Marketing and Sales, "we're there." That includes during advertisers' commercials on shows like *Baseball Tonight*, where a bottom of the screen scoreboard remains visible during commercial breaks. "We got a lot of pushback initially from advertisers," Erhardt goes on, "but we did it because we knew it really served the fan. And the advertisers accepted it, because we proved that it worked for them and for us.

"*ESPN the Magazine* is another example. Nobody had ever challenged *Sports Illustrated* successfully. Instead of copying *SI*, like everyone else did, we created the first sports magazine for Generation Y sports fans, and now its circulation is nearing two million. We were able to do that because we're fanatical measurers, pollsters, and focus groupers. We're constantly honing established subbrands like *SportsCenter* and trying out new stuff with focus groups."

ESPN's sports segmentation pays off in two ways. Its unceasing attention to sports fans has put it, Ed Erhardt says, "at the top of the food chain in brand strength vis-à-vis cable operators," from whom it commands the highest monthly fees of any nonpremium cable channel, at $2.50 per subscriber. But at the same time, he notes, with reference to the local advertising time that cable operators get to sell on ESPN programming, "We make a lot of money for them too."

ESPN itself sells the lion's share of the advertising time on its programming. Ed Erhardt said, "We astound advertisers by selling ideas, not eyeballs. Because we know sports fans. We know how they use the Web to go on ESPN.com to get scores in the office before lunchtime. We know how they relate to *Monday Night Football*. We know how they spend time with sports throughout the day and throughout the week. So we can put together integrated marketing packages that allow advertisers to participate in the way that sports fans travel the sports news and entertainment space. For example, we have had a very successful program, *Monday Night Countdown* on ESPN, as shoulder programming for *Monday Night Football* on ABC, and we can mix and match those with ESPN Radio, ESPN.com, and so on. Our special knowledge of sports fans gives us an extra edge, so that $1 + 1 = 2.2$. With ESPN Sports Poll, we've even begun to repurpose our brand and customer research for sale to advertisers and other companies."

New television rights deals for NFL games have moved *Monday Night Football* from ABC, which had aired the program since its inception, to ESPN starting in 2006. This offered the network even more direct possibilities for bundling pro-football programming for advertisers. Meanwhile the Sunday night NFL game moved from ESPN to NBC, which now found it necessary to retarget the NFL sports segment it had abandoned during the 1990s, when it was the most highly rated television network. And in November 2006 all the television networks carrying NFL games—CBS, ESPN, and NBC—were joined by the NFL's own cable channel, the NFL Network, showing games on Thursday and Saturday nights. If recent history holds, however, ESPN's ability to target profitable segments of sports fans will stand it in good stead in this new competitive environment.

There is little question that ESPN's efforts to reach and understand all major, and many minor, segments of sports fans have given it a clear sense of its competitive arena, one that is by no means limited to sports programmers. "I worry about [competition from] other sports television," Erhardt says. "But I worry more about Comedy Central and the Discovery Channel. Because even though our audience is 30 percent women, the biggest and most important chunk of it is men. We sell and market men through sports, but we're in competition with anything that commands men's attention."

• • •

Dell and ESPN are essentially single-category malls, each serving several market segments. Dell is a mall of computer and electronics stores with something for almost all computer customers. ESPN offers a mall's worth of sports programming for fans of almost every sport. If we want a similar example in bricks-and-mortar, we can find it at The Home Depot. Founded in 1978, The Home Depot was the fastest retailer to $30 billion, $40 billion, and most recently, $50 billion in sales—in fiscal year 2005, sales were $81.5 billion. With 2,005 stores in North America, The Home Depot is the world's largest home-improvement specialty retailer, and the second-largest U.S. retailer, trailing only Wal-Mart.

The Home Depot's central concept is to bring thousands of home-improvement products together under one mall-size roof. Its goal is to offer both low prices and high service, including retail floor personnel who are professional tradespeople and so can give the customer expert advice not only on what to buy but also on how to use or install it.

Segmentation and targeting have been central to The Home Depot's growth. The do-it-yourself segment grew in importance, and The Home Depot grew along with it. But the company quickly became aware of a second important customer segment. "Professional tradespeople were buying from us, because, just like do-it-yourselfers, they'd never before had access to such a wide range of products in one place and at such good prices. They could get everything for the job site—electrical, plumbing, lumber and so forth at The Home Depot," said Roger Adams, The Home Depot's senior vice president of marketing. "We nurtured that professional customer segment—it represents 25–30 percent of our business, and it's grown to around $20 billion a year."

Continual attention to market segmentation has opened up new growth opportunities for The Home Depot. To serve different types of professional tradespeople better, it now operates stand-alone Home Depot Supply, and Home Depot Landscape Supply stores. And to reach homeowners who are not wholehearted do-it-yourselfers, The Home Depot offers expanded installation services in its Expo chain stores, geared more to decor, fashion, and design.

"Since 2000, we have stayed ahead of the shifting needs of baby boomers by differentiating ourselves in home installation, one of the fastest-growing segments of the home improvement market," Adams said. "Our portfolio of installation services has evolved considerably, but we also have strong growth in traditional categories like HVAC [heating, ventilating, and air-conditioning], kitchens, countertops, windows and roofing, and newer services like interior and exterior painting,"

Equally important, The Home Depot has refined its knowledge of, and approach to, the do-it-yourself segment. "As we've grown," Adams noted, "we've recognized the need to market to different customer segments in different ways. Our goal is to continually evolve our merchandise assortment and in-store environment to reflect our evolving customer base and how they shop today."

In 2006, as The Home Depot surpassed the two-thousand-store mark, it identified other key market segments to help drive the business.

Roger Adams told me, "Industry research continues to confirm that customers are time starved and want efficient and affordable solutions. We are also paying close attention to women, who represent about half of all customers visiting our stores. Of course, they're probably in different parts of The Home Depot—men are in the electrical or plumbing store, say, and the women are in kitchen, flooring, or paint—so we pay attention to this difference as we market the different parts of The Home Depot. The Hispanic market is also an important consumer segment that continues to grow each day."

The Home Depot's data mining is intensive, because its business is so complex. Management has to understand how lot size drives a tractor purchase, or how the age of a house, or the age of the people who live in it, drives specific sorts of home improvement projects.

The Home Depot knows that if a home-owning couple have a baby, there is a fairly high probability that within twenty-four months they'll be putting up a fence. There is a high likelihood that a customer who puts in new flooring will also put up new window treatments and will probably paint as well. If you have x number of kids and y number of pets and your house is z years old, The Home Depot knows that you're a very good candidate within a certain window of time for a certain category of products.

As large a firm as The Home Depot has become, the company believes it can continue to find dramatic growth by learning more and more about its customers and continually refining its segmentation and targeting. Said Adams, "We have 98 percent consumer awareness ratings, but still only an 11 percent share of the home improvement market. There's tremendous potential for us to grow. The key to success is understanding our customer's needs better than anyone else, and then delivering on our brand promise in our stores."

Despite an ongoing serious challenge from rival home-improvement superstore chain Lowe's, The Home Depot has seen its overall business strategy and its customer segmentation continue to succeed. In August 2006 the company's website reported increasing market share in key product categories, such as appliances, and a 16.7 percent rise in quarterly sales and a 9.8 percent rise in quarterly profits.

•   •   •

Sony as noted earlier has been having a difficult time in the last couple of years, but we'll conclude this chapter with a couple of their successes—Xplod car stereo and VAIO personal computers—that were built on Sony's ability to segment the market and make the right offering to its target segments. Ron Boire, president of sales for Sony's consumer electronics, talked to us about the importance of segmentation at Sony.

Boire said, "I think that our experience with the Walkman alien campaign that we started in 2000 best captures it. We were spending tens of millions of dollars on media and I had friends say, 'You know, I've never seen the ads.' It's like, 'Good. That's a good thing that we run hundreds and hundreds of slots and you've never seen one, because you're not the target. That means I'm targeting razor sharp.' "

It's one thing to target "razor sharp," but it's quite another to make sure that the branded offer is just right. When Sony launched Xplod car stereo in the 1990s, it was very conscious of targeting Generation X and Y consumers who thought of Sony as a brand their parents bought. Boire said, "This is not a big market, so you have to be very focused, and you have to get attention. We look at the market primarily in age segments, overlaid with some behavioral segments. There are early adopters and other behavioral types in every age segment. For the young car stereo audience—testosterone overloaded twenty-year-old guys—the information we gleaned from focus groups told us we had to lead with Xplod and put Sony in the background.

"It's Xplod by Sony. It's not Sony Xplod. We made Xplod big and Sony small. We wanted to say to young people, 'You know, what's cool is Xplod and you get that from Sony.' Not 'Sony's real cool and that includes Xplod.' That wouldn't work. By putting the Sony brand in the background, we can claim the positives that are associated with it, like quality and reliability and good sound. By putting Xplod in the foreground, and making sure it has the right sense of attitude, the right design, the right colors, the right features, we renew Sony's reputation as a brand that is fresh, hip, and innovative. When you log on to Crutch-field Audio's Xplod website, you don't see anything about Sony until you click through two levels to get to the product listings. Then you see they're all Sony products. Likewise the Sony home page for Xplod has a couple of discreet Sony placements, but we continue to lead with Xplod.

"We play the same association/dissociation game with PlayStation. When our ads say, 'Live in your world, play in ours,' we mean the world of PlayStation from Sony, not the world of Sony. That approach has paid off in industry leading numbers in both units and profitability, even in the face of Microsoft's huge spend to launch Xbox.

"VAIO may be the best example. We started selling personal computers in 1996, which might not seem to be the greatest timing. The PC market was well past its first stage of maturity, and we were coming in behind IBM and Dell and HP and Apple. People heard the name VAIO and said, 'What the heck does that mean?'

"VAIO means 'video audio in out.' From the start we've worked to build a space for it in the computer world as *the* audio/video PC. By associating it with Sony, we can claim the audio/video space. By disassociating a little bit and emphasizing the VAIO brand, we bestow credibility on Sony in the PC business.

"The numbers have been phenomenal. We're growing our notebook business in an industry that's declining. We're growing our desktop business by orders of magnitude. In any given month we're one or two in the marketplace in notebooks and two or three in desktops. So it's kind of sunk in. People walk into Best Buy and say, 'I'm looking for a VAIO,' more than they say, 'I'm looking for a Sony computer.' "

•   •   •

Once again we have crisscrossed the business landscape in this chapter to stress the importance of one of our five marketing imperatives—segmenting to find the sweet spots in a market that matters. Exxon-Mobil, Nokia, Samsung, Schwab, the *Wall Street Journal*, Nestlé, Dell, ESPN, The Home Depot, and Sony all make a religion out of segmentation and targeting. But they do not all segment in a single way. Rather, the myriad approaches they use to segment markets that matter demonstrates the complexity of the segmentation process and the difficulty of executing it well.

Each firm knows that it must husband its corporate resources and target them where the possibilities of success are greatest. Market segmentation is not easy and betting the firm's resources on chosen market segments takes a good deal of guts. Nonetheless, these successful firms are ruthless in executing their segmentation schemes by focusing externally on customer needs, wants, and preferences rather then internally on company resources, competencies, and preferences.

Segmenting markets accurately and targeting the best ones for your company to compete in are only part of the battle. The best analysis and decision making will not take you very far unless you deliver real value to customers in your chosen segments and secure advantage over your competitors. This brings us to the next imperative: design the market offer to create customer value and secure differential advantage over competitors.

Design the Market Offer to Create Customer Value and Secure Differential Advantage

SIX

Meeting Customer Needs and Beating Competition

The Marketing Mavens focus fanatically on identifying customer needs and wants. Only by understanding those needs and wants, and how they are changing, can companies craft market offers that deliver value to customers and secure differential advantage over competitors. Perhaps it goes without saying that value is what customers perceive it to be. Although this may seem a recipe for the P. T. Barnum–esque fleecing of customers, the history of business shows that no company survives for long if it doesn't consistently offer the sizzle and the steak.

Critical customer value often lies hidden in the logic of a purchase. When the old IBM was enjoying its great heyday, purchasing managers or other decision makers at customer companies knew they would never get fired for buying IBM, and in the pre–Federal Express world, traffic managers knew they would never get fired for using Emery Air Freight. These beliefs gave customers psychological comfort and not only locked in sales for IBM and Emery but also enabled them to set higher prices and reap greater profit margins.

Change dethroned both leading firms—the PC revolution in the case of IBM, and Federal Express' overnight delivery for Emery. The fact of the matter is that no matter how dominant your position may be, you cannot remain on top unless you put the customer at the center of your business, and make serving the customer everybody's job.

In a market where customer value was previously defined on the basis of technological prowess, the "intel inside" campaign mounted by Intel for its computer chips was a tremendous win for everyone involved: Intel, which sold more chips and won favor from investors; trade channel customers, including both manufacturers such as HP and Dell and retailers such as CompUSA, which sold more products branded "intel inside" and had significant portions of their advertising underwritten by Intel; and consumers and other end-use customers, who found that "intel inside" gave them the psychological comfort of a reliable, high-performing product that did not have to cost them a penny more than products with a competitor's equally good, or perhaps even superior, chip. However, by the mid-2000s, the "intel inside" campaign was running out of steam, and Intel faced the challenge of renewing its brand identity, and its industry-leading position, to counter gains made by rival chip maker AMD.[1]

In this regard, every market segment you target has a dynamic set of customers with a dynamic set of value requirements and a dynamic set of competitors trying to meet those requirements. No element is static: customer demographics, customer needs, and competitor actions all change over time, often unpredictably. Customers and competitors together determine the circumstances under which you should strive to deliver increased customer value and secure and maintain differential advantage. While there is a remarkable variety of ways in which the Marketing Mavens meet this ongoing challenge, there is remarkable unanimity in the principles they follow in doing so:

- Identify those areas where they touch customers most closely, then do everything possible to deliver value to them.

- Recognize that depending on market conditions, the leverage to create maximum customer value and maximum differential advantage over competitors may be found in R&D, supply-chain and distribution management competencies, sales force and customer relationship management, and even mergers and acquisitions.

- Don't emphasize one of these areas out of proportion to the others, because no differential advantage lasts forever. Today, copycats quickly arrive from any and all quarters—so do leapfroggers who offer even greater benefits. It pays to acquire a critical balance of capabilities that enables survival and growth over time. Consistently successful firms are not lopsided organizations; rather, they tend to do most things well. And they use this well roundedness to their advantage, focusing their maximal efforts and investments in different parts of their businesses as market conditions require.

This chapter explores how to deliver customer value and secure differential advantage by considering market leaders in three different sectors of the health-care industry. Mayo Clinic, Pfizer Pharmaceuticals, and the medical insurer UnitedHealthcare have all demonstrated a consistent ability to profit by putting patients first. They are all truly customer-focused marketers that deliver value to multiple levels of customers—direct and indirect, trade and end use. These companies, and others that we'll look at from a range of industries, demonstrate that the route to delivering customer value and securing differential advantage over competitors is limited only by your creativity.

Two Heads Are Better Than One, and Three Are Even Better: Increased Customer Value and Differential Advantage at Mayo Clinic

Mayo Clinic is arguably the most well-known and powerful health-care brand in the world today. It has been delivering superb medical care to patients, providing value to many constituencies and wielding differential advantage over competitors since the late 1880s. Mayo Clinic's history continues to define its differential advantage over other direct health-care providers' brands even in an age when every major hospital and medical institution has professional marketing and public relations staffs.

The Mayo family's clinic in Rochester, Minnesota, was founded by Dr. William Mayo, a Civil War surgeon, and grew into a major health-care institution under the direction of his sons, Dr. William J. Mayo and Dr. Charles H. Mayo. The Mayo brothers, Dr. Will and Dr. Charlie in Mayo Clinic lore, encapsulated their approach to practicing medicine in two principles:

1. The best interest of the patient is the only interest to be considered.

2. Two heads are better than one, and three are even better.

If, as Peter Drucker later said, "There is only one valid definition of business purpose: to create a customer" and "What the customer thinks he is buying, what he considers 'value' is decisive," these two principles anticipated him in Mayo's health-care context and formed a natural basis for creating and satisfying customer-patients.

These principles were habits of daily life to the Mayo brothers, who began their medical training assisting their father when they were boys. "We came along in medicine like farm boys do on a farm," said Dr. Will. Their formative experiences as caregivers were thus collaborative ones, and after securing their medical degrees and specialist training they returned to practicing medicine collectively with their father. Each brother traveled at least once per year, to seek out and to collaborate with physicians and surgeons around the world who were noted for clinical innovation. Upon their return, the Mayo brothers incorporated the latest knowledge and techniques in their own practice. They continually strove to extend and refine a cooperative medical practice model, in which all Mayo Clinic caregivers served as consultants to each other and as members of multiple patient care teams led by the respective patient's primary physician.

As Dr. Will put it a century ago, "Individualism in medicine can no longer exist." Fast-advancing medical understanding made it "necessary to develop medicine as a cooperative science; the clinician, the specialist, and the laboratory workers uniting for the good of the patient." Organizing the clinic along these lines offered medical patients one-stop shopping: tests and treatments that might take months to coordinate and carry out elsewhere could be done at Mayo in a matter of days.

Mayo's model proved enormously successful, and by the 1910s the clinic's patient base had assumed national and even international proportions. Achieving this growth—which made the Mayo brothers wealthy men—required innovations not only in medical care but also in the support systems for delivering medical services to customer-patients. For example, a key early hire was Henry Plummer, MD, who devised a shared patient file system with a conveyor belt to carry files where they were needed, when they were needed. Plummer also drove implementation of the first large intercommunicating telephone system that allowed staff to talk at will either to each other or an outside person, despite the local telephone company's initial position that this was impossible. He also designed new buildings to facilitate integrated, cooperative medical care. Another legendary early hire was Maud Mellish, their editorial assistant, who developed policies and services that helped to spread the word about Mayo Clinic and its medical advances in both scholarly publications and the general press.

Right from the start, in other words, Mayo Clinic made customer-focused marketing a strategic priority.

In 1919 the Mayo brothers took the ultimate step to ensure that the "best interest of the patient" continued to be "the only interest to be considered" at Mayo Clinic. They dissolved their lucrative partnership; made the clinic a not-for-profit, charitable organization devoted to medical care, research, and education; and donated most of their personal wealth for its endowment. From then on, the Mayo brothers, and following their example all other Mayo Clinic employees, would work strictly for an annual salary.

The Mayo brothers died within two months of each other in 1939, but their pioneering collaborative care model has kept their clinic at the forefront of the health-care industry. Since then, Mayo Clinic has grown to become an organization of nearly forty-eight thousand employees serving more than five hundred thousand patients a year from the United States and around the world at three clinic and hospital operations in Rochester, Minnesota; Jacksonville, Florida; and Scottsdale/ Phoenix, Arizona. Mayo Clinic's brand awareness is extraordinary. Kent Seltman, chair of Mayo's Marketing Division told us, "Our research shows that in the United States we register over 1.8 billion consumer impressions a year—90 percent of the population is aware of Mayo Clinic, 33 percent know someone who has been a Mayo patient, and 18 percent would make us their first choice for a serious health need if there were no financial barriers." Indeed, patients from all fifty U.S. states as well as from 150 countries typically visit each of the three clinics every year.

When Mayo Clinic talks, people listen. In 1999 consumers turned irrevocably against the diet aid Phen-Fen, when the media reported a Mayo Clinic finding that Phen-Fen damaged heart valves so badly in some patients that they required surgery. "Interestingly," Steve Kopecky, a Mayo cardiologist and former chair of its marketing committee said, "the finding on Phen-Fen came about through our collaborative practice model. It was a Mayo Clinic team of physicians that put their observations together and came up with this insight. It's just like Dr. Will and Dr. Charlie said: 'in serving the patient's best interest, two heads are better than one, and three are even better.' "

Mayo Clinic's model is difficult to maintain and even harder to duplicate. More than a hundred years after its founding, Mayo Clinic remains the most successful multispecialty clinic, operating on the model created by the Mayo brothers—including salaried physicians. Several other well-known clinics, some founded by alumni of Mayo's training programs, have been created, yet none has yet been able to duplicate the model fully or the success that it has sustained. No competitor looks just like Mayo Clinic.

For example, renowned institutions such as Memorial Sloan Kettering Cancer Center, and the Cleveland Clinic, focused respectively on cancer medicine and cardiology, boast expertise within a narrower range of related specialties than Mayo. Even major medical centers, such as the networks of teaching hospitals associated with medical schools at prestigious universities, including Columbia, Cornell, Stanford, Harvard, and Johns Hopkins, find it difficult to match Mayo Clinic's national and international reputation for clinical excellence across specialties. And they have more regional than national brand power.

Equally important, no other large health-care provider has so fully committed itself to the patient-first, collaborative practice model established by the Mayo brothers. Compared with their counterparts at Mayo Clinic, physicians, nurses, and researchers at other large health-care institutions are typically relatively isolated within their departments, laboratories, specialties, and subspecialties. These tend to become rival fiefdoms battling for patient revenues or for institutional and outside funding. The differentiating Mayo model means that more patient diagnosis and care can often be accomplished in a few days at Mayo Clinic than in several weeks or even months elsewhere. Part of Mayo Clinic's success is achieved by alignment of mission and organization. Significantly, all Mayo Clinic physicians, nurses, custodians, secretaries—all employees—receive salary checks from the same account, signed by the same person. By contrast, patient care in most community and even premier academic settings is fragmented in alignment with several corporations—hospitals and physician groups— working in an environment that makes focus on the best interest of the patient more challenging. This is particularly true in major metropolitan areas where each category of care can be supplied by numerous, often competing, caregivers.

Mayo Clinic strives to extend its collaborative model to all staff. True to its founders' visionary principles, Mayo puts its entire faith as a self-sustaining, financially robust enterprise in a culture of mutual respect among all employees. Kent Seltman boasted, "I've worked in three different health-care organizations, and nowhere else have I seen the caring and respect among the staff that we have here. For example, there is virtually no tension between the administrative and operational side of the house and the physicians. In most large health-care institutions, there is constant battling between the caregiving side and the bean counters. We just don't have that. Mayo Clinic is run by physician leaders who implicitly and respectfully value the counsel and skills of the administrators who are paired with them. And the mutual respect flows in both directions."

Dr. Kopecky added, "Dr. Will said that the most important person at Mayo Clinic, after his brother, was their editorial assistant, Maud Mellish, because she did so much to show the world the great things the clinic was doing for patients. I think this organization has always acted on the philosophy that every job is important. It clearly is not just the doctor who matters. It is also the nurse, the aide, the physical therapist, the technician, the janitor, and the administrator who is making sure that we use our resources well and remain solvent. If we're going to give extraordinary care, we have to do so as a team. Great teamwork requires a high degree of mutual respect and care."

Or, as Peter Drucker urged, at Mayo Clinic marketing is every employee's job.

Rivals cannot easily emulate this collaborative care model. Distinctive people are increasingly the key to achieving and sustaining differential advantage. Developing a company-wide, customer-focused marketing and service culture is the hardest task in business, but without it today you will not succeed for long—the top marketing companies know that it is the toughest thing for competitors to imitate.

For Mayo Clinic, the difficulty of replicating its collaborative care model gives it an edge over other health-care providers. But it has also limited Mayo Clinic's growth to operations at its home base in Minnesota and newer locations in Florida and Arizona. "In the 1980s our leaders looked at population growth in the Sunbelt, and decided to put Mayo Clinic in Scottsdale, Arizona, and Jacksonville, Florida," Kent Seltman told us. "But we have no intention of expanding further. You can't be perceived as the best if there are too many of you. There's no way we could become the Starbucks of medical care. If there were a Mayo Clinic on every corner or a Mayo Clinic in every state, some of the luster that's associated with the brand would inevitably dim, because the public isn't stupid. Providing medical care is not like making coffee or manufacturing a box of soap. Health care is a labor-intensive, intellectual endeavor. It requires the engagement of the mind of the physician with the patient first as a person and then as an extremely complex organism. The brand is really about the wisdom of our clinicians, their credibility as world-class experts. The public realizes that— people know it's hard to assemble a collection of world experts. We won't serve our patients well if the intellectual component of Mayo Clinic is diffused. So we're not intending to franchise the brand. Replicating Mayo Clinic in a couple of locations was a huge challenge. It took a huge amount of work and a lot of resources to pull off."

Dr. Kopecky added, "If we open up a clinic that has a few hundred doctors, they have to be trained in Mayo Clinic's way of doing things as a team. That means they have to be trained here at Mayo, and so we are always going to be limited by constraints on how many new employees we can hire and assimilate into Mayo's culture of collaborative care."

It's one thing to build a world-class facility, to staff it with the brightest and the best, to put in the appropriate organizational design, systems, and processes so that you deliver the best customer value health care in the world. But you also want people to know about it. Following Maud Mellish's example, Mayo Clinic continues to extend its differential advantage over other health-care brands through publications and publicity. "Our clinicians and researchers publish several thousand articles, chapters, textbooks, and abstracts annually," said Steve Kopecky.[2] "For example, the Rochester Epidemiology Project, an ongoing longitudinal public health study that is one of the most important in modern medicine, has resulted in twelve hundred publications over the last thirty or forty years, many of them seminal works that have influenced therapeutic practice and subsequent research worldwide. We also publish our own peer-reviewed journal, *Mayo Clinic Proceed-*

ings, which has 150,000 physician subscribers, and *Clinical Update*, a newsletter for professional readers."

In the 1980s, in parallel with developing locations in Arizona and Florida, Mayo Clinic stepped up communications with the general public by publishing *Mayo Clinic Health Letter* and then ventured into book publishing under the mission of serving as a reliable source of health information for the general public. *Mayo Clinic Family Health Book* has sold over one million copies and has been followed by over twenty-five successful books for consumers. *Mayo Clinic Health Letter*, published in four languages, has over six million subscribers, and *Mayo Clinic Women's Health Source*, another monthly newsletter, enjoys similar success. Newsletters are sent regularly to patients, employees, alumni, and donors. And with the arrival of the Internet, Mayo's free consumer website, MayoClinic.com, has become one of the most heavily visited health information sites on the Internet. Mayo Clinic.org, Mayo's patient-care website, draws visitors who want to learn about Mayo's medical services and approach to patient care.

Mayo researchers' publications in peer-reviewed journals, the clinic's own scholarly and consumer publications, and its websites enhance the differential advantage derived from its collaborative care model by fulfilling the organization's prime marketing imperative: meet customer-patients' needs better than the competition. Every study, article, book, and website feature represents an opportunity to develop or dispense innovative patient care and to sustain the Mayo Clinic brand's high standing in the public's mind.

As in the Phen-Fen controversy, Mayo Clinic communications often spark national news stories about its research findings and patient successes. For prospective customer-patients around the United States and the world, these communications and news coverage provide powerful incentives to consider being treated at Mayo Clinic, despite the added cost when compared with being treated closer to home.

To ensure that its communications are as clear and effective as possible, Mayo Clinic continues to devote substantial attention to editorial services. For example, its communications competency includes a media relations staff of trained journalists who work with Mayo clinicians and researchers to secure publicity for patient success stories and for therapeutic and research advances.

Mayo Clinic also regularly sees itself in the news because of the

celebrated people—entertainers, professional athletes, and government and business leaders—who visit it for care. Depending on how
big the celebrity or how important the leader—Mayo Clinic often
treats heads of state—the news coverage that results may be regional,
national, or global. While Mayo staff help manage the media coverage
when it occurs, it only does so when requested by the patient. Mayo
vigorously guards the privacy of its patients and some high-profile
patients seek care at Mayo because they can do so without public
knowledge.

Let's put this in general business terms. Mayo Clinic has two sets of
communications channels, one for physicians and one for the general
public, because both are important groups of customers or potential
customers, although Mayo does not use the term. Physicians are in
one sense competitor health-care providers, but they are also potential
trade channel partners who can directly and indirectly drive customer-
patient referrals to Mayo Clinic. Likewise, communications to the general public also ultimately pay off in more customer-patients looking to
Mayo Clinic for help with major medical problems.

In addition to physicians and the general public, Mayo Clinic has
two other important customer constituencies to which it must deliver
value: insurers and its own active patient roster. Here too Mayo's distinctive collaborative care model is the main means for doing so.

The collaborative care that patients receive at Mayo Clinic drives
consistently positive word-of-mouth recommendations. Kent Seltman
told us, "Our brand studies of patients show that 95 percent of patients
feel very positively about Mayo Clinic. These patients report that they
each tell an average of fifty people about their good experience. Further, they each urge an average of twenty other people, 'You should
go to Mayo Clinic.' The bottom line is that every satisfied patient is
loyal to Mayo and brings in an average of seven new patients."

Dr. Kopecky added, "When people come here as patients, it really is
amazing how they respond to the place and spread the word about us.
Recently a physician who's referred to me for ten years from another
state called and said, 'I need to come as a patient.' He used to refer
three or four patients a year. Since he's come as a patient, he's been re-
ferring three or four a month."

Satisfied patients feed back into Mayo Clinic's communications efforts, and generate much of its media coverage. In small U.S. towns,

word of mouth about someone's good experience at Mayo Clinic frequently leads to a feature story in the local paper, or on the local television or radio news. Such stories are in turn often picked up by regional and national news services, and they can be put to good use by Mayo Clinic's own public relations staff.

"We've done a lot of research on why patients choose us," Kent Seltman said, "and there are really two factors that are the most important: a personal recommendation from a friend or relative or their physician and frustration with the medical care experienced elsewhere. Those two things are what make them willing to pay the out-of-pocket expenses averaging $1,000 to travel here, stay in hotels, and eat in restaurants. Their insurance won't pay for this.

"In Rochester we care for patients from nearly 40 percent of all residential zip codes in the United States. It's a high percentage, but very few zip codes send us ten or more patients. So we have an infinitesimal share of a huge market. In some large metropolitan markets we have .014 percent market share, but from a market of several million individuals that's still several hundred patients a year who are choosing to come here every year from each of those markets. In effect this means every other health provider is a competitor, but I prefer to think of them as potential collaborators. Both the patients and Mayo Clinic need them to have a doctor back home. Our doctors will work with—collaborate, if you will—the patient's home physician in Omaha, for example, in pursuit of the best interests of the patient. Mayo's collaborative model can create a win-win-win. When a physician or patient needs our specialty services, we're here for them. But going back to our extremely small share of a huge market, Mayo is rarely seen as a threat as we take so few patients from any geographic area each year."

Mayo Clinic's miniscule share of an enormous market also helps it remain attractive to many insurers in a world of managed care and restricted provider lists. As Kent Seltman explained, "Research shows that the greatest benefit that our brand provides is the peace of mind in just knowing that Mayo Clinic exists should patients ever need it. Many consumers find value in purchasing insurance products that include Mayo Clinic; this is, of course, strongest in the [midwestern United States]. So we can explain to insurers that having Mayo Clinic as a provider on their list offers great benefit to them as they're selling.

A few patients per zip code per year are enough to keep demand far outpacing the supply of available appointments, though Kent Seltman did acknowledge that increasing demand does create a significant challenge in managing access to appointments. So long as it continues to find ways to fulfill its founders' vision, Mayo Clinic seems well positioned to deliver increased value to medical consumers, and to wield differential advantage over competitors, for another century plus.

Mayo Clinic is a nonprofit organization. But the proof of its differential advantage is its financial success. Mayo Clinic's leading edge research and hospital facilities, its medical school, its high staff-per-patient ratio, and its roster of world-class physicians and researchers all form a going concern that counts on customers' willingness to face the inconvenience and pay significant out-of-pocket expenses to travel to a Mayo Clinic to be treated.

The Pfizer Edge: Outperforming the Competition in Sales and Marketing

Pfizer's leadership in its sector of the health-care industry is much more recent than Mayo Clinic's, and unlike Mayo, Pfizer faces numerous strong direct competitors—Abbott Laboratories, AstraZeneca, Bristol-Myers Squibb, GlaxoSmithKline, Merck, Novartis, Roche, Sanofi-Aventis, Schering-Plough, and Wyeth, among others—not to speak of focused generic drug manufacturers. Pfizer became the market-share leader in the all-important U.S. market in 1998 and worldwide in 2000. Pat Kelly, president of Pfizer's U.S. Pharmaceuticals group, believes that Pfizer's success results from its long-standing commitment to investing in marketing and, more specifically, in its distinctive sales organization.

One of the defining marketing challenges for pharmaceutical companies is that they have two distinct, yet intertwined sets of customers: prescribing physicians and their patients. There has been, as you know, an explosion in direct-to-consumer marketing and advertising of prescription medicines. Pfizer has been a pioneer in direct-to-consumer advertising. But it has also continued to rely above all on its sales force to serve the needs of customers in delivering value to both its patient and physician customers.

For all pharmaceutical companies, marketing communications

must be a dialogue with physicians to inform them about their drug products and also to learn from physicians how patients are faring with those medicines. This puts great pressure on getting sales force organization and management right.

Pfizer has the largest sales force in the pharmaceutical industry. Between 1996 and 2001 it almost tripled its U.S. sales force from roughly three thousand representatives to more than eighty-five hundred, at a time when the competition was either in a hiring freeze or laying off reps, quite a large number of whom went to work for Pfizer.

At the turn of the twenty-first century, Pfizer's sales force model had multiple reps calling on a single physician, yet detailing the same drugs. It generated prescriptions, but push-back from physicians told Pfizer that it was in danger of losing these customers' patience and trust. Pfizer knew that if it could not sell effectively to physicans, all the direct-to-consumer pharmaceutical marketing in the world could not make up the difference. So it abandoned its industry-leading model of multiple reps pitching the same products and developed a new one.

Creating what it calls a Therapeutic Area structure, Pfizer organized its sales force into five therapeutic categories: Arthritis, Pain, and Metabolic; Cardiovascular; Neuroscience; Urology/Respiratory; and Special Markets. The new structure allows sales representatives to master all the intricacies of a disease category and deepen their knowledge about the products in that category. Hence, they can deliver more detailed and valuable information to physicians not just about treatment options but also regarding general disease issues. The reps can then engage physician-customers in a much richer dialogue on the trends affecting that category. All of this frees reps to sharpen their focus on customer concerns and needs, while providing individual representatives with greater accountability for sales in their territories.

An important benefit of the new sales structure is that it clarifies sales reps' compensation. With multiple reps selling the same medicines, it was difficult to distinguish and reward the highest performing reps appropriately. The Therapeutic Area structure builds a much more direct connection between reps' individual efforts and their compensation, which obviously adds motivation to their efforts.

Pfizer also reorganized its regions to more closely match the footprint of the Medicare program, which administers its new prescription drug benefit along state lines. The thinking here is that as Medicare becomes a major customer for prescription medicine, Pfizer should conform to its customers' organization.

Of all the pharmaceutical firms, Pfizer probably has the broadest portfolio of products across its therapeutic categories. Hence it can use its advantages of scale to organize and deploy its people more effectively than its competitors.

Pfizer's experiences demonstrate that the more insight you have into customers, the better chance you have to deliver superior value and earn differential advantage over competitors by turning customer data into customer insight, then into customer value.

The market understanding that Pfizer mines from its customer data was a key factor driving its most important acquisition, the June 19, 2000, purchase of rival Warner-Lambert, whose most valuable asset was the cholesterol-lowering medication Lipitor, launched only in 1997 in a copromotion agreement with Pfizer. From sales reps' reports as well as other market data, Pfizer knew that Lipitor was the best medication on the market, the one most favored by physicians and most helpful to patients. Equally important, Pfizer was confident that its sales force could grow Lipitor's sales and justify the high price, $90 billion in stock, for acquiring Warner-Lambert. Finally, Pfizer knew that Warner-Lambert's corporate culture would meld with its own.

"Marketing and sales had crucial insights into Warner-Lambert and its value to Pfizer," Pat Kelly told us. "We were working side by side with Warner-Lambert every day on Lipitor because of our copromotion agreement, and we knew them as well as they knew themselves. That gave us the confidence not only to acquire the company, but also to keep on almost all its more than twenty-one hundred (at the time of the acquisition) sales reps in the merged company. The sales of Lipitor before and after the acquisition show that we were right. In the United States, 7.3 million people take Lipitor every day." Indeed, by 2005, Lipitor sales were over $12 billion, up from $2.2 billion in 1998, the year before the merger. In 2002 Pfizer followed up its Warner-Lambert purchase by acquiring Pharmacia & Upjohn, which added the blockbuster arthritis-fighting drug, Celebrex, and the second-generation drug, Bextra, to its product portfolio. Field data from Pfizer's sales reps also played an important part in this acquisition.

Pfizer leverages its customer insight advantage through integrated marketing of specific medicines. Viagra, now the world's most recognizable pharmaceutical brand, is a case in point. This category-creating and category-leading product—Viagra outsells copycat drugs Levitra and Cialis by 445 percent and 180 percent, respectively—began when patients in an angina medication trial enthusiastically reported that sildenafil citrate had the unexpected side effect of boosting erectile function.

Pfizer listened carefully to these potential customers, and as it developed and rolled out Viagra it listened with equal care to the varied responses the drug evoked. "Much of the brand awareness we achieved with Viagra was free of charge. It's become a worldwide consumer brand at the same level of recognition as Coca-Cola and McDonald's. That's territory that pharmaceuticals had never crossed. But we had to take the bad with the good to get there. There were times during the launch year when some things felt like they were out of control. There was counterfeit Viagra everywhere. Leno and Letterman were joking about it every night. It was a massive burst of attention all because of three letters, *s-e-x*, that people are desperately interested in. And it could all have gone terribly wrong as soon as the first media story reported that side effects had occurred with Viagra, that older men with underlying heart disease risk factors and their physicians needed to be aware of the fact that reengaging in sex would naturally put extra stress on their hearts. The fact that Viagra didn't have to be taken off the market because of bad publicity is a tribute to our marketing. Because we listened well, both to the early patients in clinical trials and to the experts in the field, we alerted every physician and every potential patient to the need for a thorough cardiovascular exam before beginning Viagra. We even included a 'users manual' with every prescription—not a users manual for Viagra but for safely reinitiating sexual activity. These and other marketing efforts kept Viagra from being marginalized or scapegoated, and we grew it to the point where, on a worldwide basis, more than six Viagra tablets are dispensed every second."

Pfizer has also secured differential advantage through compelling mass communications, as it did with its allergy medicine, Zyrtec, competing against Schering-Plough's Claritin (now sold over the counter) and Sanofi-Aventis's Allegra. "The name's the first thing to talk about,"

Pat Kelly said. "Zyrtec is not a nice name. It's tough to spell and pronounce. It means business. Those attributes bolster our consistent product marketing message, which is that Zyrtec delivers increased customer value because it is effective against all kinds of allergies, indoor and outdoor, and that it works at least two times better than anything else on the market. 'Lots of allergies, just one medicine'—that's our message. Zyrtec is just black-and-white copy and ugly lime green packaging. The Zyrtec ads, sales rep materials, direct mail pieces, and website all use the same ugly lime green. Again, it's because we think that nice, friendly visuals aren't really in line with the fact that people want their allergy medicine to do ruthless battle with their allergies. Research demonstrates that consumers think of Zyrtec in two ways: it's the one for all allergies, and it's green." It's a good example of integrating marketing and sales.

Although only time will tell how successful it will be, Pfizer also seeks to use customer insight obtained through its sales force, as well as through its market segmentation, to guide R&D for new medicines. For example, it knows from sales reps' dialogues in doctors' offices and demographic studies that physicians are facing a host of new problems in treating aging baby boomers. The increasingly large elderly population is at risk for stroke, Alzheimer's disease, and other neurological disorders for which there is as yet no effective treatment. There is great potential for growth in these areas, and Pfizer has accordingly aligned marketing and R&D to focus on them.

Pfizer shares its best practices with partners who in other contexts are, or could be, competitors. But it believes that even if GlaxoSmithKline, for example, adopted its ideas, Pfizer would maintain a competitive advantage by better execution, leveraging its first-mover advantages in terms of marketing investments, and scale.

Pfizer's recent history shows that a company may deliver enhanced customer value through its internal operations (the distinctive Pfizer sales organization and R&D), acquisitions (the purchase of Warner-Lambert and Pharmacia & Upjohn), and coventures (the deal for consumer rights to GOJO's Purell), and divestitures (the sale of the company's over-the-counter products, including the consumer rights to Purell, to Johnson & Johnson). Innovative means of delivering customer value and securing differential advantage over competitors may be found in many places but only if the search is truly guided by a desire to satisfy customer needs.

Turning Problem Customers into Profit Centers

In the United States, all health care, like all politics, is local. First, at its essential roots, the entire vast health-care industry revolves around the direct interaction of physicians and patients. Second, the fifty states have their own departments of health and insurance administering sets of regulations that each mesh differently with overarching federal regulations. In Pfizer's new sales force structure, its reps can respond flexibly to local conditions, while gaining a deeper knowledge of their physician-customers, and empowering customer communications across the entire Pfizer organization. For its part, Mayo Clinic exploits the local nature of health care by being the first and only multi-specialty clinic of its kind, so that it can draw a few patients each from a multitude of local health-care markets.

The local nature of health care creates great complexity for health-care insurers. Many traditional health-plan providers began as local entities that expanded state by state, often by acquisition. This led to a proliferation of operating systems and processes that have made it enormously difficult for large insurers to present the same face to customers and provide consistently good service in different states. Furthermore, multiple operating systems meant duplicative costs and required large expenditures of time and money to link up or replace. (An important implication of this situation is that foreign insurers such as the French giant AXA can usually compete in the American market only through acquisition.)

Another layer of complexity flows from the individual nature of insurance policies tailored to win a group-plan purchase from a small, medium, or large business, and administered via detailed certificates of coverage. A large national insurer must administer many thousands of certificates of coverage, and every little wrinkle, designed to satisfy a particular customer organization, is a customer-service mistake waiting to happen.

Finally, as middlemen between patients and caregivers, the large insurers must negotiate terms of service with America's ten-thousand-plus hospitals, and they must process claims from hundreds of thousands of physicians.

The 1980s arrival of managed care put this system under increasing pressure to control skyrocketing costs. Most insurers responded with gatekeeper behavior, restricting referrals to specialists and denying coverage for procedures that they did not deem medically necessary. These efforts did not cut costs and increase profits as expected, and they angered and frustrated customers. From 1980 to 2005 total annual U.S. expenditures on health rose from under $200 billion to over $1,800 billion.[3] From this rising tide of health-care expenditures, most insurers netted modest returns at best.

One company has outstripped its rivals. In 1993 UnitedHealth Group's earnings were $212 million on $3.1 billion revenues. By 2006 both earnings and revenues had increased twenty times or more to $4.2 billion and $71.5 billion, respectively. And its stock price had risen from the low single digits in the early 1990s (adjusted for stock splits) to more than $50 today. UnitedHealth Group's most recent growth was driven by its 2004 $4.7 billion acquisition of Oxford Health Plans.

UnitedHealthcare's CMO, Jay Silverstein, told us that the company has always based its actions on the belief that being a facilitator of customers' health care, rather than an adversarial gatekeeper blocking access to care, was the route to long-term profits. Second, it has striven to create an infrastructure that serves this role, so that a company with employees in vastly different areas of the country will have predictable and consistent service. It has ripped apart the old infrastructure, with its multiple systems and inconsistencies, and created a new standard model for facilitating care. Silverstein says, "Everywhere you go, you know what you're getting. You may not like it, but it is the same. It's predictable, it's consistent, and it's efficient.

"Where we had forty-three websites, today we have one. Where we used to have thirty-five different sets of collateral material—brochures, directories, explanations of service—for different markets, today we have one. To make sure the material would work for everybody, we engaged fifth-grade reading teachers to write it, and we hired the designers of *Real Simple* magazine to lay it out. We used to have fourteen different operating systems. Today we have two.

"It took an enormous effort, but we built information systems that let customer calls flow quickly from one call center to another to the next available staffer, each one seeing the same information on the same screens, with enough consistency across certificates of coverage to limit errors that wind up in a state department of insurance because somebody filed a complaint."

UnitedHealthcare strives to deliver customer value but recognizes that that does not necessarily mean providing the customer with whatever the customer thinks he or she may want. Delivering customer value requires the firm to think beyond the immediate attributes the customer receives at the point of sale.

"In terms of our plan offerings, we had to use a lot of sheer brute force on our own organization to get some discipline in how we wrote and administered health plans. We had to show our salespeople that it didn't make sense to have so much variation in our certificates of coverage. Because, even if the special features in the policy seem to be the ones that clinch the sale, they cause so many problems in the relationship down the line that we often wind up losing those customers when it comes time to renew. It's like expecting BMW to let customers stipulate what kind of ball bearings will be used on their car. Imagine the jerry-rigging of machinery that would entail. I guarantee the cars wouldn't come out so well.

"We moved to a model where we're like BMW in that we build plans on more of a shared platform, like building different cars on the same chassis, and where we have a manageable amount of variation at different policy price points, like BMW makes the 1 Series, the 3 Series, the 5 Series, and the 7 Series at significantly different price points, but they're all BMWs, they're all branded as 'ultimate driving machines.'

"We retained plenty of flexibility, because you can't mass average this business. But we reduced the complexity down to a manageable level. It's not that sixteen million customers in thousands of different groups are all going to have the exact same benefit package, but there's no reason they have to have ninety-two thousand differences."

Like the marketing investments at Mayo Clinic and Pfizer, the large marketing expenditures at UnitedHealthcare are driven by the desire to gain insight into customer needs. Having reengineered its systems and streamlined its offerings, UnitedHealthcare could then deploy these assets to give customers increased value and to build differential advantage over competitors. The two key elements in this initiative, which UnitedHealthcare labels plainly and simply as "consumerism," have been physician support and proactive involvement in patients' care.

"We have been the leader in physician support for some time," Jay Silverstein said. "We are leading the way right now in terms of electronically enabling physicians, and we're going to keep working to expand that penetration, making it easier for more physicians to submit, look up, and be paid for claims. We're building the logic into the system so that every claim that comes in is correct and can be paid automatically.

"We're trying to work with physicians so that every UnitedHealthcare patient is easier to treat. That translates into a better experience for the patient, so that ultimately the doctors and their patients validate UnitedHealthcare for each other.

"If we make the benefits simple, the doctor knows, 'This is how it works.' If we eliminate medical necessity review, as we did in 1999 with our Care Coordination program, they don't have to call us as many times. If we eliminate capitation and pay claims on a fee-for-service basis, as we also have done, we can mine valuable data that help us operate more efficiently and improve patient care from every claim episode. And if we eliminate referrals approval, which we've done, we eliminate a whole set of costs that don't bring value to the system.

"We were the first people to say, 'We don't need to be gatekeepers. Let's create open referral systems.' When our competitors were building restrictive health maintenance organizations, we went in the other direction. When they were scratching their heads over medical necessity review and the role of the insurer's medical director in denying care, we said, 'Let's not make that role denying care; let's figure out how to facilitate care.'

"Our competitors were slow to realize the value of these steps. Both Aetna and Cigna abandoned capitation much later than us. They were still thinking from the perspective of company costs rather than customer experience."

Unified systems enabled UnitedHealthcare to build what Jay Silverstein calls "potentially the most powerful consumer database in the world, with over fifty million person years of clinical data; it alerts us that a woman is pregnant before she tells her in-laws." With careful safeguards to protect patient privacy, this database in turn enables

UnitedHealthcare to interact with customers to improve their health care in a highly efficient, cost-effective way.

UnitedHealthcare is continuing to search for ways to deliver customer value. Those ways are only truly limited by a company's understanding of customer needs and its creativity in meeting them.

•   •   •

Mayo Clinic, Pfizer, and UnitedHealth Group show how top marketing companies deliver value to customers, and acquire differential advantage over competitors, by integrating all their operations in customer-focused marketing cultures (a subject we will explore more thoroughly in chapters 7 and 8). They also show how the most successful organizations develop offerings and hone competencies to satisfy customer needs, rather than the preferences of the company overall, or of individual company executives.

Mayo Clinic delivers customer value to both direct and indirect customers through its collaborative care model. In return it enjoys differential advantage over competition in the favorable terms it negotiates with insurers, who in turn command higher premiums on policies that cover care at the clinic.

Pfizer mines customer insight—on both physicians and patients—through its multiple dialogues with physicians and focused sales management. Greater customer insight constitutes a differential advantage over competition that is reflected in increased sales volume and market share.

The UnitedHealth Group's distinctive competence, as a health-plan provider, lies in its industry leading integration of back office claims processing with proactive patient care by its customer-service department and call centers. Cynics may argue that this appealing rhetoric simply disguises an effort to limit patients' access to physicians. But it remains true that an ounce of prevention is worth a pound of cure, and physician advocacy groups and public health authorities alike agree that the most important steps to staying healthy must be taken outside the doctor's office. Of course, the greater customer value that UnitedHealthcare's call center nurses and other staff provide—making health care easier and more proactive for both physician and patient—also allows it to limit its costs in payments to physicians and to charge higher than average premiums for its policies.

There is a pattern at work here: the top marketing companies all deliver superior customer value and retain differential advantage over competition by putting customers first. They are superb generalists who leverage a customer-focused culture across the full range of their operations in order to deliver increased value to customers. And like Mayo, Pfizer, and UnitedHealthcare, they develop distinctive competencies according to the nature of their relationship with customers. Finally, they are not content with one set of competencies but regularly acquire new ones as customer needs, wants, and preferences change and evolve over time.

Mobil achieved a differential advantage over competitors by delivering more value to convenience-driven consumers with Speedpass. ExxonMobil extended that advantage by being the first mover among the oil companies to launch a major shift to convenience stores, rather than car-service bays, behind the pumps. With its On the Run stores, it recognized earlier than rival oil companies that driver service rather than car servicing had become the crucial means to delivering increased customer value. The other oil companies eventually followed suit and adopted similar strategies of acquiring convenience-store competencies and assets, but ExxonMobil's excellent execution of the strategy has kept it in the lead. Execution is key with a less than unique strategy that several players converge on before long.

GOJO Industries exploited first-mover status in its launching of Purell as the first waterless hand cleanser in the consumer marketplace. To deliver value to retail consumers and maintain differential advantage over the copycat products that were sure to come if it succeeded, it acquired a host of new competencies. GOJO saw its brilliant execution ratified by Pfizer's acquisition of the consumer-marketing rights to Purell.

Progressive delivered increased customer value when it devised its innovative, cost-based pricing system, and it protected its differential advantage from copycats by combining lower prices with industry-leading ease of use in shopping for and purchasing insurance online, on the phone, or through an independent insurance agent, on the one hand, and with fast, efficient, fair claims service, on the other.

Dell delivers enhanced customer value by being the low-cost provider in every product area in which it competes. Earlier in the chapter, I noted that customer value may be economic, functional, or psychological. Dell has chosen to match the competition in providing satisfactory functional value but to outperform the competition in providing economic value. Different categories of customer will naturally ascribe more or less psychological value to the Dell offerings that are shaped by this choice. But Dell's revenue and market share growth demonstrate that plenty of customers find its products to their liking.

Alcoa and L'Oréal create superior customer value and sustain differential advantage over competition by integrating future-forward research and development with continual process refinement that achieves the lowest direct and indirect costs, including those for commodities, environmental impact, and worker safety. As we'll see in chapter 7, Bloomberg, Toyota, UPS, and Starbucks all create exceptional customer value, and wield differential advantage over competitors, by integrating their operations in rigorous alignment with customer needs.

An increasingly critical area for delivering customer value and securing differential advantage is in product design. In both business-to-business and consumer arenas, many firms offer products that function effectively. They do the job they are supposed to do. But what separates the winners from the losers in many cases is the ability to enhance the customer experience through innovative design that supercharges a product's performance, value, or aesthetic appeal. As we saw in chapter 3, Alcoa and L'Oréal in their different ways have long excelled in this area. In the consumer electronics and computer markets, Apple's brand identity is first and foremost a design identity: the company sells an operating system software and products that march defiantly apart in manner of use and looks from products in the PC computer world.

Until recently the vastly greater customer population of the PC world has meant that Apple's Macintosh computers and ancillary products could never dominate the industry, no matter how innovative their design. All that changed with the iPod, Apple's brilliant MP3 player and its first product to be made PC compatible.

The iPod's capabilities were impressive, but rival MP3 players soon duplicated those capabilities at significantly lower prices. Yet despite the apparent performance-for-price edge of rival products, iPod sales took off fast and kept climbing because of Apple's ergonomic design and intuitive interface, including a patented thumb-operable click wheel control that reviewers and consumers alike loved. In fiscal 2006, with sales over thirty-nine million units (and twenty-one million in the first quarter of fiscal 2007),[4] the iPod had transformed—and significantly expanded—the entire MP3 sector of the consumer electronics business. For Apple, the original iPod had morphed into an entire line of iPods at several profitable price points, and numerous companies had plunged into the business of making ancillary products for them.

Companies that place a premium on great design often in turn enjoy a premium price for their products. We've already seen the important role that design plays at Nokia and Samsung, as well as Alcoa and L'Oréal. Certainly, Sony has had some recent stumbles; nonetheless, it has a well-deserved reputation for design excellence. Ron Boire, president of consumer sales for Sony Electronics USA, told us,

"I think one of the true powers of Sony is great design. I think the fact that we think about the human interface—not just from a 'how do things work' standpoint, but how do they fit and feel in human contact—is a strategic advantage and it's something that we've invested in through our design centers and R&D and product planners for decades and we've become extremely good at. If you go into a store to look at computers, the Sony VAIO looks, feels, and interacts with you differently than any other laptop on the shelf. Some people have copied parts of it. But they're always going to be a few iterations behind because they don't have the design teams that we have in New York and San Francisco and Tokyo and around the world that are really driving the idea of the total human experience when you're touching a product. And that's an advantage that's very hard to copy."

Sony's design advantage helps it command a higher-than-industry-average price for its computer, as for many of its other products. Ron Boire explained, "The target customer is kind of a differentiated customer to begin with. You know, we're not selling VAIO computers at $2,000 a piece to the masses. We're selling to that top 10 percent of the population that can afford to appreciate the design and the differentiation.

"The most exciting thing about Sony to me is when you're in a lineup review and they're showing you product and you get this twenty-eight-year-old product planner and this thirty-year-old designer and they walk into a room and they pull back a piece of cloth and they show you a product and you go, 'Oh my God, it's perfect.' And when you get into those moments, you know, it's about the passion that this organization has for great products. This organization really believes in creating the best possible product that you can create. That's ingrained in the organization. And the areas in which we're making the greatest progress build on that. The subbrand power of PlayStation and Xplod car stereo, our improved channel management and better alignment with trade customers all build on that.

"The core strength of this company is passionate designers and product planners and senior marketing managers who just absolutely love what they're doing. And there's this one designer in Tokyo that typifies that for me. When you first see him, you think, 'Oh my God, a street person has wandered in and is loose in the building.' Because he's got pants that are four sizes too big, and his clothes just hang off him, and he looks like he hasn't slept in a week. But when he pulls back the drape on the new product he's designed, you're blown away.

"I took our newly hired marketing VP to Tokyo for product lineup meetings. We're looking at products all day, some market ready, some that still need to be tweaked. About 4:00 in the afternoon they had all the CD players out there and this one designer came in. I had told our VP about him, and as soon as the designer walked in our VP said, 'That's him, isn't it?' The designer took the cloth off his new CD player and the VP looked at me and said, 'I just love this place.'

"Cause the stuff was perfect. It was just perfect. That line of CD players sold six million units in the United States alone. And we didn't have to touch it, it was perfect. So that's the strength of Sony, somebody with passion designed that thing."

•   •   •

We have by no means exhausted the impressive number of ways in which top marketing companies deliver superior customer value and achieve a profitable differential advantage over competitors. But it is a healthy sample with some shared strong patterns:

- Understanding that customers are a company's reason for being, the most successful companies find differential advantage through superior customer insight.

- Armed with a better understanding of customer needs than competitors, they frame offerings that deliver superior customer value—and they profit accordingly.

- Marketing Mavens recognize that they may have several different layers and levels of direct and indirect current and potential customers throughout a supply chain for a good or service, and they seek the customer insight that is appropriate to each.

- The more levels of customers a company recognizes and serves appropriately, the more profitable it will be. In other words, multiple customer sets—direct and indirect, trade channel and end user—multiply profitability.

- Marketing Mavens look wide when it comes to customer needs, but they also look deep. They want to find ways to pull value through a whole chain of suppliers, vendors, partners, distributors, and end users. That means they must gain insight into the economic, functional, and psychological needs of customers in every category.

- Marketing Mavens communicate to customers the value that they create in whatever is the most effective manner. In some cases, the appropriate vehicles will be mass communications like advertising and public relations, and increasingly Web-based methods. In other cases, interpersonal communication methods using a sales force or newer organization forms like strategic and global account management will be most effective. We see examples of several communications approaches throughout this book.

Of course, the flip side is also critically important. If you fail to recognize customers you can serve profitably, do not understand their needs, and/or fail to serve them appropriately, the entire system will break down. Products that you may sell in at one level will not move through the channel, and your sales will atrophy. After all, a chain is only as strong as its weakest link.

Above all, excellent marketing companies rely on human resources and core staff competencies to deliver appropriate value to every level and category of customer, and to do so in a way that beats the competition over the long term. In several cases, the crucial human resources are embodied in an iconic product design. But that should not distract us from recognizing that the success of the iconic design depends on the designers' creative responses to changing customer needs. This high level of design competence is hard to achieve for innovators or copycats, and hard to sustain. No design dominates forever, so a company's human design resources must regularly be renewed and refocused around new customer needs.

The same can be said of all a company's essential human competencies for meeting customer needs. Processes and designs can always be copied, imitated, or improved on. But as we'll see in some detail in the next two chapters, customer-focused, company-wide marketing cultures that produce successful processes and designs can be imitated only with difficulty and can never be duplicated exactly.

Integrate to Serve the Customer

SEVEN

Structuring Systems and Processes to Serve Customers

Crafting a compelling offer to secure differential advantage over competitors is one thing. Execution—delivering the full value of the offer to more and more profitable customers—requires aligning a line organization and a robust infrastructure of systems and processes with customer needs and devoting a dynamic set of collective human resources—a unified corporate culture—to serve the customer.

The challenge of integrating the firm's operations and culture to execute a strategy that delivers value to customers can take many forms. You not only have to integrate internal operations to serve the customer but reintegrate them to keep in step with technological advances and evolving customer needs. A special challenge is to reintegrate internal operations following mergers, acquisitions, or even divestitures that may dramatically alter operational competencies and brand assets. Many's the acquisition that failed because of incompatible corporate processes and cultures—of course, this is an especially severe challenge in the increasing number of cross-border mergers like Daimler and Chrysler, and Alcatel and Lucent.

Integrating with the systems of a customer can be an order of magnitude more difficult. Going one step further, a true customer focus may involve helping your customer company reengineer its own systems and processes to align them the needs of its own customers. For example, the engineers in 3M's coatings business offer considerable value to boat builders in helping them to improve their entire boat-building processes, including but not limited to those process that use 3M's coatings.

Any one of these initiatives inevitably stresses the customer-focused, company-wide marketing culture required to implement them. But it is only on account of such cultures that the initiatives can succeed. The most successful companies we talked to bear witness to this. They all out-execute the competition in aligning their company cultures and their line organizations with customers' needs.

Mayo Clinic has deployed and integrated innovative systems to support its collaborative care model resulting in a unique corporate culture within the health-care field. As we saw in chapter 6, over the years these systems have included specially designed buildings, the first internal telephone exchange to allow speedy consultation by physicians and nurses, and data sharing that gathers all caregivers' notes and observations into comprehensive patient files that are immediately accessible to everyone involved in a patient's treatment. The data-sharing system, which began in the 1920s with mechanical procedures to move physical files around Mayo's campus, has been continually updated and now incorporates advances in digital information technology.

But again, more important than the sophistication of any single business system is their integration into a customer-focused, in this case patient-focused, whole. A corporate culture is the ultimate means of integrating systems and processes to serve customer needs. The Marketing Mavens show that when a firm's people all join together to serve customer needs, the results tend to be extraordinarily successful. Of course, sustaining such an organization culture demands a lot from a company and its employees. Kent Seltman, Mayo's Marketing Division chair and Brand Team leader, told my colleagues and me, "Mayo Clinic's corporate culture is extremely strong. And you ultimately have to buy into our patient-centered, teamwork culture or leave the organization."

•   •   •

Auto insurer Progressive transformed the entire U.S. car insurance industry with its pioneering pricing schemes. To keep that differential advantage from evaporating when larger competitors played copycat, Progressive had to refine its pricing process, including the ability to calculate competitors' pricing, to continue offering customers both appealing premium rates for its own policies as well as trustworthy comparison shopping. But anticipating that these marketing features would be duplicated by rivals, Progressive integrated other services to deliver value to customers.

Progressive had to extend the industry-leading ease of use advantage of its comparison pricing service throughout all its operations, by developing a customer-centric claims adjustment system. It was then able to handle customer needs, at the customer's discretion, equally well through all channels: via Web, phone, and independent agent. Progressive encapsulated this approach for customers in its slogan, "Think easier." Such steps sustain the company's unique market identity in customers' eyes, and they are especially effective at building customer loyalty and retention. By integrating services and delivering customer value through claims adjustment, Progressive developed perhaps the best Claims Department in the industry. Certainly no one ever wants to deal with a car insurance claim, but when that fateful day arrives customers want to get their claims processed efficiently and effectively.

• • •

Effective integration of operations and other assets to serve customers, enabled and implemented by a company-wide, customer-focused marketing culture, can see an enterprise through tough times. In 2004 Pfizer saw its share price battered by regulatory and ethical concerns over the safety of COX-2 inhibiting arthritis drugs, aggressive direct-to-consumer advertising for Viagra, and the conduct of its direct-to-physician sales efforts. Many of its rivals faced similar problems.

In the midst of a hard-fought battle to keep Viagra the number one drug in its category against impressive market share gains by Levitra, the product of a joint venture among Bayer, GlaxoSmithKline, Schering-Plough, and Eli Lilly's Cialis, Pfizer had to withdraw a television ad campaign that failed to specify that Viagra was for erectile dysfunction and left the impression, as the FDA saw it, that the company was marketing the drug for recreational use. The television ads for Cialis, Levitra, and Viagra all looked like would-be trailers for a hot scene in *Sex and the City*, one episode of which featured the recreational use of Viagra, a "product placement" that Pfizer did not seek and did not want. The only substantive difference in the advertising for Viagra, as opposed to that for Cialis and Levitra, was that it failed to include the words *erectile dysfunction*. Pfizer also came under scrutiny when it was reported that some of its direct-to-physician sales teams might be making unethical payments to physicians to encourage so-called off-label prescribing of the company's medicines.

Yet preserving present and future profitability through these difficult times has clearly depended on the vitality of Pfizer's direct-to-physician sales efforts and their integration with the company's other marketing systems, from the R&D phase to direct-to-consumer advertising and the final delivery and sale of the company's products. Pfizer's ability to switch its sales force model from multiple salespeople calling on the same physician, to a new structure based on five therapeutic categories, whereby individual salespeople have deeper knowledge and therefore greater value to physicians, has positioned it to weather a storm over the pharmaceutical industry's ethical issues that has also engulfed Merck and other rivals.

•   •   •

As we saw in chapter 4, Alcoa uses its Alcoa Business System, spearheaded by Market Sector Lead Teams that puts Alcoa engineers, designers, managers, safety experts, and even accountants to work in customers' plants, to carry Alcoa's company-wide focus on "make for use" directly to its customers. Alcoa has credited this systematic integration of operations and culture for its continuing market share lead, its low lost workday rate due to accidents, record cost savings, and increased profitability for each of its six main business segments: alumina, primary metals, flat-rolled products, extruded and end products, engineered products, and packaging and consumer goods. In 2006 Alcoa's revenues reached $30.4 billion. In an enviably well-balanced revenue picture, engineered products ($5.5 billion) were 18 percent of the total. This marks Alcoa's success in building, as the firm's 2004 annual report put it, "a coordinated approach to markets and customers [that] migrate[s] our value proposition from materials and components to higher-value, customer-centric engineered solutions."[1]

The fact that Alcoa not only talks a good game but also walks the walk has been vouchsafed for by Airbus, one of its key global customers. Alcoa, it said, "won a strategic position on the Airbus A380 by applying its integrated product approach."[2] The A380 features more new Alcoa materials and products than any other aircraft the company has worked on, including a new, highly damage-tolerant alloy for the fuselage skin. The signature Alcoa product on the A380 is its XPL lock-bolt, which has a titanium collar that is both strong enough to handle the great size of the airplane's wing and compatible with the composite and aluminum materials it has to link. Every A380 contains about a million XPL lockbolts.

As chapter 4 touched on, Dick Melville stresses safety as one of the hallmarks of the Alcoa Business System in everything from basic smelting to final products. He credits his Aerospace Market Sector Lead Team's design of a "safe process for delivery" of materials and products to Boeing for cutting delivery times by 80 percent and dramatically reducing accidents with a "uni-train concept." Work that once required a large crew for several days is now done by one person in a few hours. Likewise Alcoa's aluminum bats "cut down lawsuits [from splintering of wooden bats] for our customers [bat manufacturers] by orders of magnitude." As chapter 4 also noted, there is concern about traumatic head injuries caused by the greater speed with which a baseball flies off an aluminum bat, but aluminum bats remain the preferred choice for all competitive baseball except the professional leagues, because they are seen as safer overall, as well as aiding hitting and home-run production.

As Dick Melville puts it, "A safe plant tends to be laid out much more intelligently than a nonsafe plant. When we walk our customers through our facilities, they can see cleanliness [and] instantaneous feedback on quality. They can see people who are well trained and care. They can see their product coming through with a great deal of thought and attention." In other words, for Alcoa safety is one of the key ways of measuring and extending its operational integration and customer focus. A drop in accident rates for Alcoa or its customers is a drop in concomitant human and other costs that makes the relationship of Alcoa and its customers more valuable for both of them.

There is, of course, no way to make the relationship between customer needs and your systems and processes perfect. It is a constant struggle to keep company and customer interests aligned, and the relationship between the two will always be buffeted by change. In dealing with this challenge, Alcoa, like all Marketing Mavens, will continue to rely on the rigorous integration of operations to serve customer needs, and on a company-wide, customer-focused marketing culture.

•   •   •

Once a company acquires important new competencies, they must be integrated into ongoing operations and melded into the corporate culture. That was the case when ExxonMobil acquired retail convenience store competencies and assets to achieve success with its On the Run stores. Its Retail Centers of Excellence help instill the "face to the customer, back to the company" attitude throughout the world. Operationally they are, of course, a means for assiduously honing retail convenience-store competencies: the look and layout of the stores; category management; and most important, employee training, motivation, and retention. Its strong systems ensuring a high level of performance was the key reason that *Convenience Store Decisions* selected On the Run for its Chain of the Year Award in 2003.

Recall that Hal Cramer stressed the importance of hiring and training "the right people that touch the customer." When I questioned him on this, given that the rival convenience-store chains are basically drawing on the same labor pool, he elaborated, "You've got to start with employees. Because unless . . . employees get it, unless . . . [they] understand what they're supposed to be doing . . . [and] feel good about presenting your brand image, you can't win the hearts and minds of the customer. It's the difference between knowing what to do and wanting to do it." Thus, Cramer said, ExxonMobil's strategy is to motivate On the Run employees "through training, through culture, through rewards and consequences."

Convenience Store Decisions noted ExxonMobil's "extensive support system" for franchises, especially its category management and its "workplace audits" and "people system, [which] helps it connect with front-line employees." U.S. sales director Mark Shore, told the magazine, "We are the pacesetter in [workplace safety]. Our vision is 'Nobody gets hurt,' and our employees value that." ExxonMobil's workplace audits go hand in hand with reward schemes that compensate and acknowledge franchisees and direct employees for sales performance in the On the Run stores. The result has been a decrease in employee turnover at On the Run that is the envy of rival chains. For ExxonMobil as for other top companies, treating employees and staff appropriately in terms of safety, compensation, and other human resource issues is a critical means of aligning company operations to deliver customer value.

•   •   •

Dell's direct model continues to pay off in growth and profitability, despite recent gains by Hewlett Packard. Dell rigorously hones an asset base of systems and processes that extends seamlessly from component manufacturers to end-use consumers. From its home base in Texas the asset base has grown into a worldwide network of factories and other facilities, all integrated together to serve Dell's direct manufacturing model. Rigorous integration of global supply capabilities to serve a truly global customer base means that Dell can continue to win on price against all comers, including the cheapest outsource supplied rivals.

Dell maximizes its operational cost advantage through a major ongoing investment in employee communication and training. Describing Dell's corporate culture efforts, vice president for global brand strategy Scott Helbing told us, "We do regular communications [with employees] via the Web and through the different marketing groups. We'll attend regularly scheduled meetings around the company on a quarterly basis to present the whole concept behind the business model and keep that conversation going, because our best salespeople are all the people who work here. If they're at the dry cleaner or the kids' soccer game and someone says, 'What's the deal at Dell? What's the direct model all about?,' we want them to be able to say very quickly, 'It's every machine configured to the individual customer on the lowest cost basis.' "

Michael George, Dell's CMO and vice president for corporate strategy, also stressed the company's efforts to keep all employees focused on using the direct model to meet customer needs. Customer knowledge is an explicit criterion in evaluating all employees, whether or not they have customer-facing jobs. It doesn't matter, George said, "whether they're in [human resources], finance, or manufacturing, they should know their role in serving the end customer."

The best sign of this, George proudly noted, is that everyone at Dell shares "a wonderfully healthy paranoia . . . [We] assume that any day someone could catch us and beat us." With increasingly aggressive rivals like HP and Lenovo, that paranoia should stand Dell in good stead as it deals with competition-driven erosion of pricing and profitability in all its product sectors, a challenge we'll revisit later in the book.

•   •   •

L'Oréal's position at the head of the worldwide cosmetics market depends as much on a complex chain of research and development and industrial operations as it does on creative packaging, advertising, and promotion. The company has to create a thorough-link from lengthy

R&D efforts, through materials procurement and processing, to fast-moving consumer health and lifestyle trends.

Outsiders often miss the complex integration of operations that is necessary on the industrial side of the cosmetics business. L'Oréal consistently tries to refine its integration efforts in order to drive cost out of the business. From 1993 to 2003, despite vast growth, L'Oréal succeeded in cutting water consumption in its manufacturing operations by 28 percent and energy consumption by 7 percent, while increasing recycling, reuse, and clean incineration of industrial wastes by 23 percent. Over the same time period, its conservation efforts and eco-friendly approach formed an increasingly important part of L'Oréal's brand identity, as customers in every market region became more environmentally and socially conscious. For these customers, L'Oréal's commitment to operating as efficiently and cleanly as possible constitutes an additional form of customer value beyond the utility and aesthetic appeal of its products.

To draw the general point: taking pains to integrate your operations in line with customer needs pays off in multiple ways. L'Oréal's eco-conscious approach both saves it money and enhances customer loyalty and brand appeal. L'Oréal reinforced this aspect of its image when in 2006 it acquired the Body Shop, the well-known socially responsible cosmetics retail chain with a portfolio of over two thousand stores in fifty-three countries around the world.

Growing at twice the rate of the cosmetics market as a whole in the 2000s, L'Oréal hopes to sustain that market-leading growth by continuing to integrate its R&D systems with demographic trends both in developing markets in eastern Europe, India, and China and in the increasingly diverse societies of western Europe and North America. In 2003 it established the L'Oréal Institute for Ethnic Hair and Skin Research in Chicago, and it has seized the industry lead in a new business segment, "nutricosmetics," that is part of a mammoth customer trend, the growing interest in healthier lifestyles and products.

The company has also taken a number of steps to ensure that its culture remains marketing driven and customer focused. As part of an ongoing effort to identify, hire, and foster a diversity of talent among employees that reflects the demographic mosaic of its global customer base, L'Oréal conducts two annual contests for teams of undergraduate and MBA students, the L'Oréal Marketing Award/Brandstorm and the L'Oréal E-strategy Challenge, and regularly hires from the pool of contest entrants. And a new Web-based distance-learning program, "L'Oréal Marketing Basics," has become part of employee training worldwide.

The result of these coordinated efforts in systems, processes, and culture, Carol Hamilton told us, is that "everyone at L'Oréal is a brand manager, no matter how high up you are. Everyone knows the texture of Revitalift, and if they opened up a jar they would know instantly if the texture was off."

●   ●   ●

With all these corporate examples as context, let's now look more closely at how the top marketing companies achieve excellence in both corporate systems and processes and corporate culture.

Toyota's Systems for Premium Quality Volume

Since the mid-1980s, Toyota's vehicle production system has likely been the most discussed and praised industrial operation in the world. *The Toyota Way: 14 Management Principles from the World's Greatest Manufacturer, Inside the Mind of Toyota,* and *Notes from Toyota-Land* are a few of the scores of books that have been written about the Toyota production system. Advocates of total quality management (TQM) have so embraced Toyota as a signature example that casual observers might easily think that TQM stands for Toyota quality management.

Toyota's manufacturing system deserves great praise. Springing from the dearth of resources in post–World War II Japan, its guiding principles of lean thinking and continuous improvement—the Japanese term for the latter, *kaizen,* literally means chance (*kai*) for the better (*zen*)—have made Toyota the unquestioned leader in just-in-time supply and inventory management and innovative, low-waste production processes. Toyota implements these principles by distributing authority to intervene on customers' behalf down to the factory floor, where the lowest-echelon worker can stop the production line for any reason. Japan's other carmakers have also succeeded in global markets by adopting similar principles, but there is no disputing the fact that Toyota leads the world in building high-quality vehicles on a low-cost basis.

Year after year Toyota automobiles rank at the top of industry and consumer ratings for initial and ongoing quality. They are built so well that many experts routinely recommend that the best new car value consumers can buy is a used Toyota, because it will run like new for the foreseeable future. Indeed, Toyota's program for marketing "Certified Pre-Owned" vehicles, once solely the province of luxury car makers, is perhaps the most successful of any volume car maker. The program reinforces the value of Toyota's new cars and allows it to set higher prices than other well-regarded Japanese brands like Honda and Nissan, because of Toyotas' high resale prices.

Yet Toyota's manufacturing system is just one of three integrated, market-driven systems for meeting customer needs. Preceding it comes Toyota's research and development system, and after it comes Toyota's dealer management and customer service system.

Toyota's R&D process begins with extensive research into customer demographics and lifestyle trends. Steve Sturm, Toyota's vice president of marketing, explained, "We start with a broad look at the demographic trends over a twenty-year span. What has been happening in the lives of baby boomers, Generation Xers, and Generation Yers? What lifestyle changes are gaining momentum?"

To which one might say, "So what? Every automaker does that." Indeed, they do. But as in so many aspects of business, execution is critical. Toyota's ability to gain in-depth insight in its customer research studies is best exemplified by its creation of the Lexus and Scion brands.

To develop the Lexus, for example, the chief engineer and his team lived for several months in Southern California's upscale Laguna Hills and visited many similar metropolitan areas around the United States—from Coral Gables near Miami, to north Lake Shore Drive in Chicago, to Westchester County, New York. On each visit they talked with luxury car owners, learned how they drove and treated their cars, how they dealt with valet parking, and figured out the role these cars played in their lives.

These sort of data give Toyota a sense of the sorts of new features that may be desirable in current models and the sorts of new models that will appeal to consumers a few years down the road. To go further in both renovating existing car models and designing and building new ones, "We have to narrow that and say, 'Okay, when someone is looking for a product that's going to give them capability, versatility, and value, what are the needs and wants of that customer?' And we do that in general and fundamental research. And then at that point we kind of let the designers go at it."

For Toyota, letting the designers go at it means initiating a competition among the company's five research and design studios: in Tokyo and Toyota City, Japan; in Newport Beach, California, and Ann Arbor, Michigan, in the United States; and in Nice, France. Toyota's worldwide product planning process allows it to bring the best developments in the world to any particular market of interest. A few Toyota models are sold around the world in all markets, but otherwise the lineup changes considerably from market to market. There are Toyotas the consumer can buy in either Japan/Asia, North America, or Europe, that are not available in the other two regions. But this does not restrict the design studios, each of which has won competitions to produce designs for cars sold outside its "local" market. "They all compete for what is the best look," Sturm said.

Toyota's R&D systems cover more than the look of the company's vehicles, however; they explore the entire car-owning experience. This comprehensive approach was crucial to the success of the Lexus.

In the 1960s and 1970s Toyota established itself in the North American market by selling economical, yet supremely reliable cars to young baby boomers. In the 1980s, watching the boomers reach middle age and become increasingly affluent, Toyota dreamed of selling them luxury cars. As Steve Sturm told us, the company's research was encouraging.

"We surveyed American consumers who owned luxury cars—American and foreign made—and found a big gap in customer satisfaction. Dealers sold luxury cars at high markups above the recommended retail price, yet overall the cars were also very unreliable and very expensive to maintain. People bought products they liked and then became frustrated because the car was always in the shop and repair charges were astronomical. The most disturbing thing for customers was that warranties were not uniformly honored from dealer to dealer. If a customer brought a car in for service, most of the time the dealer said, 'Sorry, it's on your nickel not ours.'

"So there was a lot of dissatisfaction among luxury car owners. There was also a gap between lower-priced luxury and higher-priced luxury. We believed this was a significant segment that we could come into and take advantage of. That was the number one question which Toyota needed to be able to answer yes.

"The second question was, were there important product needs that were not fulfilled by either American or European luxury carmakers? The answer to that was also yes, because technologically many of the existing luxury carmakers were resting on their laurels.

"Third and last, could Toyota do better on both counts? Could we sell customers a better luxury car and back it up with better service?"

Toyota already had experience making luxury cars for the Japanese market, so it knew it could deliver the right car at the right price point. And it was confident about its ability to deliver industry-beating service. But the company's research also indicated that it would have a tough time convincing American consumers to pay luxury car prices for a Toyota, which was firmly identified in their minds as an economy car.

That recognition triggered the company's decision to position Lexus not as a new Toyota model, but as a stand-alone brand. Honda had already made the same decision, launching the Acura brand in North America in 1986. But Toyota was not overly concerned about Honda's bringing the first Japanese luxury car to the American market. It was focused on becoming the best luxury carmaker in consumers' eyes, bar none, and the early news on Acura, successful though it was, showed that the field still lacked a clear winner.

As the first step to establish a Lexus dealer network and integrate with other operations, Sturm told us, "We mapped the United States and Canada into what we called primary market areas. Basically each PMA was a major metropolitan region. We determined that there should be two dealers in a PMA, except in the biggest cities, like Los Angeles and New York, which could obviously support more. Then we identified target locations and the best dealers in every PMA."

Significantly, Toyota conducted its search for the best dealers without prejudice as to whether or not they were Toyota dealers. The decisive factors were the dealers' track records with customers and their financial resources (they would have to spend heavily to establish their new franchises).

"If the local Toyota dealers were doing an excellent job, they had first choice. But in Dallas/Ft. Worth, for example, the two best dealers were selling Cadillacs in one case, and BMWs and Mercedes-Benzes in the other. As experienced luxury car dealers, they knew the gaps in the market and recognized the opportunity we represented, they had the money to build new dealerships, and we chose them. In Los Angeles we invited the cream of existing Toyota dealers to establish Lexus dealerships in separate facilities, and we also had dealers who had never sold Toyotas."

In the run-up to the first Lexus models going on sale in 1990, Toyota made another crucial decision, one that no other carmaker had made before: not only would every Lexus dealership have to be a stand-alone facility, on separate premises from any other dealerships the franchisee might have; they would all have to be built with the same facade and the same signage. "It was like McDonald's," Sturm said, noting that some thought imitating the strategy of a mass-market franchise was counterintuitive for a luxury product. But for Toyota, ensuring the consistency of the dealerships' appearance was an important way of communicating to consumers that the Lexus experience, in contrast to the erratic performance of previous luxury cars and dealers, would be consistently satisfying.

First-year sales for Lexus exceeded Toyota's expectations. But mechanically there were teething problems, as with any new car, even one built by Toyota. This was the acid test for Lexus, and it stands as proof that a superb production system alone does not explain Toyota's remarkable record of success.

"We had a couple of quality issues. So we were tested pretty quickly as to how we were going to deal with the warranty and recalls. We went beyond what any other car manufacturer and dealer network had ever done, and we set a new benchmark. We took back every car. In some cases we went to the customer's home. We checked the whole car and fixed everything, not just the things we recalled it for. Then before we gave the car back, we washed it and filled the tank. Minor things, maybe. But they blew people away, and they motivated tremendous word of mouth. Lexus owners were boasting about us and our service to their friends, 'You know, they just don't talk about standing up for their product—they actually back up their comments.'

"We didn't rely on recalls from headquarters to alert us to problems either. For the first ten years, each of us in management called four Lexus customers a month to find out how things were going with the car and the dealer."

To ensure that both Toyota and Lexus dealers provide Toyota-quality service, their franchise agreements, which run for three to five years, include what Steve Sturm called a "strong set of guidelines." No doubt other carmakers have similarly strong guidelines. The Toyota difference is the degree to which the company takes action to support its guidelines. As Sturm elaborated to my colleagues and me, "If the dealers don't meet those guidelines, their franchises are not renewed. It happens quite a bit. We have strong regional organizations in both Lexus and Toyota that call on the dealers weekly, if not daily. We monitor every aspect of a franchise. We see the financial statements. We get customer satisfaction scores for every car we sell.

"The completed surveys go to us and the dealers. If we see a trend that shows a deteriorating service environment or customer satisfaction environment, we go in and counsel the dealers as to what's wrong. It could be a people issue. It could be a process issue.

"Bad, unscrupulous salespeople will not survive at Toyota or Lexus. Either they will not survive by not selling the right cars or their surveys will come in so poor, the dealers will say; 'You're not working. Good-bye.' And if the dealers are slow to catch that, we are there to make sure they do.

"That requires consistent, continual training programs for everybody—for internal and external people. We provide that with our training group, which we call the University of Toyota."

Toyota's faith in integrating operations to meet customer needs, rather than company or industry preferences, can also be seen in its advertising and promotion, Steve Sturm maintained. "We don't follow the rules of the conventional, cyclical nature of the car business in our promotions. Because we basically are building products that customers need and want. Even in the worst years, the industry's still selling fifteen million cars. You know, you're not going to see it go below fifteen million probably ever again. Regardless, if you provide the right cars you do well in bad economies and good economies. We actually do better in softer economies [because] there's less competition.

"To support that, we have a consistent advertising dollar budget in the market at all times. Because the media companies know we're going to do that, we tend to get great prices all the time. Maybe even more important, we get the great properties. You know, it's not just about being on television a lot, it's about being on the most-watched programs."

A few weeks before we first spoke to Steve Sturm, Toyota announced that it would launch a new brand for young customers, the Scion.

"We're doing very well," Sturm said. "But if we sit on our laurels and relax and enjoy the tail wind, we'll lose. What keeps us focused is that we have to continue to reinvent the way we do business, the way our products are promoted, the way our dealer service is handled, to make sure that we raise the bar and not just sit on our reputation. And that we continue to attract younger buyers so that when people reach their elder years and buy their last cars, we have people in their twenties coming in. We want to continually seed the market with new conquests, as well are retain current ones. Scion will target the hip-hop generation."

The 2003–4 Scion launch reprised the Lexus launch at the opposite end of the price spectrum, although not all Scion dealerships were the stand-alone variety, and some were established within existing Toyota dealerships. Again, there were teething problems with the cars; again, Toyota went the extra mile to fix them. And once again, Toyota hit a marketing bull's-eye. In the midst of a national craze for customizing cars among younger drivers, manifest in such television programs as MTV's "Pimp My Ride," Toyota was the first carmaker with a line of products targeted at that market. Every prospective Scion purchaser is invited to "personalize your ride" with a full array of factory or dealer-installed and after-market accessories, and Scion's sales collateral—both its online and in printed brochures—speaks the language of the hip-hop generation. To maintain Scion's hip brand image, Toyota plans to restrict U.S. sales to 150,000 units in 2007.[3]

When GM tried to revive Oldsmobile with a revamped model line and an advertising campaign centered around the line "Not your father's Oldsmobile," consumers didn't buy it. But Generation Yers are buying Scions—in seven months of 2003, 10,898 with two models; and in 2004 and 2005, 99,259 and 156,485, respectively, with three models—because it is so plainly "not their parents' Toyota."

Meanwhile, sales of the Toyota and Lexus brands continue to rise. In 2006, with anticipated annual sales of 8.85 million cars—a 9 percent year-to-year increase—Toyota was poised to overtake General Motors as the world's top automobile company. Toyota sustains growth in all major markets anticipating 4 percent in Japan (for 44 percent market share), 9.8 percent in the United States, and 60 percent in China. Toyota's consistent sales increases and operational efficiencies produced a net income for the fiscal year ending March 2006 of $11.67 billion—for the comparable period, General Motors' profit number was similar at $10.6 billion, but it was a loss! These results are reflected in stock market valuations where Toyota's mid-2006 valuation of around $170 billion was ten times greater than GM's.

Showing once again that it is not content to rest on its laurels, in January 2005 Toyota announced that Lexus, with sales of 2.4 million cars since its debut in 1990, was finally coming to Japan. The company forecast that the line would achieve profitability there within two years. This represents a considerable risk of Toyota's brand equity in its home market, but given the vitality of its integrated marketing systems— R&D, production, and dealer management/customer service—I wouldn't bet against the company's completing its plan to make Lexus a truly global luxury brand, on or ahead of schedule.

UPS: Synchronizing Customers' Commerce with Synchronized Systems

Integrating complex systems is UPS's stock in trade. Regularly ranked at or near the top of *Fortune*'s annual lists of the most admired United States and global companies, UPS plays the leading role in the burgeoning global logistics industry. Firmly established as the world's largest package delivery company, UPS looks to specialized transportation and third-party logistics services to continue its phenomenal success into the future.

At the UPS Atlanta headquarters, we spoke with three key people. One was senior vice president of Worldwide Sales and Marketing John Beystehner—not long after our conversation he was promoted to COO of UPS, president of UPS Airlines, member of the UPS Board of Directors, and second in command to chair and CEO Michael Eskew. The second was vice president for Brand Management and Customer Communications Dale Hayes, now vice president of Marketing. Third was vice president for brand and product management Gary Mastro. In two extended conversations, they shared their experiences in deploying a global integrated network of logistics systems to deliver value to their customers and their customers' customers.

Since its founding as a local messenger service in Seattle in 1907, UPS has grown steadily through organic development of its businesses and by acquisition. Important recent acquisitions include its $185 million purchase of Mail Boxes Etc., whose United States and Canadian locations have been rebranded as The UPS Store; two large freight-forwarding companies, Fritz and Menlo; and most recently the trucking carrier, Overnite. Integrating large-scale acquisitions into UPS systems has been a major recurring task.

Along the way UPS has also had to respond nimbly to changing regulatory situations in the United States and abroad. For example, Canadian regulations once meant the company had to use taxicabs to move packages across provincial borders. And it has met the challenge of competition from both government-subsidized national postal services in Europe and North America and rival companies, especially of its fellow most admired company, FedEx.

Since the 1980s, UPS and FedEx have been converging on the same market targets. FedEx's breakthrough in overnight air delivery stimulated a major push by UPS to expand its own air services. Likewise, UPS's purchase of Mail Boxes Etc. undoubtedly helped influence FedEx's purchase of the Kinko's chain.

"FedEx started out air based and then drove down to the ground," John Beystehner told us. "We started out ground based and then worked up the other way."

Despite FedEx's remarkable success over the last thirty years and its number one position in overnight air delivery, UPS remains a substantially larger company in overall package volume and revenues. "FedEx Ground handles about 1.6 million pieces per day. We handle about 10 million ground pieces," Beystehner said. "FedEx Air handles around 3 million pieces per day. We're around 2 million."[4] FedEx's 2005 revenues and profits were $29.4 billion and $1.4 billion, respectively; comparable UPS figures were $42.6 billion and $3.9 billion, respectively. Most significant, UPS claims a clear lead in the areas it considers most important to future growth—third-party logistics, freight forwarding, and international trade services.

UPS believes that its fundamental advantage is an integrated network that is not only across North America but the world. For over 90 percent of its volume, customers upload the data regarding their shipments. This not only increases the efficiency with which UPS can

handle those specific shipments but enables it to do consultative selling and marketing.

The vehicle for that is UPS's own version of customer relationship
management. UPS employs technology-enabled relationship management. It can drill down on large accounts to the individual decision
makers, whether they're in the mail room or the executive suite, and
offer them tailored solutions that provide security, flexibility, and
accountability.

As an example, Beystehner cited UPS Campus Ship that by 2006
had 650,000 active users in twenty-two thousand companies. "UPS
Campus Ship is a system designed for a large corporate environment,
to allow all employees to arrange shipments from their desktop computer. But it also allows the customer to set controls, so that different
employees have different degrees of freedom in using the system.
Maybe you want everybody to be able to ship Next Day Air; maybe you
only want some employees to be able to do that. And then the system
gives the customer a bill that captures all this clearly and that the transportation manager, say, can use to charge back and allot costs to different groups and divisions."

Dale Hayes added, "Another benefit is that the customer doesn't
have to separate packages at the loading dock. You give us everything;
we take care of it. Plus we make as much information about the packages available to you as you need. That's the heart of another product
that dovetails with Campus Ship called Quantum View, which we developed over the course of a few years. We tested it first with some of
our biggest global and strategic accounts, and they helped us match
needs to services. Quantum View scans the horizon of everything that
is coming into your enterprise or leaving your enterprise, so that you
can track everything upstream and downstream."

Although these products are aimed at UPS's largest customers and
executive decision makers, the company knows that it cannot take its
eye off the small fry. "Even if we gain access to the CFO, the CIO
[chief information officer], or the CEO," Dale Hayes explained, "we
still have to have relationships with the mail-room manager, who's
maybe deciding which company to ship letters and small packages
with, we still have to have the small business owner's and the personal
shipper's trust. If we fail to deliver day in and day out, to the full spectrum of our customers, big and small, the time-definite delivery that is

our core service, then our entire infrastructure will begin to crumble, because we will no longer have reliability in customers' minds."

In the previous chapter we explored how Marketing Mavens craft offers that have enhanced value to customers and thus offer differential advantage over competitors. Integrating company operations to serve customer needs is a necessary means to delivering that enhanced value and achieving that differential advantage. For UPS this marketing imperative has often taken the form of developing systems that empower customers with knowledge, tools, and decision-making capabilities that were once its alone. These efforts have built substantial equity for UPS in the form of customer trust and loyalty.

The trust UPS earns with customers, Gary Mastro said, is the key to "our 75 percent to 80 percent success rate in showing new products and services to them."

Speaking to the same point with reference to UPS's "What can Brown do for you?" John Beystehner noted that this advertising campaign is really where UPS wants to get to, going in and finding out what issues are facing customers and how we can help resolve them. "Reverse logistics—returns—are a great example of that. In 2001 we introduced five new return products to address the fact that every year over $60 billion worth of goods are sent back to companies, who spend $40 billion handling them. That's a $100 billion issue facing business.

"If a company getting returns is connected to us, we make it possible for their customers to print out a label on their home or office computer that has all the information we need to move the returned packages through our automated facilities."

One of the most interesting things about such UPS services is that they often happen directly on the customer company's website. If one of UPS's customers, say Firm X, sends a package to its customer, Y, both employees at Firm X and Customer Y, can track its progress. Firm X can provide this information as a ready resource while Customer Y is already engaged on its website.

UPS did the same thing with the returns that it did with tracking: it developed an open platform and gave it to its customers. Amazon. com's customers can then do tracking on Amazon's website. The end customer never goes to UPS.com. UPS did not seek to have the customer relationships transfer from Amazon.com to it. UPS enabled Amazon.com to continue to own and grow its customer relationships on the Amazon.com website, using UPS tools that their customers see as part of the Amazon.com brand.

UPS did that for companies with enterprise resource planning (ERP) systems as well, creating an entire suite of UPS online tools for larger customers on an open-platform architecture, to directly integrate UPS information into customers' ERP systems. Rather than taking data from UPS in a way it prescribes, customers can take the code in several formats to customize it in any form they want. Then they can make it available to different areas of their business processes such as order management, accounting, customer service, and distribution, or directly to their customers for ready visibility.

In short, UPS has developed and integrated its systems to the point where they are equally adept at aggregating and disaggregating packages for efficient shipment, and aggregating and disaggregating the information connected with them, including financial flows. The security, flexibility, and accountability of these systems have enabled UPS to do the following:

- Create a new process for laptop computer service for Toshiba. Toshiba customers can drop off laptops needing repair at one of over four thousand UPS Store locations, where they are carefully packed and sent not to Toshiba but to a UPS facility, where each is repaired and packed for direct return to the customer, all in half the time of the previous process.

- Guide Honeywell Consumer Products Group, a leader in the automotive aftermarket, to move from five distribution centers down to two and to decrease the average number of shipments per purchase order from three to one, while increasing order fulfillment accuracy to nearly 100 percent.

- Enable Hitachi Global Storage Technology to blend in the assets acquired in the purchase of IBM's storage technology division efficiently, decreasing the required number of facilities locations from seventy-two to fifty-two and, as with Toshiba, using The UPS Store's four-thousand-plus locations as customer drop-off points for service repairs.

- Dissuade a major medical equipment manufacturer from trying to bypass its more than two hundred distributors to its hospital customers by identifying the value the distributors add, especially in managing hospital inventory, and showing the manufacturer how to leverage its relationship with them.

- Design a flexible service parts logistics network for a Fortune 100 telecommunications provider with forty-five million customers, which meets service demand with 85 percent less field inventory and increases annual turns of spare parts inventory from one to six, with a positive return on investment within the first year of implementing the new program.

- Reengineer a European supply chain for Cisco Systems, which cut transportation carriers from 150 to 6 and streamlined customs clearance, documentation, and billing.

- Cut costs for National Semiconductor by 15 percent to 20 percent and improve cycle times for the supply chain from its manufacturing facilities in Southeast Asia to its global customer base.

At the beginning of the chapter, I noted five major challenges of operational integration for companies. As these examples show, UPS regularly achieves excellence in all five: integrating its own operations to serve the customers; reintegrating or reengineering its operations to keep in step with technological advances and evolving customer needs; reintegrating its internal operations following mergers, acquisitions, and divestitures; integrating its internal operations with those of a customer company; and helping a customer company to reengineer its own systems and processes with its customers' needs.

In delivering solutions to customers, UPS's systems pay off for the company in lower operating costs, better profit margins, and increased customer loyalty. These examples also show how UPS continually focuses its line of sight into future customer needs. As Gary Mastro told us, "Package delivery is going to carry UPS for some time. But down the road we will ultimately become a very different company, with more of our operations devoted to logistics and supply chain management and consulting. Of every logistics dollar, only $.06 are spent on transportation; $.94 are spent on warehousing, inventory management, and distribution. We are continually refining the precise engineering that we can apply to those areas."

UPS is addressing that $.94 by taking advantage of its expanded capabilities across the supply chain. For example, UPS Trade Direct is a new multimodal service that combines the firm's air, ocean, and ground freight transportation, customs clearance, and international express and package delivery services to improve supply-chain efficiency. Initially a cross-border service among Canada, the United States, and Mexico, UPS Trade Direct now operates around the globe. Goods at the origin are individually packaged, labeled for delivery, combined into one freight shipment, and shipped for rapid customs clearance in its destination country. Individual parcels or less-than-truckload lots from the deconsolidated shipment bypass costly distribution center stops for final delivery. UPS maintains shipment visibility throughout the supply chain for better inventory management.

As this future takes shape the UPS Marketing Committee will continue to be the company's key forum for new product development and acquisitions. "At UPS," John Beystehner said, "the Marketing Committee comprises the CEO, the COO, and other members of the Executive Management Committee, as well as members of our Sales and Marketing departments. It is not focused on day-to-day things like pricing. It is entirely focused on what the strategic opportunities and challenges are for UPS. For example, our acquisition of Fritz in a $450 million stock swap, was driven by discussions in the Marketing Committee about what our customers want, need, and desire."

Let's look at this evolution of UPS capabilities and systems in terms of its competition with FedEx. As already noted, the two companies have converged on the same market targets from opposite directions, FedEx starting with overnight air delivery and UPS starting with ground transportation. With two such well-run companies, it did not take long before they had at least rough parity in delivery systems and cost control. This put a premium on adding additional services, such as package tracking and return products, before the competition and thus honing a distinctive brand identity in the minds of customers.

We can see the same dynamic at work in other industries. Which automobile makers had cup holders first, and then more of them in more convenient places? Detroit was famously late on cup holders, and the Japanese carmakers, including Toyota, were famously early. Which cosmetics manufacturer established the strongest environmentally conscious brand identity? L'Oréal's purchase of the Body Shop chain consolidated this crucial element of its brand identity. Which aluminum maker gets in sooner and tighter in product development with key customers? If its role with both Airbus and Boeing in airplane development is any indicator, it is Alcoa, not Alcan. Companies that slight the importance of steadily evolving their systems to integrate them with customer needs will soon be left behind. If you don't continually raise the bar by adding new customer value, you can be sure that a competitor will.

The System Behind the Starbucks Experience

Over the last twenty years, Starbucks has earned recognition as one of the world's great experience brands. Currently more than forty million customers per week frequent the over eleven thousand Starbucks locations in almost forty countries around the world. Even more astounding, the most loyal customers treat Starbucks as what the company calls the "third place" in their daily lives (the first two being home and work), visiting the chain an average of eighteen times a month to repeat their experience of its distinctive coffees and ambience.

Anyone who begins to examine the Starbucks story will soon see that largely one person, Howard Schultz, the founder, has shaped Starbucks as we know it. I say "as we know it" because there was a Starbucks before there was a Starbucks.

In 1971 Starbucks Coffee, Tea & Spice, named after the *Pequod*'s first mate in *Moby-Dick*, opened in Seattle's Pike Place Market as a specialty coffee emporium and attracted a fervent local clientele. In 1982 twenty-eight-year-old Howard Schultz joined Starbucks as its director of retail operations and marketing. His first efforts concentrated on providing Starbucks coffee to Seattle restaurants. In 1983 Schultz visited Milan on a buying trip. Inspired by the vitality of Milanese espresso bar culture, where he saw people gathering not just to buy and drink coffee but also to read the daily papers, converse, and socialize, he persuaded the owners of Starbucks to let him try to transplant the concept of a "third place" to a new location in downtown Seattle. The success of the venture, which opened in 1984, emboldened Schultz to found his own company, Il Giornale, "the newspaper," the next year, and in 1987 local investors joined Schultz in buying the Starbucks assets and renaming their own company the Starbucks Coffee Company.

Then the growth of Starbucks really began, growth as dizzying in its sustained ascent as anything on the modern global business scene. The company added twenty, thirty, forty, fifty, then hundreds, and then thousands of new locations a year, with seemingly no end in sight.

Our freewheeling conversation at Starbucks waterfront headquarters in Seattle was interrupted only by a telephone call. It was from National Basketball Association commissioner David Stern (then chair of the board of trustees of Columbia University and, ultimately, my boss) about the Seattle Supersonics' previous night playoff game in San Antonio (at the time Schultz was chair of the Basketball Club of Seattle, LLC, owners of the Supersonics and the WNBA's Seattle Storm—but they were sold in 2006). I asked Schultz about the operational systems that support the Starbucks experience and ensure its consistency from location to location.

Before he would begin answering that question, however, Schultz insisted, "The keys are the culture and values of our company that allow our people to feel the way they do about Starbucks, so that they genuinely want to convey the attributes, the characteristics, the aspirational qualities of what we offer the customer."

We'll look closely at the issues of corporate culture and employee training at Starbucks in the next chapter, but well-integrated operational systems are also crucial, as Schultz enthusiastically explained. The first piece of the answer is structural.

"Early on we had very good local competitors. But when you begin to have multiple locations, consistent execution becomes extremely difficult. Starbucks is a real anomaly in that we are a completely vertically integrated company. We buy and roast all of our own coffee. We distribute it ourselves to our stores. We own and operate almost all our own stores—the only exceptions are in foreign countries, where we have partnership and licensing agreements with local businesspeople, and in licensed locations in the United States, such as campus bookstores and airports, where it is not possible for us to own and operate the store outright."

All the people in the company-operated stores work for Starbucks. "That has given us a very large competitive advantage over the control of the quality of the product, the training of employees, and the supply chain. There are cost benefits of managing supply chain operations well. Wal-Mart wrote the book on how to do it well. Because we grew quickly, efficiencies of scale early on also gave us competitive advantages. Finally we were competing in most cases with the franchise model, and the experience that the franchise operations created in their stores never could measure up to what we were doing."

Starbucks' ownership and operation of its stores — it achieved major success well before expanding overseas — enabled the company to integrate the stores' look and feel at a level that competitors reliant on franchisees and outsourcing could not. As Schultz elaborated, "We took things so fastidiously in terms of creating the visual, non-verbal cues of what it means to be in a Starbucks store. In 1989, when we had only fifty stores, we decided that we were going to bring all of our architecture and design work in-house. There are more than two hundred architects on one floor in this building, probably making us one of the largest architectural firms in the West Coast. And then we have more people in our own design studio.

"What we decided early on is that the equity of the brand is linked to all of the nonverbal cues of the brand experience, from the overall look of the store and subtle visual cues to the senses of aroma and the sound of the music that we have playing. We viewed the nonverbal signals and environment of every store as a very significant component of the customer's experience. And that became a very, very large competitive advantage, because there wasn't a competitor around that was willing or able to spend the amount of money that we spent on these things and that we continue to spend.

"When someone walks into a Starbucks, we want that person to be swept away. The visual cues, the design motifs, the colors, the smell of the coffee, the music — they all have to blend as well as the taste of the coffee. And now that we open five new stores a day somewhere in the world, we have to ensure that there's incredible consistency to that without having every location seem to be stamped out of a machine like Taco Bell and McDonald's and the other fast-food franchises. That I think is part of the genius of Starbucks. All the stores are similar, yet they're also all different. A Starbucks on Wall Street in downtown Manhattan doesn't look exactly like one in Berkeley, or one in Barcelona for that matter, but they all have the same spirit."

Successful entrepreneurs characteristically have egos as large as their ambitions, and it is clear that everything about Starbucks bears the stamp of Howard Schultz's dynamic personality and individual sensibility. Yet Schultz almost always speaks about Starbucks in terms of "we, us, our" and almost never in terms of "I, me, mine." We'll touch on this again in the next chapter's look at the Starbucks culture, but in this context it is worth noticing that Starbucks has avoided a pitfall that turns many an entrepreneurial success into failure, being straitjacketed by the founder's insistence on doing things "my way or the highway" and refusal to listen to associates, or more important, to customers. Schultz spontaneously offered one example of a message from customers that Starbucks had to heed, and I pressed him on another.

"Ten years ago we were in the morning part of the business. And we had no business to speak of in the afternoon. Our stores closed at seven o'clock at night, and we were done for the day. The customers started driving a new business for us by using our stores in multiple day parts. All of a sudden we had to create an afternoon beverage business and an after-dinner dessert business. I was starting to look at day-part analysis for one of the stores and I was stunned . . . 'From seven to nine we're that busy? It's got to be an anomaly. Let me go see that store.' I went to that store and saw that it was across the street from a college campus. All these students were in there with their laptops studying and comparing notes with their friends. Sororities and other student groups were meeting there."

In effect, Schultz was discovering that Starbucks had a greater number of important customer segments than he first thought, and that the company had to find ways of reaching out to those additional segments.

"As we looked into this, we saw that lots of our stores were becoming meeting places for book clubs, poetry readings, I mean everything. We saw people starting to play chess and Scrabble. And so we said, 'Is there something we could do to support that? Maybe we could create a game.' Well, game creation was not one of our competencies, but the customers' use of our stores for all sorts of activities eventually led to our incredible success with the game Cranium.

"The way that came about is that socially I met a phenomenal entrepreneur named Richard Tate, a Scottish guy who had been part of the early team at Microsoft. He started and ran something like seventeen different businesses for them. One day Richard said, 'I've been out of Microsoft a year now, and I know what I'm going to do, and I want to talk to you about it.' He was in the early stage of incubating Cranium and he used me—as well as probably twenty other people—to test its appeal. I said, 'That's very interesting. My view is do not sell this game in Toys "R" Us; you're going to blow it. This has to be a top-tier game.' And he said, 'If that's the case, where should it be sold?' I said, 'Well, you should sell it at Amazon.com and Barnes & Noble.com.' And he said, 'Or it could be sold at Starbucks.' I said, 'Well, I don't know. We've never done this before.'

"I knew that if I carried the Cranium game to our people, it would never happen or it would happen for the wrong reasons. So I said, 'Richard, this is who you need to go talk to. I'll open the door, but you've got to make it happen on your own.' And Starbucks loved it. And he created exclusivity for Starbucks. We were the only bricks-and-mortar retailer to have it at first (Target soon added the game to its product mix), and he introduced it on the Web with Amazon and Barnes & Noble. And we created the Cranium brand for him, and the numbers were staggering. It was the fastest-growing game in the history of board games and won Toy of the Year. It beat Xbox, which was great for Richard as an ex-Microsoft guy. And now he's developed several different generations of the game."

The benefit to Starbucks of integrating Cranium into its offerings lies in its enhancement of the Starbucks brand experience and the sense of community that it offers customers.

"[Cranium] has also spawned a new category for Starbucks, where different store managers created Cranium nights and, springing off from that and from customers' interests, poetry readings, open-mike nights for local musicians, and so on. It's been a win-win for three constituencies: the Cranium company, Starbucks, and most important, our customers."

Pursuing this line of thought, I asked Howard Schultz about his continuing to insist for some time that Starbucks only serve whole milk in its coffees, although great numbers of customers were clamoring for low-fat or skim milk. For Schultz, this was antithetical to the genuineness of the brand experience he wanted Starbucks to provide. For customers, it was plain common sense that they should be able to choose what kind of milk they wanted.

"I think there's always going to be tension," Schultz said, "between the standards we envision and the evolution of what customers want and will accept, between who we think we are and who customers want us to be. I think the perfect example is that we have not wavered on creating artificially flavored whole-bean coffee for home consumption, when that is the most significant growth in the category of coffee. Forty percent of the growth in the specialty coffee industry is in artificially flavored coffees. We don't sell those coffees. I think the question is, how do you balance the conscience of the brand and the product with the overwhelming consensus of what the customer wants. And, you know, this is not in the textbooks. It's intuitive. And in the end, we answered the question a little differently on skim milk than we have on artificially flavored coffee. We realized that the answers fell on different sides of the fence."

In the end, then, Howard Schultz demonstrated his true devotion to his customers' needs by listening to them and letting their functional "ownership" of the Starbucks brand experience modify the systems that he and his colleagues had created. Or, in the terms of chapter 6, Starbucks let customers define what they really value and then delivered that value in an enhanced form. So now you can have your Starbucks latte with skim milk. But don't bother asking for artificially flavored coffee.

Since we spoke to Howard Schultz, Starbucks has set its sights on China as its next significant growth market and reaped enhanced profits and an enhanced customer experience of community in the Starbucks brand by marketing music CDs that become available from traditional music retailers only after an exclusive on-sale period at Starbucks. In 2004 Starbucks "became a force in the music business with the success of the Grammy-winning album of Ray Charles duets, *Genius Loves Company* . . . sell[ing] more than 750,000 copies of the album," and in 2005 it made similar offers of CDs by Alanis Morrisette and Bob Dylan. In March 2007, Starbucks announced the formation of its own record label with Paul McCartney as its first artist. Ken

Lombard, president of a new Starbucks Entertainment division within Starbucks said, "We're focused on providing our customers unique opportunities . . . We want the music customer to think of Starbucks as a destination."[5]

What it is vital to notice here is how seamlessly Starbucks integrates Cranium nights and music CD marketing (it has since had major success with book sales as well) into its business plan. Howard Schultz founded Starbucks based on a vision of offering a new kind of community to coffee drinkers. If community is the true selling point, the real mark of difference between Starbucks and its competitors, then it behooves the company to recognize every possible way of binding customers into a shared Starbucks experience. Given the role that music has played in unifying groups of people in every known human culture and society, it makes perfect sense for Starbucks to elevate the music it plays in its stores into a substantial marketing initiative of its own. It may not hook a coffee drinker on its new exclusive CD the first time they hear it in the store, but an average of eighteen store visits per month for their most loyal customers provides ample opportunities to do so—or to listen to customer feedback and change the CD that's playing to one customers like more, further enhancing both CD sales and the customer experience of being part of the Starbucks community.

The Founding Customer:
Michael Bloomberg and His Interactive Success Terminal

Like Starbucks, the financial data services and media company Bloomberg L. P. bears the strong stamp of its founder. Michael Bloomberg started up the company in October 1981, when he cashed out of the Salomon Brothers investment bank as a general partner. During his time at Salomon Brothers, Michael Bloomberg ran the equity-trading desk, headed sales operations, and oversaw systems development. In a nutshell, he intended his new company, first named Innovative Market Systems, to provide real-time data on financial markets, instruments, and transactions for the customer he had just stopped being.

In December 1982 Bloomberg installed its first data terminal on a trading desk at Merrill Lynch. Two decades and counting later, the Bloomberg Professional service, Bloomberg L. P.'s core product, is an interactive desktop system with many thousands of functions offering instant access to millions of financial instruments and integrating data, news, analytics, multimedia reports, instant messaging, video telephone, and e-mail on a single platform. Suites of services on the Bloomberg Professional service are tailored for every market player including equity traders, bond traders, currency traders, hedge fund managers, legal professionals, merger and acquisition specialists, industry analysts, commodities traders, institutional money managers, and financial planners for high net worth individuals, as well as customers at the world's central banks, government agencies, and corporations in every industry. In addition to providing data, news, and analytics, the Bloomberg Professional service incorporates trading systems, order management systems, and Bloomberg Tradebook that allows customers to conduct transactions in any currency in any of the world's financial markets.

By mid-2006, Bloomberg boasted over 260,000 users in over one hundred countries around the world. Its users' monthly subscription fees together with spending on Bloomberg Tradebook and media advertising generate Bloomberg an estimated $4 billion annual revenues. Indeed, as an outgrowth of its subscriber services, Bloomberg has become a media company serving the larger public interested in financial news. Just as we saw in chapter 5 how ESPN surrounds the sports fan with sports news in all channels: television, radio, print, and the Web, so Bloomberg surrounds its customers with financial news through its integrated multimedia operations. Bloomberg's media services include the global Bloomberg News, with over 1,900 professionals in 126 bureaus worldwide; Bloomberg Television, a twenty-four-hour business and financial network produced and distributed worldwide on ten separate channels in eleven languages; and Bloomberg Radio, providing up-to-the-minute news on WBBR 1130AM in New York, XM, Sirius, and WorldSpace satellite radio. Bloomberg also operates a highly trafficked website and publishes Bloomberg Markets (magazines) and Bloomberg Press (books for business and financial professionals).

At Bloomberg's headquarters on Lexington Avenue in New York City, Judith Czelusniak, Bloomberg's global public relations head, spoke to us about how all of the company's systems are integrated to serve the users of its terminals. First there is the nature of the data. It provides raw data feeds and sophisticated analytics integrated on a single desktop product with news, charting, trading systems, messaging, and multimedia. Bloomberg's proprietary analytics, databases, and charting tools are not available anywhere else, including the Internet. It adds new functionality so that its unique single-platform product allows Bloomberg to keep its customers ahead of the markets with product enhancements that are transparent to the user.

Bloomberg delivers this information on a proprietary Intranet of high-speed phone lines with a feature called Bloomberg Anywhere so that users can also access Bloomberg Professional service from any PC with an Internet connection, including their own data, messages, news, and information. With a special triple data security system that is unique to each user, Bloomberg is again one step ahead of the curve in providing on-demand, on-the-go tools for its busy users.

Because Internet e-mail can be a very leaky sieve for information that a company may want to hold in confidence, many of Bloomberg's customer companies do not use Web-based e-mail. "For security reasons," Czelusniak explained, "many brokerages don't allow access to Internet e-mail on their trading desks. But the Bloomberg Professional service had Bloomberg e-mail and instant messaging with robust security before there was Internet e-mail. And so Bloomberg messaging is one of the main channels of communication across the global financial services industry."

Bloomberg's telephone-line based Intranet also allows it to deliver blindingly quick customer service. All user guidance and service goes through the telephone via live, in-your-language global customer support twenty-four hours a day—from a representative who is using the same product as the customer on the other end of the telephone. Support is also provided on Bloomberg Professional service itself instantly via live chat.

Bloomberg's integration of services through its interactive terminal is its chief means of delivering enhanced customer value and achieving differential advantage over competitors, and we could well have looked at the company through that lens in chapter 6.

The real differentiator at Bloomberg is customer service, delivering what that customer needs or might need as his industry evolves. If he is looking at Swiss franc pricing, something might pop up that lets him look at Swiss news or tells him how to go to Swiss equities.

Bloomberg's continual product enhancements, reflecting up-to-the-minute changes in how the markets operate, and new functions to enhance its business are almost always a result of conversations with customers.

In addition, Bloomberg employees regularly call subscribers to check on their satisfaction. "That's something Mike Bloomberg borrowed from Lexus. When Lexus called him three months after he bought one of their cars to make sure he was happy with it, he said, 'This is a brilliant idea. We have to apply this to our business.' And so we do," said Czelusniak.

By crafting services for the customer he once was, Michael Bloomberg created a company that threatens to displace Reuters as the world's leading brand in business and financial news publishing. The result is a company made very much in the image of its founder. As in the case of Starbucks, however, both founder and company know that it is ultimately present and future customers who decide the fate of the brand. Bloomberg learned this lesson the hard way when it developed a service that allows users to access their Bloomberg terminals through their mobile phones.

"[This is something] that Mike Bloomberg absolutely loves and uses constantly, and that we basically built around his personal needs. If you have a Bloomberg terminal and a cell phone, it allows you to get messages, worksheets, and so on from the terminal or your cell phone. Everybody has a cell phone, right? So you would have thought 80 percent of our customers would want this. Well, we developed it, we spent money on it, we promoted the hell out of it, and only a few thousand people in the world use it. What we discovered is that most of our customers, when they log off their trading desks, they don't need to know. The trading book moves from New York to Tokyo, say, and the guys in New York have gone out to dinner."

In other words, Michael Bloomberg, with the personal wealth and global interests his business achievements have earned him, is no longer his company's prototypical customer. But so long as Bloomberg the company recognizes this, it can continue to meet the needs of all the traders and brokers who, to borrow from Gatorade's Michael Jordan commercials, "wanna be like Mike." And so the company can continue to prosper even though Mike Bloomberg stepped away from day-to-day operations to become mayor of New York City, where his abilities to direct and manage systems and processes are tested every day.

•   •   •

The discipline we found for crafting systems to meet customer needs is impressive. It cuts across all industry categories, all products and services, from product manufacturers like Alcoa, Dell, L'Oréal, Pfizer, and Toyota to service businesses like Bloomberg L. P., Progressive, Starbucks, and UPS. An argument might be made that the integration of systems and processes is even more critical for service businesses than it is for product businesses, because in the former quality "manufacturing" must occur in real time as the firm interacts with customers. There is no question that integrating operations and systems to serve customer needs is a key to out-executing the competition. Your operations and systems are only as good as the people who implement them. With that in mind, it's time to see how Marketing Mavens foster a company-wide marketing culture.

EIGHT

Creating a Company-Wide Marketing Culture

Integrating your business to serve the customer is not just about systems and processes but also about developing a unified corporate culture. It is a task comprising many elements: CEO leadership, management buy-in, hiring, training, and compensation, and internal branding and communication, a group of practices that in some companies includes devising office layouts and protocols that force face-to-face encounters across divisions and departments.

Out of Three, One: Verizon Learns to Speak to Customers and Employees with One Voice

Verizon's formation and growth can be traced to the 1984 breakup of AT&T into a single national long-distance company and several regional companies. It faced significant challenges yet has succeeded in integrating elements of four large merged companies that came together in the following order: Bell Atlantic, NYNEX, GTE, and MCI. The acquisition of GTE in 2000 by Bell Atlantic, into which NYNEX had merged in 1997, was one of the largest in U.S. business history, priced at more than $52 billion. Taking the name Verizon, the merged company became one of the dominant players in its industry, and perhaps the most profitable. Verizon weathered the shakeout in telecommunications with its accounting integrity intact and, in early 2005, added MCI to the mixed company stew, integrated largely as Verizon Business, a unit dedicated to supporting large business and government clients, cashing in on the former MCI's strengths. The MCI acquisition also brought Verizon valuable long-haul lines outside

Verizon's stronghold in the eastern United States. (The original MCI had been purchased by WorldCom in 1998, but in 2003, because of accounting scandals, WorldCom had changed its name to MCI. In 2005 former CEO Bernie Ebbers was sentenced to twenty-five years in prison for accounting fraud.)

Both the Bell companies and GTE faced a fast-changing telecommunications environment in the 1990s, thanks to the deregulation pursued by the Clinton administration. The Baby Bells had to adjust to a nonmonopoly competitive environment, in which customer needs rather than company preferences immediately became the number one driver of the business. For its part GTE now had to position itself not just against a single behemoth but also against a host of sizable competitors, including MCI and Sprint (previously divested by GTE), as well as a formidable group of regional Bell operating companies (RBOCs)—hence the driving rationale to merge with Bell Atlantic to form Verizon.

This round of reamalgamation developed two major national players: Verizon and SBC. But having achieved comparable national size, the two companies followed quite different branding strategies, with SBC's marketing separate constituent brands—PacBell in California, SBC in the Southwest, Cingular for wireless—and Verizon's, as Bell Atlantic became after acquiring GTE, pursuing what Jody Bilney, Verizon's senior vice president for Brand Management and Marketing Communications, termed a single "master brand" strategy with subbrands all branching off from the same tree: Verizon local, Verizon long distance, Verizon wireless, and then Verizon DSL. In 2005 SBC acquired AT&T long distance, the last vestige of the original Ma Bell, rebranded itself as at&t, but continued to market Cingular as a stand-alone brand.

"One of the most interesting things about Verizon is that we chose to compete as a single brand right from the start," Jody Bilney said. "The master branding strategy and renaming the company grew out of a study of the equity that was resident in GTE and the equity that was resident in Bell Atlantic. GTE meant nothing in the Northeast, and Bell Atlantic meant nothing in California and Hawaii. We tried various combinations, GTE Bell Atlantic and so on, but nothing worked particularly well. So we decided we had to have a new name, although it was painful for many of our people who had spent their whole careers working for these companies to let those names go and embrace a new one." (Interestingly, another company that was part of the research for this book, Vodafone, pursued a similar branding strategy in Europe.)

Giving the pieces of GTE, Bell Atlantic, and NYNEX a single new brand name was an important first step in the integration campaign. "We included representatives from every level of the company in the renaming process," Bilney said. "Salespeople, technical people, marketing people, employees that are on the phone, entry-level sort of employees as well as senior VPs and people all over and in between— wireless, directories, everybody. Everybody was represented. Everybody owned it." The result combines the Latin word *veritas*, or "truth," with horizon, a name Verizon management saw as appropriate, given its ability to provide customers with clear, true signals across the full horizon of their locations and channels.

Uniting the brand equity of GTE and Bell Atlantic demanded considerable effort. "But we feel that we've been successful," Bilney said, "because we took great care in transferring the equity of each brand to Verizon. As soon as the merger was complete, we immediately ran ads that said, 'GTE is now Verizon,' and 'Bell Atlantic is now Verizon.' Everything that's been good before will still be good. After we felt customers were comfortable with that, then we began to tell them about the extra benefits of working with Verizon, ensuring that they understood the breadth of our product line with DSL and so forth."

Verizon was betting, Bilney said, "that if we predisposed people favorably to the brand on a local basis, that would open doors and enable us to sell more effectively the current and next generation of products that we will have continuously coming out: DSL, wireless, and whatever comes next."

Crucial to making this bet pay off was matching this intensive external branding with equally intensive internal branding. Verizon not only had to tell customers what it could do for them, it also had to tell the employees of GTE and Bell Atlantic what the new company was about and where it was going, and engage them in the process of getting there.

This required changing cultures that had long thrived inside GTE and Bell Atlantic. Bilney said, "We knew we had to move from a culture of reactive service to one of proactive service."

An important part of this move was Verizon's hiring of many new marketing people with the skills to operate in an environment that's customer-choice driven, not regulatory driven. When you're no longer the monopoly provider, there has to be a better understanding of customers and better ways of communicating with them.

After Bilney was hired, she was supported by bringing in people from the airline and insurance industries who had experience in marketing services to customers based on very sophisticated databases, as well as the intellect and credibility to articulate what was needed to Verizon's IT people. "It was vital that everyone saw that it was okay to have these strange marketing people around, these alien social contaminants, and not only that, to involve them in all kinds of decision making," said Bilney.

Fortunately for Jody Bilney and her team, the people who had been working at GTE, Bell Atlantic, and NYNEX were curiously open to change. Verizon knew that it needed to do more sophisticated marketing. When customers began having choices about who would provide their local service, their long-distance service, and their cell-phone service, then Verizon had to learn a lot more about them, not just their addresses as in the old monopoly days. What Verizon had to do was create a data warehouse that would be useful for marketing.

"Then," said Bilney, "we had to take our legacy systems and reinvent them. The billing system needed some sort of polishing, so we could put individually tailored messages to customers on the bills. We influenced that, and we began to get marketing considerations into the daily operations of the business and work our way into IT, sales, the call centers, and so on. One by one we were able to influence the critical areas and have the investments that would allow us to talk to customers about their needs and serve them better."

Verizon's internal branding campaign mandated marketing department participation in all its requirements gathering sessions for new products and services, and even for internal technology choices that at first glance may seem insulated from customer considerations. With marketing department representation in these sessions, Jody Bilney told us, "We could say in relation to a new systems enhancement, 'As you're making this adjustment, let's make sure it preserves and enhances our ability to communicate with the customer.' "

Making the marketing department a presence in formal decision-making routines also stimulated many informal interactions between members of the department and other employees. "It's become routine enough," Bilney noted proudly, "that in many cases there doesn't have to be a formal meeting with fifteen people," because the decisions are being made in real time in daily interactions.

In addition to the marketing department's formal and informal roles in operations, Bilney told my colleagues and me, "We embarked on, and we have continued, a full-court-press on employee education and internal communications for all of our 250,000-plus employees. Branding is even more important internally than it is externally. If the customer experience doesn't match what you say externally, it sets you back. If we don't bring our brand promise to life internally, if it isn't our mantra and if it isn't what we do every day, we've missed the boat."

To keep employees involved in conversations about the brand, Verizon uses several vehicles. "We adopted the goal of having every employee hear about new brand initiatives seven times prior to their being launched with customers, through internal e-mails, voice mails, the company newsletter, our internal television system and internal Web, official meetings, or more informally. We try to develop an idea that resonates powerfully among employees, something that can hold us all together in terms of a shared purpose to serve the customer."

●　　●　　●

Like Verizon, the other top marketing companies routinely credit much of their success to culture-building employee education and communications, often explicitly dealing with it as a form of internal branding. Although these companies have many different styles, some hard edged, some softer, they tend to deal with employees in ways that are encouraging and empowering, rather than dictatorial or adversarial.

Customer-service expert Hal Becker spoke with my research team and pointed to the opening of a Nordstrom's store in Cleveland, where the in-place competitors included Dillard's, Kaufman's, JCPenney, and Sears, as an example of how to create a truly customer-centric culture.

"Nordstrom came to Cleveland and blew everyone away," Becker said. "Where do you think the people who did this worked before Nordstrom opened up? Do you think Nordstrom brought them in from Seattle? They were in Cleveland working at Dillard's and Kaufman's and [Penney] and Sears. Nordstrom hired the good people from those stores and gave them better tools. The same people could have made any of those other stores the best department store in Cleveland. Only Nordstrom had the infrastructure and the training." Nordstrom both held employees accountable, and set a tone of encouragement, empowerment, and respect.

Using a sports analogy, Becker spoke to the need for company leadership constantly to coach employees, with training as an ongoing activity aimed squarely at increasing customer satisfaction.

"Look at Target. They made a commitment to upgrade their inventory, to upgrade their training, to listen to customers. And now they are the most successful retailers in America along with Wal-Mart.

"To have that kind of philosophy in a company, it all has to start top down. Be reminded every day and practiced every day. It's like any athlete or any sport. Whatever you want to be good at, you have to practice. And you have to practice being good at customer service within a company.

"Everything starts top down. If the CEO's committed to it and the general management's committed to it, senior management, and it goes down. You can't train attitude. You have to model enthusiasm, integrity, empathy and sincerity directly. How do you know what people are going to do unless you're there? Keep it simple. Show your people how to do things and observe the process—coach them through their mistakes. Spend time with them. Observe them. Talk to them, not at them. Show them respect. They'll do the same in return." Hal Becker also observed, "All the great companies do what Starbucks and Target are doing."

The Human Resources Difference

Recall that Starbucks founder Howard Schultz told my colleagues and me that the key to his company's phenomenal success "is the culture of our company." There is little debate in the business world that culture is one of the toughest things for a company to get right, and Schultz acknowledged the enormity of the challenge:

"I think it's very difficult to wake up one day and say, 'I'm going to create a culture' or 'I'm going to change the culture.' You have to recognize early on the attention to detail and the concern that you must have about building intimacy and trust with your people. The ongoing relationship that we have with our people, how often the management of the company is in the field, in front of people, is really extraordinary. And you can't use technology as an excuse for getting out in the field. You have to connect with people."

•   •   •

Starbucks' success depends on ensuring that its employees' attitudes and behavior transfer seamlessly into positive customer experiences. To nurture a culture of customer service, Starbucks routinely spends more on employee training than on advertising and it famously has extended benefits, including health insurance coverage, to part-time workers. As an example of Starbucks relationship with its people, Schultz described how the company decided on the morning of September 11, 2001, to close its locations nationwide.

"On September 11, an hour after the event we were one of the few or only national retailers to close our stores. We made a decision in that moment about the safety of our people. But more importantly, we knew we wanted to be home with our families and our kids. And we sent everyone home to do that.

"We closed every store. We lost millions of dollars in sales. There was never a flinch. I called the CEO of another national retail company to kind of calibrate what they were doing, and I mentioned what we were about to do. He said, 'You're closing every store? Why? Are you really going to do that?' I said, 'Yeah, this feels like the right thing to do.' He was surprised. I think it's those kinds of defining moments when you're in the eye of the storm where reputations are made and respect and dignity are built."

This was certainly a dramatic expression of Starbucks' concern for its people, but offering comprehensive health-care coverage and stock options to part-timers, as well as full-time employees, was Schultz said, "the transformational event in the culture of the company," bringing all employees into one company-wide conversation about serving customers better. Starbucks works hard to sustain that conversation, Schultz explained.

"We had our first global conference, where it was like the UN at Starbucks—thirty countries represented. In addition to going through the strategic plan for the next few years, we had a mini-Starbucks trade show with booths for every country to show their best practices. The people from Japan showed us how to utilize small spaces. The people from the Philippines, our best food market, shared how they achieve such high-quality food. And so on. Right before our eyes, we could see the company coming of age in a way in which we believe that we're growing big but staying small."

It probably goes without saying that a company has to be honest in assessing its culture. At Starbucks, Schultz said, "We do a cultural, internal audit every year where we go to our people and we ask them to evaluate our behavior and practices and their trust and confidence in management. And we share those scores with the company every year."

Like thinking underlies ExxonMobil's at first surprising penchant for sharing undesirable practices as well as best practices, which we heard about in chapter 3 from Hal Cramer, president of the company's fuels marketing division. When ExxonMobil receives complaints about customer service, "we filter them right back through our marketing territory managers to the dealers," Cramer said, "and we tell them, 'This is a poor level of service. Think about the consequences for your business.' "

The continuing growth of Starbucks worldwide will primarily depend, Howard Schultz maintained, on how it treats its people, communicates with them, and gives them the tools and motivation to serve customers well. The question, as Schultz put it, is "whether we can sustain the soft side of Starbucks with our people, and ultimately with our customer. We now have over one hundred thousand people working with the company. We're in thirty-seven countries. No company that we can track has been able to do what we're doing—not economically but culturally. That's why I travel around the world, help select partners and connect with as many people as I can. Our challenges are not access to capital or real estate. They're all human resources [HR]. I think the most important discipline in building a great company is HR—not IT, not marketing, although I think HR is marketing."

• • •

As at Verizon, so at Starbucks and ExxonMobil. We heard echoes of this idea over and over again—that to unify a company culture and integrate operations to serve customer needs, a company's internal marketing to employees must be consistent with its external marketing to customers.

Hitting the Bull's-Eye at Target

Focusing an entire company culture on customer needs is not only important in service and retail businesses. In chapter 7 we already saw how hard-goods producers like Alcoa, L'Oréal, and Dell benefit from company-wide marketing cultures. But the issues surrounding creating such a culture are particularly salient in retail organizations, where so many employees have direct daily contact with customers. As I observed in chapter 7, a service company's interactions with customers can be seen as manufacturing and delivering a service in real time.

Target offers another dramatic example of a company culture built around empowering employee training and internal branding that is in sync with external branding. Since the first Target store opened in 1962, Target has promised customers, "Expect more, pay less." From interviews at Target headquarters in Minneapolis with vice chair Jerry Storch and executive vice president of marketing Michael Francis, we learned that it puts as much effort into communicating that message to employees as it does to the customers whom it religiously refers to as "guests."

Michael Francis described how Target has nurtured a company-wide marketing culture through its employee training and internal communications:

"We have a set of cultural guidelines, 'Fast, Fun and Friendly,' which really says how we want people to feel as Target team members. Just as 'guests' says how we want people to feel about the experience of shopping with us. I know that working as a team can sound kind of randomly imposed when many organizations talk about it. But that is organic here."

For Target, "Fast, Fun and Friendly" is a cultural device that creates opportunities for its team members to talk about the Target brand. It continually reinforces this culture in national meetings, internal communications, and product development. Target wants both its "team-member" employees and its customer-guests to enjoy the service interaction. It recognizes that unhappy employees cannot delight customers with great service.

Allowing for many differences of tone, all top marketing companies strive to serve and empower their employees, because even in the most carefully worked out manufacturing operations, employee behavior on behalf of customers can be modeled, studied, and practiced, but it cannot be defined in advance. In chapter 7, we saw how Toyota integrates its vaunted manufacturing system with its R&D and customer-service systems. In its manufacturing plants, the lowliest employees are empowered to stop the production line for any reason, and do so frequently, using their individual initiatives to maintain Toyota's high quality while building a car in fewer worker hours than any other manufacturer.

At Target, Michael Francis explained, great effort goes into coaching and communicating with employees at different levels, from company-wide messaging to department and division communications to one-on-one interactions. The desired outcome of this training is creative teamwork to meet individual customer needs. Target obviously cannot script every interaction with guests. But it can model the principles of good customer-service behavior in action. Accordingly, its main vehicle for training is a constant flow of new stories about guests' experiences.

"An important part of how we communicate is we use field stories to train the rest of the organization, as opposed to some abstract model that we impose," Michael Francis said. "We use DVDs to show what team members and guests are thinking in situations where service was handled poorly and then appropriately. We role-play and we deliver on-the-spot coaching to help leaders ask better questions. We train with a bias toward simulation and application, using actual scenarios that lend themselves to the situations our team members will experience — the constant focus is a form of practicing how to serve guests. And we have our team members submit guest-service stories to include in our storewide news magazine. When you're trying to deal with something as abstract as how you want guests to feel when they're in your store, you can't accomplish that without personalizing it. You have to capture the emotion of the experience and the tone. And the only way you can add texture is by telling more human stories that answer the important questions. What are our guests saying? How are they reacting to what they find in the stores and how we treat them? What are we feeling in the stores?"

Interestingly, several top marketing companies share this reliance on stories of customer experiences to train employees, notably Starbucks and ExxonMobil, as we have already seen. "We literally have stories from around the world," ExxonMobil's Hal Cramer told us, "that show we've succeeded in creating a customer-service mind-set. People who got a 'wow' experience, where we've exceeded their expectations."

Target's Michael Francis said, "We bring all these best practice examples to more than fourteen hundred stores. But it's not a situation where we say, 'Here's the rule. Don't deviate from the rule.' The people in every store have to be empowered to figure out how to extrapolate those examples into their own guest space, so that everybody owns part of serving the guest."

The same principle applies in Target's corporate giving. "Seventy-five percent of our total giving, the individual stores review the needs of their communities and determine how those dollars are spent. So it keeps the people in the store very connected to their individual guest base."

Fostering company culture in such directly customer-focused ways, and doing so consistently, is a top-down process that requires senior management to lead, and listen to, employees. At Starbucks, Howard Schultz sets the tone of employee interactions, HR practices, and how the company strives to serve customers. At Target, Michael Francis said, "It starts at the top. Our chairman and CEO is the brand czar, and you only get that kind of consistency from the top."

Echoing Jack's Welch's approach at General Electric, Target's Jerry Storch spoke to us in a similar vein, stressing the determination to operate without internal barriers. "It's a concept of boundarylessness," he elaborated. "We work together very tightly as one company, from product development to merchandising to logistics. We do that formally. But even more important are the informal collaborations across the company in these areas. People will not thrive here if they don't collaborate."

Collaboration naturally implies shared responsibility. A notable example at Target is the expectation that everyone will participate in trend-spotting, which is a form of prospective customer service. Even those Target employees who normally do not deal with customers in the store are expected to see the world in terms of meeting customers' needs for new and exciting products.

"If you go back twenty-five years ago," Jerry Storch said, "discounters tended to take trends that were developed elsewhere and then milk them at the declining end of their product life cycles. Target now leads

all retailers in the introduction of new trends." Michael Francis elaborated, "We identify trends with a dedicated trend group that travels the
world to find new trends in everything from apparel to home decor to
food, and we use a tool called the trend curve to segment the life cycle
of trends. This helps us determine when it will be hot, so we can get it
into our stores at the right time for our guests. But we also involve the
rest of the company.

"When anyone in our corporation is traveling abroad, the expectation is that they will carve out time to go and understand what is happening in London, Berlin, Antwerp, Prague, Tokyo, or wherever they
are. We want to know, what's emerging? What is the cool restaurant?
What are the teenagers wearing? What are the young artists showing?
We have an excellent trend department, but we also have people in
every area of the company who have carved out the niche of being
trend czars, because everyone has that role to play. Everyone is expected to cultivate an eye."

Once a trend has been spotted, Target credits its integrated operations for enabling it to act more quickly than other discounters.
Michael Francis said that a "competitive advantage of the way we're
structured . . . [is] . . . our ability to bring an incredible in-house design
team together with sophisticated merchants, cutting-edge logistics, and
a worldwide sourcing operation. Our ability to go from observation to
execution is probably one of the shortest in the industry, so, for example, we can have cashmere in Target the same season that specialty
stores and full price retailers are featuring it.

"In response to the rising importance of premium denim in the
marketplace, we created a quick-reaction testing process to determine
which denim washes and styles would be most popular among guests.
Then we launched our own label, Premium Denim by Mossimo, with
advanced speed to market to ensure it hit stores when guests wanted it
most. And in response to the growth of pharmaceutical sales we can-
vassed our guests and learned that they were frustrated by bottles that
were difficult to read and companion materials that often became
separated—they were concerned about mixing up medications. Ultimately we developed our own medications system called Clear Rx that
provides greater surface area for information, built-in pockets to con-
tain supplemental information, and color-coded rings for each member of the family."

Target's trend-spotting doesn't just stop with customers. It's always on the lookout for what other competitive and noncompetitive organizations are doing via its benchmarking initiative. Target's "horizontal councils" in each merchandising and functional area meet regularly to share best and worst practices, but senior managers always ask council members, "What did you find out from other firms about this?" Answers to these questions are required!

Target's efforts to sustain a customer-focused corporate culture have paid off in higher profit margins than its rivals. Target has become a discount retailer that doesn't have to offer the lowest possible price to survive, and it thrives on the slightly higher premium it is able to charge. "We've turbo-charged our brand over the last decade to the point where we're reaching a more affluent consumer who wouldn't normally be caught dead in a discount store," Michael Francis said. "We've been able to change the profile of our core guest segment compared to what our competitors have done. That is what has created the phenomenon of guests pronouncing our name as 'Tar-zhay,' as if we were a chic boutique. We've earned this beautiful kind of organic response from guests to what they find in our stores that they don't find anywhere else."

• • •

Now let's examine the experiences of two rival companies, SAP and Oracle, that see themselves as being, and that in many ways clearly are, quite different from each other. Yet in their efforts to foster an effective corporate culture, they have much in common with each other and with the other high-performing companies in our survey.

From "Sapanese" to "One Voice" Marketing

SAP, the business software giant, is based in Walldorf, Germany, but its global marketing organization is based in New York City, headed by CMO Marty Homlish. Before joining SAP, Homlish ran Sony Computer Entertainment America, which launched PlayStation in the United States. At SAP's Global Marketing New York HQ on Manhattan's trendy Lower West Side, Marty Homlish spoke to us about his perceptions when he joined SAP. I had directed and taught some executive-education programs for Marty when he was at Sony, and it was good to meet up with him again.

When Homlish arrived at SAP, its products were coherently organized in industry specific solution sets for twenty-seven industries, from aerospace to retailing. But he did not believe that SAP presented these solution sets in a way that was coherent to customers.

His assessment was that SAP was winning the product battles but really losing the perception battle. No one really understood what the SAP brand stood for. There was a great deal of confusion. What is SAP? What does SAP do? Where and who is SAP?

"SAP was not disciplined or focused enough to speak with one voice to the marketplace," said Homlish. "There were over four thousand individual printed pieces of sales collateral literature that lacked cohesive branding. There were business cards with over twenty different styles and logos. And in different countries around the world, there were different ad campaigns being run by different ad agencies," Homlish continued. "These multiple voices were confusing to the marketplace."

Homlish speaks of a time when the Internet and tech stocks boomed. Many firms were promising both business customers and consumers tailored service through a "myCompanyName.com" website. So SAP grabbed the opportunity to brand a new offering "mySap.com" and "the City of E" for the new e-commerce sphere.

Homlish's challenge was to transform marketing and reposition the SAP brand. Said Homlish, "I saw SAP as a marketer's dream: great products, a strong history of innovation, and a loyal customer base—all we needed to do was to transform marketing." He faced three core challenges for repositioning the SAP brand globally: communicate the brand consistently, align the organization, and create a brand flexible enough to support challenging business objectives in a dynamic industry. One of the first things he did was to kill an exciting idea for using the most high-tech blimp ever made, with Porsche engines and GPS tracking, to fly from Palo Alto to SAP's global headquarters in Germany. The mySAP.com logo would light up the blimp.

"I said, 'Look, guys, when I think about a blimp, I think of something slow and ponderous and old-fashioned. The most famous blimp experience in the United States was the Hindenburg, and that went up in flames.' We went back and forth for a couple of weeks, and then one day I opened up the *New York Times*. There was an article headlined 'Deutsche Bank—Old-Fashioned Blimp or Streamlined Jet?' with a picture of the Hindenburg in flames. I sent that article to everyone, and that finally stopped the blimp conversation."

As Marty Homlish saw it, "SAP in the 1990s was a brand without much humanity and warmth. That was okay because it was providing mission-critical software for core business operations. But then SAP decided to move the brand 180 degrees in the other direction, with mySAP.com. The idea was to create new, hip, young brand attributes. But this was not really believable to the customer when they thought of SAP. The slogan, 'You Can, It Does,' was confusing. You can what? It does what? And no one knew why they should travel to the City of E."

But Homlish believed that the strategy had some strong points. "It was correct in some ways. Many of the solutions that were being provided through a server-based technology had to be made Internet accessible. But the brand implication was much more complicated. There was no clear understanding of what mySAP.com was supposed to deliver to the customer, so the customer didn't understand it either.

"The most important thing," Homlish concluded, "was that SAP never really tied its technology features to business benefits. MySAP.com was speaking Sapanese—the internal language of the developers and engineers. The site focused on features—but our customers wanted benefits. SAP had four thousand brochures, but a lot of these were really technical white papers. There was no filtering mechanism, and no process for establishing priorities in how the company communicated."

By 2000 SAP CEO Hasso Plattner concluded that SAP's messaging, for the overall firm and individual products, was sprawling, inconsistent, and confusing. He set out to radically change SAP's marketing organization.

Plattner had the vision and the courage to take SAP's entire corporate marketing organization out of Germany, move it to New York, and put a former PlayStation guy in charge—a CMO with fresh eyes from outside the tech business. That was a very bold move for a European firm. He did it because he was highly frustrated. He knew SAP had the best solutions, but he knew it had to change its *face* to the customer. Plattner knew SAP had to move to an outside-in view that focused on the benefits to customers. SAP could no longer operate on an "If you build it, they will come" mentality.

Facing the need to build a company-wide marketing culture virtually from scratch, Marty Homlish made several important decisions early on. To start, he stopped all the advertising, collateral, and events, working down the budget line by line, freezing everything until he could figure out what to do. Then he set about defining the SAP brand attributes and positioning through extensive interviews with SAP's board of directors and its top fifty managers. He also sought input from partner and client companies in all twenty-seven industries SAP serves, including, the end users, the people who sit in the client companies and actually use its software. With CEO, senior management, and customer contributions to a new brand vision, he then tackled the problem of getting SAP's more than thirty thousand employees on board. And he consolidated all of SAP's marketing business with one global advertising agency, Ogilvy and Mather.

Homlish said, "The single most important thing we did is we created a living, breathing document called the *One Voice Marketing and Positioning Handbook.* This became the internal SAP bible. One Voice was our way of publishing internally and externally with one set of guidelines. And the way we built One Voice is we put together cross-functional, cross-cultural, cross-country teams of key stakeholders, and in many cases key skeptics, from throughout SAP. Everything we did, we did it in such a way that we involved SAP's people. We explained in great detail why we were changing, we explained the value of the brand, and we didn't want to do anything in a vacuum."

Change is difficult in any organization, and Homlish encountered stiff resistance. "It was a difficult educational process for some of our technical people. But I had the advantage of a track record in marketing and branding. I told them, 'I don't know a lot about software development and engineering. But I do know that 90 percent of our customers are really interested in business benefits.'

"Before One Voice, when we would talk about a successful implementation, for example, we would talk about the technological side of the implementation. 'Customer XYZ implemented SAP supply-chain management. They had to do it within one hundred days, and they went live in ninety-nine days and they only had one critical crisis.' But that was not the issue. The real story was, 'Customer XYZ implemented SAP's supply-chain management solution and as a result they reduced their on-hand inventory from 2.8 months supply to

2.1 months supply. They reduced their on-the-water inventory from one month's supply to two weeks' worth. And they saved $500 million.' "

One of the first channels for SAP's One Voice marketing was its website. "We had to reinvent the website," Homlish said, "because that was our external face and it wasn't doing a good job. It was difficult for customers to get basic information. We identified a vision, a mission, and a strategy for the website. The payoff at the end of the day was SAP being awarded in 2001, the prestigious International Web Page Award for Technology and Science."

Other accolades for SAP's marketing efforts include the ACE Award and *Forbes'* Best of the Web. In 2004 Homlish was named Chief Marketing Officer of the Year by *BusinessWeek* and the CMO Council. This inaugural award recognized marketing visionaries based upon the strategy, leadership, and creativity employed to build value, momentum, and uplift for their organizations. Homlish was also named a Top Marketer by *B to B* magazine in its "Best of 2004" issue.

"One Voice became the mantra for everything from the SAP logo and letterhead to business cards to our templates for PowerPoint presentations to the corporate Christmas card. For example, in the first year we went from four thousand brochures to four hundred brochures. Everything is on brand, everything is customer-benefit centric, not technology-feature centric. Everything is integrated to serve customer needs through a company-wide marketing culture.

"One Voice talks about everything that we do, but it talks about it in a way the customer understands. It talks about what we do in the language of business, because at the end of the day it's the businesspeople that are buying our solutions. It's the CEO, it's the head of Sales, it's the head of Marketing, it's the Production people."

The process of canvassing SAP management and employees, as well as partner and customer companies, to create the One Voice framework had a wide-ranging impact. In defining the brand's core attributes, it helped identify best practices and syndicate them throughout the company, and helped eliminate suboptimal practices. This had as much relevance for product planning as for product marketing.

Homlish went on, "As I said before, we got some push-back, but I had a mandate from the CEO and senior management, and input from clients about what they wanted and needed. So I said to the skeptics,

'Okay, if you guys are doing everything that should be done, that's great. But let's first determine who's doing what.' In the process, we in fact identified several duplications and a number of gaps that needed to be filled.

"The result," Homlish said, "is that the role of SAP's Marketing Department has dramatically changed. In parallel with *outbound marketing* to customers, the company has begun to do *inbound marketing* that is directly linked to the development organization. We are now providing an outside-in view of product management."

Along with the change in marketing came a culture change throughout SAP, and a change in the way SAP is viewed by its customers and the business community. "Once SAP's people saw some positive results," Homlish said, "this thing took on the momentum of a freight train. A year after we started the campaign and began to prove that brand perception can drive reality, Hasso Plattner told me, 'So nothing has changed, but everything has changed. Our product is the same, our people are the same, our customers are the same. But the perception is 180 degrees different, and now that we have everybody speaking with One Voice, we're the darlings of Wall Street, we're the darlings of the analysts, we're the darlings of the press.' "

When the technology stock bubble burst, it did not burst for SAP. At that time SAP was one of the few high-tech companies to achieve increased sales revenue and profitability. According to *BusinessWeek/* Interbrand's influential annual study of the top one hundred global brands, by 2006 SAP's brand value rose to over $10 billion, up from $6.1 billion in 2000, and at number thirty-four was ranked above long-established brands like Apple, Canon, Xerox, and Volkswagen.[1]

Sustaining the culture change that made this possible is not easy. Homlish said, "This is an ongoing educational challenge." But to illustrate that One Voice has indeed taken hold within SAP, he proudly shared two anecdotes with my colleagues and me.

"At SAP's headquarters in Walldorf, Germany, I got on an elevator and a gentleman got on with a bag emblazoned with a mySAP.com full color logo from the late '90s. And he recognized who I was and he kind of looked down in an embarrassed way. And then everyone in the elevator was staring at the bag and going, 'Rrrrr,' and he was clearly extremely uncomfortable about carrying something that was off-brand.

When we reached his floor he hustled off the elevator. It was a very special moment.

"Another time I had to give a speech to a large SAP audience. We were going to be in a very big hall, and when I stepped to the back of the hall I realized that the One Voice compliant template that I was going to use didn't work in such a large space. So I made a decision the night before the speech to change the template.

"I announced the change when I began to speak, and said, 'I've made the decision to use a different template today.' The next week I was in Germany for a town hall meeting with employees, and I heard, 'How could you do that? You changed the template.' That was another special moment that showed me how much progress we've achieved in bringing all of SAP together under a common vision and a truly powerful global brand."[2]

In Oracle's Japanese Garden

Thanks in large part no doubt to its famously aggressive cofounder and CEO, Larry Ellison, Oracle has an in-your-face style that was on ample public display as it steamrolled to a hostile takeover of People-Soft in 2004 and then quickly integrated PeopleSoft's operations into its own. We saw the same style inside Oracle headquarters in Redwood Shores, California. During a freewheeling interview, CMO Mark Jarvis said, "We don't see SAP as doing anything special," boasted about "hijacking" IBM's e-business advertising, and drew a pointed contrast between Microsoft's charging outside developers for access to source codes and tools and Oracle's providing them for free.

Behind the bravado, Oracle takes all three companies seriously. Its press release on completing the PeopleSoft deal stated that the acquisition had been undertaken to "make Oracle more competitive against Microsoft, IBM, SAP, and others in the enterprise application market and the broader technology stack." And the seriousness with which it takes SAP was demonstrated by its filing of a lawsuit against SAP, as this book went to press, alleging "corporate theft on a grand scale."[3]

Oracle's "take no prisoners" approach has plainly served it well, just as SAP's more buttoned down approach to achieving consensus has served it well. Before the PeopleSoft acquisition, Oracle had about

$9.5 billion in annual sales revenues and SAP about $9 billion (€7 billion). The acquisition of PeopleSoft pushed Oracle's revenues to the $12 billion mark, and its early 2006 acquisition of Siebel gave it another boost. For 2006 Oracle ranks at number twenty-nine on the *BusinessWeek*/Interbrand Top 100 Global Brands Scoreboard, five slots above SAP, and its brand equity is valued at just under $11.5 billion.

This may give Oracle the edge in bragging rights, although SAP could boast that its organic growth strategy brought it 60 percent of the global enterprise software market and 44 percent of the U.S. market in 2006.[4] The point is that there are many paths to an effective company-wide marketing culture. And despite genuine differences, Oracle and SAP also have much in common. For example, both strive to speak to the customer in a benefit-centric way and to do so in the customer's language, and both strive to match internal branding and communications with external branding and communications.

Mark Jarvis said that Oracle follows a "Japanese garden philosophy of marketing." As in a Zen garden where a few carefully sited rocks and plants evoke an entire landscape, Oracle takes great pains "to crispen everything down" to the essentials.

"The technology industry is completely filled with gobblety-gook and technical terms designed to confuse the average buyer," Jarvis elaborated. "So our goal has been very simple, very consistent. How do we get rid of all the gobblety-gook? How do we dissolve these messages down to something that the average guy can understand?

"That's what we talk about with Japanese gardening. Whenever we do reviews [of any communications materials], I become the customer from hell. I immediately put myself in customer mode and I look at everything and I go, 'What the hell does that abbreviation mean? What is the word *solution* doing there?' Our industry uses the word *solution* a great deal. *Solution* is banned in Oracle. We don't have any solutions. We have products.

"We play this game called Bullshit Bingo, where we actually have a formal template that has a whole bunch of very techie words like infrastructure, systems integration, solution, footprint, and all this crap. We play the game in meetings, and every time someone says a word you mark it off. And the first person to go 'Bingo,' by having a vertical or a horizontal, wins.

"What it forces everyone to do is crispen their language. And it forces everyone to come to the point where they say, 'This is the one thing that matters.' " This effort serves both internal and external communication. Like Verizon, Starbucks, and other leading marketing companies, Oracle makes the conversation with forty-two thousand employees a mirror image of the conversation with customers.

"It has a huge benefit," Mark Jarvis said, "which is that the customers and the sales force both understand what the message is for our database. It's one word: *Unbreakable.* What does our database do? 'It's unbreakable.' And then underneath that, we explain why it's unbreakable in terms that even the average person understands. 'Won't go down if your server fails. Won't go down if your site fails. Fourteen international security certifications.' I can see the ads in my head. So can every sales rep. The crisper the language, the simpler the message, the less words you use—the better it is. Same applies, by the way, to our website. On our Web pages typically there's no scrolling and it's all charts, bulleted lists and, to keep pages loading fast, minimal pictures. And we notice that people spend a lot more time on our Web pages than they do on the average Web page."

Internally, the responsibility for keeping all Oracle employees talking the same language as customers belongs to the marketing department. "We really have three key divisions at Oracle," Mark Jarvis said. "We have the sales organization, we have the development organization and we have marketing in the middle. It's marketing's responsibility to link between sales and development. Marketing is the ultimate source of truth, and the marketing message doesn't represent the product, the product represents the marketing message."

In other words, a customer focused company-wide marketing culture is ultimately what integrates Oracle's parts into a whole. The product, which is always being upgraded, is not an end in itself, but is a way of embodying Oracle's core brand promise.

"This integration is complete on a systems level, also," Jarvis asserted. "Our HR database is the same thing as our finance database, our sales database, our marketing database. It's one unified database organized by customers and products, and so it can serve product development and customer service as well as product marketing."

Jarvis emphasized that "most of the people that are in the Marketing Department we took from product development. It's part of the career path here. You start off in development, you then become a product manager and manage what goes into the products, and ultimately you'll be turned into a marketing person."

With regard to Oracle's unified internal database, it is fascinating to note how the company links it to online services for the four million registered users of the Oracle Technology Network (OTN). It has become a crucial tool for Oracle for communications and delivering customer value. Jarvis explained how OTN both "violently increases customer loyalty" and joins employees around the world in the same marketing conversation. "OTN subscribers are all developers and database administrators, the geeks of the industry. They go online to get information and software for free. There are forums and chats, which allow them to interact with their peers, and discussion groups so that they can ask questions and get answers."

The "geeks of the industry" who use OTN "don't necessarily buy Oracle software. But they definitely influence the person that does buy it. And that community now is pretty much the way we do all our technology marketing. So we can do high-quality marketing to technologists at zero cost because it's our website, we run our own banner ads on it, we run our own e-mail marketing blasts."

True to its freewheeling persona, Oracle does not police the discussion of its products on OTN customer forums. They are reviewed but only for politics, religious slander, and sexual innuendo—topics that might be personally offensive. "Otherwise," says Jarvis, "we'll let anyone post anything. Which means that sometimes you'll get a guy who says, 'Oracle on Linux sucks.' We allow that to go into the forum, because we know that within twenty minutes, ten people will have told him that he's wrong. Instead of our having to respond to that guy, our users respond. Generally, they help him solve the problem, and at the same time they tell him that it's not right, that the product is actually great. So it has promoted incredibly violent loyalty in our products, which is all great."

OTN not only provides a wonderful channel for customers to reach into Oracle and extract value as part of a community of Oracle users, but it also enables Oracle to reach out to customers. OTN has become the medium for running marketing across Oracle, because of the way it links to its internal database. When a customer registers online for a technology seminar, he is tracked online; that includes individuals, provided they have opted in. If a user attends a seminar or downloads a product, then Oracle knows that they may have a certain interest in something it's about to do. Someone from Boston will be sent an e-mail about a technology day being held there. If that has huge value to that person, it increases loyalty to Oracle, which at some point leads to buying a product or influencing the purchase decision maker in their organization.

"It all goes into one database," says Jarvis, "that has become the ring that unites sales and marketing. And everyone in the company has access to that information. So we can track a marketing idea around the world.

"For example, someone on my staff might say, 'Why don't we build a technology seminar?' In order to do that technology seminar, we enter it into the marketing system. That determines the budget allocated to it. It determines the entire plan and that system is then used to communicate with the whole world what this seminar is going to be. Every Oracle person around the world sees the same plan and they also then can sign up to run that in their local place. So, you know in Prague, they may say, 'Oh, the technology seminar is great. We'll do one too.'

"Then at any point in time I can say, 'How many seminars are we running on this technology next week?' I can pull it up and see, 'Ah, there's fifty-five next week. And here are the cities that it's in.' So can the sales force. They can go and tell their customers, 'Hey, there's a seminar in your city. Why don't you come to it?' "

The work-flow management features of Oracle's common platform also facilitate integration. "All the approvals of budget get handled by the system. All the execution of the marketing program. Ultimately at some point we will take a count of a number of interactions with the customer. We've done a dialogue with them electronically that grades them into the system for developing leads, and the information gets handed over to sales, who decide whether it goes to a field salesperson or whether it goes to a telephone sales rep. And the salespeople then can track that whole thing through to the end.

"We can down to the dollar tell you, 'This marketing campaign cost this amount of money and generated this amount of sales. Therefore our cost per sale was this.' Marketing is totally a science in Oracle. Yeah. You know, we can sit down and someone will say, 'Why don't we do this?' And we can statistically prove whether it will work or not. And it all flows from that Japanese garden philosophy that we spread throughout Oracle. And my job is to be the pain in the ass to everyone, where I continually force them to think differently and to garden. That's why everyone here loves me and hates me for the same reason."

• • •

As we've seen, the top marketing companies all have distinctive styles—Oracle has "take no prisoners" imprinted in its DNA, not just its rhetoric—yet from their different starting points they converge on remarkably similar strategies for building a company-wide marketing culture. These strategies all share the following key elements:

1. Top management makes a company-wide marketing culture and employee training top priorities for everyone from the lowest-echelon worker to the highest.

2. Employee training and other means to develop the corporate culture are ongoing.

3. The company understands the importance of speaking to employees as it does to customers, doing so in language that is clear, consistent, and inspiring.

4. Internal branding to employees and external branding to customers are not only both equally clear, they are conceptually in sync, as closely intertwined as the two strands of genetic material in every piece of DNA.

5. Employee performance measures and compensation support the goal of aligning the company to serve customer needs.

• • •

The fifth common element of company-wide marketing cultures brings us to the last of the five core marketing imperatives of our time: measure what matters. In the next chapter we'll explore that imperative in depth.

Measure What Matters

NINE

Measuring Enterprise and Market for a Custom Fit

Company performance measures fall logically into three categories: input, output, and intermediate variables. Input variables essentially measure what the firm does, such as expenditures on the production of goods and services, human resources, advertising and sales, and increases or decreases in product quality. Typical output variables are revenues and profits, market share, return on capital, customer satisfaction, and customer profitability. Intermediate variables occur after inputs, but before outputs. Typical examples are sales pipeline measures, planned activity in the distribution system, and changes in customers' beliefs and behaviors. Although there is much talk these days of balanced scorecards for company performance, too few managers focus in a balanced way on input, output, and intermediate variables.

"If you can't measure it, you can't manage it" is a wise old business maxim. In practice most companies manage the things that are easiest to measure in hard numbers, the inputs and outputs, and give only intermittent attention to intermediate variables and underlying market trends. At the world's most successful companies, Marketing Mavens do not ignore inputs and outputs by any means, but they also strive to manage the things that are most uncertain and most difficult to measure, especially those that indicate changes in customer beliefs and behaviors.

Market trend data commonly receive little attention under the umbrella of company measurement, but Marketing Mavens are obsessed with getting the most precise insight possible into emerging market segments, and customer preferences and behaviors. These data are the missing link in measuring what matters, the key to producing customer-focused action throughout an enterprise, from research and development to current sales and customer service. If your business is like most, you are measured on sales, market share, and/or profit contributions. What is often missing are the factors that drove these results. Your measurement system must produce information that fuels the creation of customer-focused action throughout the enterprise, from research and development to current sales to customer service.

How ExxonMobil Measures the Needs of Drivers and Its Ability to Serve Them

ExxonMobil's "Life on the Move" strategy of combining gasoline and convenience retail is based on a comprehensive segmentation study that identified the most profitable potential customer groups for it to serve, those whose purchases are motivated more by convenience and speed than by low price. For Hal Cramer, president of ExxonMobil's Global Fuel Sales, measuring what matters to the most profitable market segments begins with inputs. "Operationally, you've got to start with measuring, monitoring, and continuously helping your own employees," Cramer said. "Because unless your own employees get it, unless your own employees are aligned and understand their objectives and feel good about what they do, they can't present and deliver your brand promise. If they get it, then you can reach through them to the customer level. You can't simply start with customers. If you can generate desired behaviors by employees, they will take care of your customers, and then you can deliver maximum value to shareholders."

ExxonMobil also takes great pains in measuring customers and their behavior at the pump and the convenience store counter. It mines "the tremendous amount of information we get from focus groups and market surveys" and strives to marry that data with trends in output measures such as sales figures and with other intermediate variables such as shifts in customer attitudes to the products sold in On the Run stores or relationships with the distributors of those products. Accordingly, Hal Cramer explained, "We have a system that incorporates a balanced scorecard at the global level, the regional level, and the individual business unit level. You can't look only at sales figures. You have to have a host of leading and lagging indicators: safety, security, environmental performance, sales, credit, costs, and customer satisfaction, among others. They all combine to drive our performance going forward. Balanced scorecards are not unique to us. Most companies have them one way or another. The trick is driving them down throughout a worldwide functional organization. Making sure everybody's aligned and understands where they're going is absolutely critical."

This brings up a critical general point in the way the world's top-performing companies fulfill the imperative to measure what matters: they consistently and effectively link company performance to employee compensation. Surely this is any company's most important operational measurement: are you paying your people what they're worth?

"You need to dissect the business," Cramer said, "so everybody's accountable, and everybody's measured and rewarded for what they contribute as individuals and as part of the team. ExxonMobil's a large corporation with many affiliates around the world. Employees can't be left to think that their actions are insignificant in relation to such a huge enterprise. Each individual must know how he or she contributes, because it's thousands of individuals working together who deliver the overall earnings. Make sure there's individual accountability. Reward people and rank people accordingly. And it's as simple but as complex as that."

Measuring Customer Behavior and Employee Performance at Nestlé

Earlier we saw how Nestlé Prepared Foods (NPF) uses focus groups, surveys, and other market research to align its Lean Cuisine division with major consumer lifestyle trends, such as time pressure in two-earner households and a general decline in culinary skills. NPF has grown Lean Cuisine to close to a billion-dollar brand and maintained its lead in the frozen food category over ConAgra and other competitors. Most recently that success has hinged on an alert response to a measurable shift in consumer concern from low-fat to low-carb dishes through qualitative research, a combination of one-on-ones and focus groups, tracking perceptions of its brands and products, and maintaining quality by renovating its products based on what it learns from and about customers.

NPF senior managers subject their own behavior, a key input variable, to outside measurement. "We have to lead with good teamwork from the top," Stephen Cunliffe told us. "My direct reports and I work very well as a team and we work at working as a team. Periodically we bring in consultants to scrutinize our teamwork and enhance it. And if you can get that bunch of bandits to work together—because they're strong people with strong characters—it flows down through the organization."

NPF grounds desired employee behaviors by linking them as transparently as possible to three company performance measures: "market share, EBITA [earnings before interest, taxes, and amortization], and most significant, real internal growth. We're all on the hook for all of those."

Matching Company Inputs and Market Outputs at Pfizer

Pfizer has maintained a number one position in U.S. and global pharmaceutical sales by precisely tracking the link between sales visits and prescriptions. Pfizer's Pat Kelly told my colleagues and me, "We're measurement intense. 'Metrics 'r' us.'"

Recall that Pfizer organizes its data in accordance with its return-on-sales investment model, so that it can precisely map the effect of company inputs on market outputs. Having structured its measurements intelligently, Pfizer has the courage to act on them. To take an operational example, in Pfizer's analysis there are thirty-two steps in the prescription process and a hundred additional steps between prescription and sale. This makes measurements of direct-to-consumer marketing more difficult than direct-to-physician marketing, so Pfizer identifies surrogate markers, like patient requests of a product as a result of direct-to-consumer marketing. Based on history, Pfizer knows that a certain level of patient requests will in turn generate a somewhat predictable level of physician compliance with those requests. Then it works backward by tying degree of call to action in advertising to percentage of patient request, to percentage of physician compliance, to number of prescriptions. Kelly acknowledges, "The numbers get a little squishy because of all the variation and noise in the system, but we can demonstrate to our satisfaction that there is a significant positive return to our business from direct-to-consumer marketing."

In general terms, Pfizer takes copious intermediate measures of customer perceptions and behavior and then links them to company inputs on the one hand, and market outputs from the customer's perspective, on the other. In the specific example here, Pfizer's inputs are its direct-to-consumer advertising; its outputs are the number of prescriptions written. Continuous, not intermittent, monitoring of intermediate customer behaviors and perceptions enables the company to adjust company inputs to produce maximal market outputs.

Operationalizing Market Measures in Real Time at Amazon.com

For Amazon.com, measuring what matters primarily means tracking customers' purchases and treating the resulting data with predictive algorithms that enable it to influence future purchasing within and across retail categories. The trends in purchasing patterns for both individual customers and customer segments drive everything that Amazon does, and the company takes advantage of these measures in near real time, adjusting promotions and other marketing communications on the fly with the feedback represented by millions of customers' click-throughs or click-offs.

Amazon advertises in traditional media such as Sunday supplements, employs traditional focus groups to learn about customers, and assembles user groups for alpha and beta testing of new technologies and website features. But the company makes its own website and e-mail the primary channels for learning about customers, selling to them, and serving them when they have a problem. It reaps economies of scale in data capture from its relationship with around sixty million unique customers, who make hundreds of thousands of unique visits a day to its website. Of course, much of this effort is automated.

Amazon collects data by asking random samples of customers on the website a pop-up question, such as what motivated that day's visit. Was it the result of an e-mail promotion, an ad, or previous shopping on the site? "Likewise," Amazon.com's Lance Batchelor told us, "We go back to a cross section of recipients of pretty much every e-mail promotion and survey them, via e-mail, about what they liked and didn't like."

The company also randomly surveys customers having contact with customer service. It monitors the customer service department's performance by automatically tracking total contacts per day, cost per contact, response time by e-mail, and response time by telephone. "We keep all these threads on our system, and if contact with an unhappy customer escalates past a certain point, the system automatically alerts us," Lance Batchelor said. "Then a senior supervisor can step in, go back through the whole thread of messaging, fix the problem, and coach the customer-service rep on addressing the customer's need better and faster."

The story is much the same in marketing promotion. "In four or five different spaces on the website we'll have multiple messages stacked up for different Amazon.com stores or partners. We randomly serve the messages in each set to customers, and the information technology we've developed tracks the click-through rates on the messages and weights them accordingly. It's a real-time feedback loop that continuously updates and tunes itself. Within a couple of hours we're showing messages that are very attractive for most people. And then the next day, other partners or other of our own stores get their chance to be spotlighted.

"We measure the click through rates on different e-mail messages the same way. Typically we're sending out twenty million e-mails over three days, and within an hour or two or three we're getting a feel for which messages work best and how to tweak the remainder.

"The result is that every day 10 to 20 percent of our customers are being shown a different treatment of some kind. Almost the only thing we don't do this automated testing on is price. We've found it's best to stick to our everyday low-pricing strategy, and to vary our offers in other ways."

Amazon's skillful use of its technology creates myriad opportunities for cross-selling. "A classic example," Lance Batchelor said, "is when someone has just bought travel books, and our system launches an invitation to click through to our partner, Expedia.com. Our virtual mall of Amazon stores and partner stores has enough range that we can suggest something of interest for everyone."

Automated website and e-mail monitoring keeps the cost of data capture low. But it also helps lower other operating costs. "There's a purity of linkage from the customer through Amazon to the supplier. It happens in minutes that a publisher knows we're selling its book or an electronics company knows we're selling its DVD player. That means we can stay very lean on inventory and have the advantage of low working capital, so long as our predictive algorithms get it right on the forecasting side."

As an Internet retailer, Amazon.com naturally takes advantage of the way Internet and other computer technologies can automate many monitor-and-control functions, shifting between macromeasures and micromeasures, and between long and short cycles, as necessary to compile a balanced operational scorecard. Top marketing companies in many other industries do the same, aggressively seizing opportunities to automate customer-focused measurements. And no top marketing company fails to concentrate substantial resources on finding and implementing appropriate measures of customer needs and customer satisfaction. Now let's look at a few more cases in greater depth.

Measuring Wow Power: Building the First All-Digital Consumer Electronics Brand at Samsung

Few companies have so astutely leveraged their brand value upward in recent years as Samsung, the giant Korean semiconductor, telecommunications, and consumer electronics and appliance manufacturer. In doing so, Samsung has relied extensively on intelligent measurement of the firm itself, its competitors, and its customers—both trade channel and end user. Above all, it has focused on one measure that matters most to its brand value: design excellence.

The 1997 Asian financial crisis threatened Samsung with extinction. Since its founding in 1969 the company had expanded steadily by following a high-volume, low-price strategy that was endorsed, and subsidized, by the South Korean government. Relying on large capital loans to finance its operations, Samsung strove above all to lift market share. In consumer electronics, increasingly its key battleground, the company manufactured components for high profile brands, yet its own products occupied the low end of the market in price, prestige, and profitability.

Eric Kim, Samsung executive vice president of global marketing operations, told my colleagues and me, "The Asian financial crisis triggered a catalytic change at Samsung. Continuing to increase market share on borrowed capital was no longer a viable option. Even scarier than the debt crisis, and the underlying reason why we couldn't count on riding things out, was that our commodity manufacturing competencies were losing value, because the number of contract manufacturers was exploding, especially in China. If we stuck to our old ways, we were faced with going out of business sooner or later."

As a result, Samsung decided to embrace a truly market-driven change, a fundamental change of mission, processes, and the way it measured its performance via a consistent, systematic, and information-rich manner. Samsung's measurements shifted from a volume, market share and cost-centered approach to a customer-value and profit-centered approach. It divested a lot of areas that were not core to its business and significantly improved its balance sheet by moving away from debt financing and focusing on internal cash generation. Every product group became responsible for its own profits and losses (P&Ls).

To move its products up the value chain in customers' eyes, Samsung established a system of measurement that translates into "right price-positioning system." The idea was to figure out the best retail price position for each product category and product in terms of performance, features, image, promotion, and competition.

A central element in the strategy was Samsung's decision to go all out with digital products, stealing a march on industry-leading Sony and nearly all of its other competitors. This required different measures from the traditional approach.

Samsung decentralized financial responsibility for the P&Ls, but it simultaneously centralized brand management. That way it could migrate from a commodity brand to a lifestyle brand, targeting consumers who wanted leading-edge products with great value. To accomplish this transition, Samsung set out to design and build products with "wow power," that, as Kim said, "would make consumers say, 'Wow, look at this,' because they're fun, stylish, and a perfect fit for contemporary lifestyles." Designs that failed to measure sufficient "wow power" would no longer be brought to market.

Samsung adopted the slogan "Samsung DigitAll" to convey the idea of all digital products, and especially the convergence of digital products like the mobile phone, the personal digital assistant, the camera, and the MP3 player, for everyone. And it moved its positioning upmarket, striving to do so in a friendly rather than snobbish way.

Measurement was critical to Samsung in its new strategy. It invested heavily in market research to understand consumers and their lifestyles. It also invested heavily in design and measured its product groups on how many hit products they delivered. With focus, hard work, and good measurement, Samsung went from nowhere in design to being the second-most awarded design company in its category.

Stressing the measuring and sharing of best practices is another critical factor to Samsung's success. It encourages employees to adapt and invent new best practices. Once a year it goes through an extensive evaluation process, picks the top best practice innovations, and flies the individuals and teams responsible for them to headquarters for a celebration with a lot of fanfare where the CEO gives the grand prize and runner-up awards. Such a focus creates a tremendous drive to better practices throughout the company.

"Applying that best practices vision was probably hardest for the manufacturing guys," says Kim. "For years they had been charged with maximally utilizing capacity. When we set the new corporate agenda, they could no longer do that. They had to adjust to making lower-volume, higher-ticket items, and either get rid of the excess capacity or find other products to make. If they had dug in their heels, we couldn't have achieved the transition we wanted to make."

Externally, Samsung demonstrated its brand-changing resolve by jettisoning high-dollar-volume customers who didn't measure up to its new strategy.

"We wanted to get out of the low-end, commodity-oriented channel and into a higher-end, premium-value channel. So we had to leave places like Wal-Mart and Kmart, which were a big source of our revenue, and flow into channels like Best Buy, Circuit City, Sears, and regional electronics specialists. In tandem with this we transformed our field marketing and sales operations based on a CRM [customer relationship management] paradigm."

Note that except for Sears, Samsung's preferred retailers specialize in consumer electronics. A specialist retailer in any category naturally carries brands at a greater number of price points than a general department-store-like retailer and thus attracts customers who are more

sophisticated about the product category and more likely to buy products at higher price points. It would surely be difficult to quantify exactly the demographic difference between a Wal-Mart and a Best Buy
customer. Both are attracting value conscious consumers, and people
who shop for consumer electronics at Best Buy may well shop for
many other things at Wal-Mart. But Samsung was confident that there
was a significant, if difficult to measure difference between the two customer sets, and it had the courage to act on its reading of this crucial
variable. As for the inclusion of Sears among the preferred retail outlets for Samsung products, the legendary mass-market retailer still
looks relatively upmarket in some parts of the country, despite its troubles. In any event, the strategy worked beautifully.

Eric Kim told us, "There's a strong commitment at Samsung to continue to push forward to fully establish us as a premier brand in the
consumer electronics category." Since the strategic overhaul began,
Samsung has leapfrogged past most of the competition to vie with
Sony as the premier consumer electronics brand. Among other Asian
manufacturers, only Sharp has kept pace with Samsung, mainly because of its design- and technology-forward Aquos LCD televisions,
and it's surely no accident that its "From Sharp minds come sharp
products" slogan bespeaks a similar strategic approach to "Samsung
DigitAll, Everyone's Invited."

Samsung has been dubbed the "fastest-growing brand in the world,"
continually edging up *BusinessWeek*/Interbrand's annual measurement
survey of the Top 100 Global Brands, reaching twentieth position in
2005 and 2006 with estimated brand equity respectively of just under
$15 billion and just over $16 billion. In June 2004 Samsung proudly
announced that over the prior five years it had received nineteen Industrial Design Excellence Awards (IDEA) from the Industrial Designers
Society of America, tying Apple for first place. In 2004 five Samsung
products received IDEAs, and in 2006 it won twenty-five prestigious
International Forum Design Awards (Hanover, Germany), in both
cases more than any other company. But Samsung has yet to develop category-defining products like the Apple iPod or the Sony
PlayStation.

These results were reflected in its financial results. From 2001 to 2005
Samsung's revenues more than doubled, from $35.4 billion to $79.8
billion. Net income more than tripled, from $2.3 billion to $7.6 bil-

lion, and even reached $10.4 billion in 2004. From the perilous days of 1997, when Samsung faced the threat of extinction, the company has fully justified its transformational strategy and the hard and soft measures it chose to implement it.

In recent years the competition in mobile phones among Nokia, Motorola, and Samsung continued to be fought largely in terms of design. In 2005 Nokia finally released its first clamshell designs in the U.S. market and stabilized its number one U.S. and global market share through renewed design excellence. Meanwhile, Motorola regained the number two market share position, the *Wall Street Journal* noted, thanks to "a slew of cool devices and ads, featuring Motorola's trendy 'batwings' logo. Its ultraslim RAZR mobile phone has become the must-have handset since it was introduced, serving notice to Nokia that things are changing at Motorola."[1]

Samsung has no choice but to redouble its design efforts to develop products that score well on "wow." At the same time, as we will see in the concluding chapter, it formed common cause with its archrival, Sony.

Keeping a Lead: How Sony Uses Metrics to Counter Old and New Rivals

Hard as it is to reach the top, business history shows that it is even harder for a company to stay there for an extended length of time, as Sony has done in consumer electronics. For the global market leader in this major consumer products category, success carries special vulnerability: immense size and the profitability of existing product lines make it difficult to stay on the leading edge of consumer preference.

Since we interviewed Ron Boire, president of sales for consumer electronics, this core business, which accounts for more than two-thirds of Sony's total revenues, has had a fairly rocky time. Sales have been mostly flat, and Sony has lagged in bringing important new product features to market, such as making the CD Walkman compatible with MP3 music files on CD-R/RW. It introduced Network Walkman, its first portable audio product with a hard drive, only in August 2004, two years after Apple introduced the category-defining iPod. Sales of PlayStation2 have declined sharply in a market share and price war with Microsoft's Xbox that has hurt profitability for both products. In addition to fast growing Samsung, Sony faces stiffening competition from Dell, which now sells flat-panel televisions, and from Canon, Sharp, and NEC, leaders, respectively, in digital imaging, LCD televisions, and LCD displays.

Despite these difficulties, I can't imagine counting Sony out since it has had significant successes. Sales of its flat-panel televisions and digital cameras have seen strong growth, and Sony Ericsson cell-phone sales have been another big plus. Thanks to these gains, and hopes for the PlayStation 3, Sony climbed from twenty-eighth to twenty-sixth on the 2006 *BusinessWeek*/Interbrand rankings of the Top 100 Global Brands.

Given its large size and many mature product lines, Sony is a remarkably nimble marketer. Although it must continue to navigate difficult waters, it nonetheless remains the benchmark against which Samsung, Sharp, and other rivals measure themselves. To address its challenges, Sony measures what matters in every area of operations from new product development to rebranding, or retirement, of existing products and sales force policies, and uses its measures to drive real organizational change.

"Sony is really driven by the concept of 'If you can't measure it, you can't do it,'" Boire said. Perhaps the most telling example of Sony's ability to market through measurement that connects company inputs, customer behaviors and perceptions, and market outputs lies in its revamped sales operations, where it changed the parameters of its interactions with its retail trade channel customers. As Boire explained, "With national customers like Best Buy, Sears, Circuit City, Wal-Mart, and Target, or a strategically important regional chain, we used to do classic sales compensation: budget versus sell-in. If you had a budget target of a million dollars for a category and you sold at 1.1 million, you did a great job, you made a good bonus. Regardless of what was stuck in the barn at the end of the month or the end of the year. Regardless of whether or not they could pay for it. Regardless of whether you delivered it to them on time. We were paying our people to stuff the box.

"Sony moved to a process in which 50 percent of salespeople's compensation and up to 70 percent of its entire inventory management/asset management group's compensation is based on customer scorecards with metrics that are agreed on individually with national and strategic customers. Most of the metrics focus on simple things like on-time delivery, in stock, gross margin return on inventory [the key retail performance metric], forecast accuracy, and a number of other top-line metrics that are driven by hundreds of little activities that lead up to them."

Boire told us, "To set the metrics we ask each customer, 'What's important to you? What are your targets? What are your strategic concerns?' Best Buy's target currently is 90 percent on-time delivery, plus or minus one day, and 95 percent in stock. We may or may not hit that metric due to a variety of reasons, but the point is everybody's got the same goal in mind. Depending on their size, we track retailers either monthly or weekly. And our salespeople are given bonus compensation twice a year based on their customer scorecards.

"As the saying goes, 'People do what they're paid to do.' When you change the basis of people's paychecks, it really is remarkable how fast they change their behavior. We've seen a tremendous shift in the behavior of the organization, and a very positive reaction from the marketplace. No one else in the consumer electronics industry is doing this. And in most of the industries that our customers do business in, whether it's appliances or software or consumer electronics or computers, all the sales forces are compensated on sell-in.

"It's a revolutionary change for the consumer electronics industry to have a salesperson say, 'No, I won't take your purchase order, because you have too much inventory.' Everybody talks about aligning with your customers, but if you're paying your salespeople to stuff the box you can't be aligned, it's impossible."

Sony's revolutionary sales compensation scheme aligns its salespeople's short-term desire for healthy bonuses with the company's long-term desire for profitable customers. In implementing the scheme, Sony's huge size, relative to competitors, gives it a market stabilizing function that it can ill afford to shirk.

Sony may represent 30 percent or more of a national consumer electronics customer's revenue. This gives Sony a considerable role to play in establishing and maintaining trade confidence for the consumer electronics industry. Boire said, "As a market leader, we very carefully monitor the way we deal with customers, because we don't want to be the ones that push a customer past the tipping point. At the same time we have to remain profitable; we have to maximize our position with the most profitable customers and limit our risk with customers whose businesses are in trouble. We probably overinvest rather than underinvest in most of those situations. Historically, we've had some winners and losers over the years.

To support the market as a whole while cultivating its own interests, Sony has to be a keen judge of its customers' future profitability so it can be proactive and intervene with a customer well before they reach the tipping point.

Sony measures customer profitability from a contribution margin point of view. "For example," Boire said, "when Sony's movie *Men in Black* was released in the United States, we had an exclusive program in place with Best Buy, a multimillion-dollar investment by us, multimillion-dollar investment by them; it's a form of event marketing that we really push hard on here. Our baseline program with Best Buy says we should do x amount of business in this period, so we're looking for x-plus: incremental revenue and incremental contribution margin for them, incremental revenue and incremental contribution for us— based on tie-ins with the movie.

"Marketing has P&L responsibility on these major customer accounts. The only thing we load into the customer's P&L are direct costs attributable to that customer. We look at the contribution margin in dollars per customer, we project midrange contributions some years ahead, and we calculate a net present value (NPV) with a conservative termination value.

"Sony has had several customers experiencing financial difficulties. It asks: 'what's the contribution margin of this customer?' If they go away, the fixed cost at headquarters doesn't go away. But there may be $30 million in contribution margin that goes away. The contribution dollars and the NPV give us balance points to ask, 'What should we invest in this customer to try to help them stay healthy?'

With one customer, Sony hired outside consultants to go in as a crisis management team to work with them on process reengineering, on inventory and supply-chain management, and on advertising productivity. Sony focuses on its at-risk number, the annual contribution margin. "If we invest up to that point," Boire says, "and the customer turns the corner, we're not going to claim sole credit for saving them, but we certainly didn't help them go down, right? On a day-to-day basis, this grounds management as to the relative value of any customer. Because we can say, 'You know what? The net present value of this customer is $600 million. That's what this relationship is worth.' "

Sony does have customers where the contribution margin is significantly below what it would like. It tries not to use contribution margin to make product allocation decisions or strategic position decisions, because that could be dangerous. It has, for example, a retailer with a very high-end brand position in a very upscale community. It's where affluent consumers go for a home-theater room, and maintaining a strong selling presence for Sony products in that customer's business provides an umbrella effect to the local marketplace. Sony can take a lower contribution margin in that retailer because it's strategically important to Sony.

Sony has less influence outside the consumer electronics channel. If a major national multicategory retailer is in difficulties, Sony is such a small percentage of its total business that it wouldn't matter what it did, it wouldn't avert the inevitable. What it does do in those cases is manage its risk well, as was the case with Kmart where, Boire says, Sony predicted in advance the day Kmart would file for bankruptcy protection. "We took some losses, but we managed our receivables with Kmart probably better than anyone in the trade."

Sony is also developing metrics for advertising productivity, both for itself and its trade channel partners. "The next great frontier is the black hole of advertising productivity," Ron Boire says. Because Sony delivers hundreds of millions of dollars in advertising to the channel, it's been able to demand agreed-upon goals up front, and then do postmortems to try and get its arms around how to move the needle on the dial at every different customer. For Customer A an end-cap in-store display may work, whereas for Customer B it's more about getting the right size box in their catalog, an inside right-hand page versus an inside left-hand page.

Sony's customer scorecards obviously have to be transparent to both Sony and its retail trade customers. No less important, Sony has to resist withholding information from them to aid its own direct-to-consumer retailing on the Web. If Sony chose, it could aggressively undercut its trade channel customers by manipulating the release of changes in its inventory and pricing. But as Ron Boire told us, "More than anything else, customers want to know they're being treated fairly. They want to know that when product is tight, it's tight everywhere.

They want to know that when a price moves, it doesn't move online for us a month before it moves for them. You can't say anything to earn trust in a competitive relationship. It's what you do. We can't just talk the talk, we have to walk the walk. And we've been doing it long enough that most of our customers say, 'They're playing the game fairly; we'll keep doing business with them.' "

Low Concept, High Content: Prudential Financial Writes a Brand Renewal Policy to Fit Customer Need

Well-chosen, well-applied metrics can also help save a brand that has fallen on hard times, as was the case with insurance and investment services giant Prudential Financial. Michael Hines, Prudential Financial's senior vice president for Global Communications and Marketing said, "I came from Fidelity to Prudential in July 1996. At that time, Fidelity's brand image ratings were off the charts, and Prudential's were at their low point. Prudential had been charged with using improper sales practices, and it was in danger of becoming a brand that everybody knows but nobody does business with, like Woolworth."

Prudential, though, still had tremendous inherent strength and a huge customer base. It also had a lot of good products, perhaps the best-balanced product lines in consumer financial services, with strong insurance, investment, and real estate offerings. The challenge was to turn the company's image around, internally as well as externally, and have it become something new in people's minds.

Prudential's new leadership team concentrated its strategic and operational attention on five key measures:

- Market supply and demand

- Customer profitability

- Consumer concerns and purchase patterns

- Aligning company offerings, employee behavior, and customer need

- Customer satisfaction with the entire marketing offer, from messaging and product to customer service

Market Supply and Demand

In consumer financial services, as in most industries, there is more supply than there is demand from the most profitable customers. Prudential recognizes, as Michael Hines memorably put it, that "people don't have to do business with us," and it accordingly focuses its resources on winning market share and customer loyalty in two key market segments. The first segment comprises affluent baby boomers—not all baby boomers, mind you—who have recently started retiring and will continue to do so over the next twenty-five years. The second segment comprises those younger customers who are the "emerging affluent" and who will follow the last of the baby boomers into retirement.

Of course, every other financial services firm wants to penetrate the same market segments. The way to profit now is having affluent baby boomers as customers. The way to profit tomorrow is having the affluent members of the next generation as customers. As we'll see, Prudential Financial positions itself to reap those profits by the way it measures what matters to affluent consumers.

"We all want the affluent baby boomers forty-five years old and older. They're the ones you can possibly sell multiple products to and have multiple relationships with today. For financial-services marketers, the emerging affluent are less cost effective to pursue at present. But if . . . individual[s are] younger and [are] entering their peak earning years, they have the potential for good companies to build very long and profitable relationships."

Customer Profitability

In an ongoing effort to match their offerings to a range of customer segments, many consumer-oriented firms in financial services and other industries have invested heavily in CRM technology. By contrast, Prudential espouses a single, all-embracing offering—"Grow and protect your wealth"—and eschews segmenting its services to suit vastly different styles of customer behavior. Michael Hines told us why he and his colleagues remained skeptical about current CRM technology's usefulness in consumer financial services.

"If you're a broker, agent, or financial adviser at the grassroots level, and let's say you've got five hundred customers, you are probably making yourself and the company more money on the top fifty than the bottom three hundred. The ones in the bottom three hundred have a smaller relationship with you, and you probably don't give them as much of your attention as you do your best customers. What you don't know about any one of those three hundred smaller relationships is: who is in a trial mode with you? Maybe they have major relationships with your competitors, but they may become one of your top fifty as they become increasingly satisfied with you and the firm.

"CRM will look at all the customers' zip codes, length of relationship, products owned and maybe a hundred other things, and then tell you to pay attention to some and ignore the others. The algorithm tells the firm how hard to pursue the customer—whether to let the phone ring twenty times at the call center or pick it up within three rings.

"The more you understand about this sophisticated database stuff, the more you realize how inaccurate it can be. At the best, you're going to get 40–60 percent of the relevant information. If a customer has a small relationship and you treat them like a nobody, and they have a big relationship someplace else, they will think, 'Well, I guess they didn't want my business.' The algorithm didn't pick up their dissatisfaction with another firm, and the potential to vastly deepen the relationship. There are so many ways of getting it wrong when you're doing it that way, that it's really not worth doing it. You get all these marketers from the biggest companies, and they all go to the same business schools, work at the same four or five companies and they think that CRM is the only way. Customers generally feel that companies neither know nor understand what they want. Billions have been wasted on this in the last twenty years.

"As I said, we all want affluent and emerging affluent customers. But in terms of trying to come up with an algorithm that quantifies it, that you can take to the bank, you can't do it, in my view. Most marketers think you can do it. I don't think you can do it. Whether you're a direct marketer or whether you use a sales force, you have to look at who the customers are in a more subtle way. I have always thought the most interesting aspect of marketing or branding is when the algorithm goes curvilinear, that is, when the variables no longer work because of one small change. In the early '90s, the *New York Times* rated a wine from a small Napa Valley winery better than wines costing ten times as much in a very small story. The winery owner told me they had calls from Australia based on that one little story and that they could have sold fifty times what they had produced. Their brand forever changed because of that one piece of PR. If they had been doing CRM instead of focusing on the grapes, the algorithm would have turned on its head."

Prudential Financial's experience is clearly not the only word on CRM, but it is a cautionary note that however sophisticated measurement tools may be, they can really only be as sensitive to what matters in a market as the people using them.

Consumer Concerns and Purchase Patterns

By understanding its most desirable customers' concerns and purchase patterns with sufficient precision, Michael Hines told us, Prudential could increasingly behave in a way that appealed to them and win their loyalty. Key to this effort were effective measures of customer behaviors and perceptions.

Prudential observed that the consumer buying process in financial services usually takes several months. During this period, people think about a product they want to buy, like long-term-care insurance, look for information about it in magazines like *Money* and *Consumer Reports* and on the Web, scrutinize everyone's ads, and get referrals from people they know.

"I've watched many focus groups," Hines said, "and the pattern holds every time. People will describe what I call 'stalking' the product. In the process, they look at a company and they say, 'Would I buy that product from Prudential? The article I read mentioned GE and Prudential. Would I buy long-term-care insurance from Prudential? I wouldn't buy it from No-Name Life Insurance Company, because I can't fool around with my financial future, but I might buy it from GE or Prudential.' So two companies get considered.

"Then customers scope in closer. They don't want to be stupid. They're not going to buy a long-term-care policy from either Prudential or GE just because they have brand names that have been around for a hundred years. That's meaningless at that point. They look at the two companies' brochures. They go on the websites and compare how they look and feel, and they discuss the product with an agent. They want high content at that point. This is an important decision. So they scope in. They compare. They try to make a rational decision. Then they make a purchase decision."

Through focus groups, Prudential assessed the extent to which customers want to simplify their financial relationships and have multiple relationships with one trustworthy company. It also saw that affluent, Internet-savvy customers want to transact all their business as simply and painlessly as possible. "They want to be able to interact with you via any channel they choose: in person, over the phone, or on the Web," Hines observed. "If they're going to give you their business, they want you to simplify it.

"That's where you need a good technology infrastructure, to handle people's information sensitively and not barrage them with multiple mailings. And to greet them the same, no matter how they come in the door. So they don't say, 'How come you don't know who I am?'"

Recognizing that it must integrate its operations to speak to all customers with one voice, Michael Hines told us, "We are agnostic about how we reach customers. We want to serve all channels everywhere. I think every oligopolizing firm over the past ten or fifteen years has been trying to become all channels and all products everywhere, globalizing with the broad range of financial products sold over the kitchen table, the phone, or the Internet. However you want to buy it, we'll sell it. That's the positioning that all companies have been trying to effect: all relevant products, all relevant channels everywhere. It's an important goal when supply is unlimited and demand is limited."

Company-Customer Alignment

To align its offerings and behavior with customer need, Prudential had to see itself accurately and act on the inherent strength of its balanced product portfolio. Prudential was an insurance company, but the new leadership team from 1996 on saw itself differently, as being in both investment and insurance. It wanted to participate more in the biggest bull market in history, and the new focus helped. Fortunately, the decision to give equal marketing emphasis to insurance and investments also positioned the company to appeal to customers in the anxious, postboom environment that soon followed. For affluent baby boomers looking at their assets after the tech bubble burst in spring 2001, security became at least as important as growth.

In May 2001 Prudential evolved its offering to growth and protection. Insurance and investment became the linchpins of presenting itself as growing and protecting wealth. Most competitors were not emphasizing protection but were stuck in go-go growth pitches. In offering an equal balance, Prudential differentiated itself from even those companies with a similar range of products. Prudential has the double-sided strength to do it in insurance and investing. Sometimes insurance products grow wealth, and sometimes, usually, they protect it. Sometimes investment products protect wealth, like a money market fund, and sometimes they grow it, like an equity fund. Trying to meet the needs of the same affluent boomer clients is what everybody is trying to do, but Prudential has differentiated itself by doing that as two pieces of business that come together around customers' two most fundamental concerns.

Prudential's strategy succeeded so well that it was able to demutualize in 2001 and become a public stock company at an impressive valuation, amid sinking investor confidence in the market. Since demutualization, Prudential's stock price has tripled, and in 2006, net income was $3.4 billion on $32.5 billion revenues, up from $1.3 billion net income on $27.9 billion just three years earlier. Prudential's "growing and protecting your wealth" offering has gained increasing traction with consumers, as witness the copycat marketing by rivals such as Fidelity, which now highlights retirement planning above investment choices, a significant departure from its positioning before the technology bubble burst in 2000, Genworth Financial, and Lincoln Financial, which promises to help customers "create, protect, and enjoy" their wealth. But interestingly, the first payoff for Prudential was internal.

Hines said, " 'Grow and protect' was not just an advertising slogan, but an organic development that helped focus all our people on who we are and the value we offer customers."

As we saw with both manufacturing and service companies in chapter 8, so with Prudential. A company's marketing culture is a necessary outgrowth and engine of integrating operations to serve customer needs.

Customer Satisfaction

"Growing and protecting wealth" provided good strategic alignment with customer needs. What affluent boomers most wanted in the early to mid-2000s was exactly what Prudential was best positioned to deliver. To support that strategy operationally, the company uses the information it derives from customer satisfaction measures to refine its offerings and practices. If Prudential hopes to sustain its leading position in financial services over the long run, it will also have to track how the drivers of high customer satisfaction among affluent baby boomers match up with the wants and needs of the emerging affluent in younger generations.

"We measure customer satisfaction in the investments business and the insurance business. We want everybody selling Prudential products to understand, 'These customers rate you this way and here's your profitability on them. These other customers say they never hear from you, and here's your profitability on them.' That's a powerful tool. And we've done a lot of work internally to improve how fast we respond to customers, how long it takes to process an insurance claim.

"If the customer scopes out a product from different companies and you get the nod, it's the simple things that customers value: answering the phone in a friendly, helpful way, sending the bill on time, and so on. If you perform well on these simple measures, then you will win an opportunity to cross sell that customer. You don't have to surprise and delight today's customer, once you have someone as a customer. Answer the phone, send out the mail, go away when they want you to go away, don't insult their intelligence. When they begin the search for the next product they need, they'll scope in on you. Over time, if we keep serving them well, they'll pull back and say, 'I do financial stuff with Prudential,' like they say, 'I drive a Ford,' or, 'My phone company is Verizon.' "

Prudential's commitment to adjusting its behavior in accord with appropriate customer satisfaction measures had its most immediately visible impact in a dramatic change in the company's advertising, from high concept to high content.

Prudential fired all of its ad agencies and brought everything in-house to unify its focus and cut costs. It knew that its brand equity had been deteriorating in the bull market and that it had limited resources, so it had to get control over the messaging and put a unified effort to redefine the Prudential brand. Prudential produces advertising at about a fifth of what it cost to produce outside. Said Hines, "The ad agency system is geared to producing a few million-dollar-plus commercials loaded with high-concept creative, and running them over and over again in prime time with heavy network media buys. That's how the agencies make their money."

Prudential wanted to do lots of ads to tell people as quickly as possible about the new Prudential. Each ad might only run a few times, so it had to produce them at a low cost. The advent of digital video established a situation where they could make television commercials much less expensively.

"Along with low cost," Hines said, "we wanted to go low concept and high content. Madison Avenue goes high concept and lowest-common-denominator content. Before the rest of the new leadership team and I got here, one of the outside agencies was doing television advertising that was very cool, very Madison Avenue hip, and it was quite separate from the image that Prudential actually had. The advertising was way off from where the image was. And it was also out of step with our target customers, the affluent boomers who want to make sure they don't make a mistake with their kids' college education money or their retirement funds.

"Madison Avenue's typical commercial for a financial-services product like long-term-care insurance may be funny and memorable, but it diminishes what customers think about the company. Show a room full of people the commercial and they say, 'That was hilarious, a talking dog cracking jokes about long-term-care insurance. I love that spot. But I'm not interested in long-term-care insurance.' The people who are really interested in long-term-care insurance are bothered by that spot. This is where winning an advertising award is absolutely meaningless.

"Our approach is straightforward, high-content advertising. It's not going to win advertising industry awards, but we don't care; we're not producing it for awards. High-content advertising is conveying a serious message to the consumer in thirty seconds. The proof of the pudding is in our image ratings. Those numbers have gone basically straight up since they hit bottom in the mid-1990s. Right after that we began to change the advertising, first print and then television, and our ratings began to head back up. They are now among the highest in the industry.

"We also save money and increase our effectiveness by having our own in-house media buyers. I have a deal sitting over there right now, to buy this weekend's football games at a very attractive price. The networks come to us because there's no time-consuming middleman to go through and the deal won't be leaked. You come and you tell us; it stays with us. So we get a tremendous advantage that way."

In measuring the effectiveness of its advertising and other operations, Prudential, like all the top marketing companies, is committed to unflinching honesty in its research. It does image ratings three or four times a year and is prepared to change direction at any moment if its advertising is not working. Hines opined, "Most marketing and advertising research boils down to: 'Find something that shows the campaign is working.' We don't ever do that. Our numbers have been very good, but I said we had to get them verified independently, because we're not going to fool ourselves."

Finally, Prudential's clear focus on measuring what matters allows it to stay the course and give its strategies time to succeed.

"There were a lot of naysayers when we changed the advertising. I said, 'This is what we are going to do. We are going to stay with this format, it's high content, and it's going to work.' Fortunately I was allowed to do that, and not have to change things a year later because one person said, 'Gee, I don't like it.' You change it and then you lose your identity. You don't have that sense of purpose. It takes years to build your identity and years to change it as well."

•   •   •

Prudential illustrates how the five marketing imperatives reinforce each other. We've looked at Prudential's handling of them in terms of measurement, because measurement provides the information that is the basis for picking markets that matter, segmenting markets, crafting offers that provide enhanced customer value, and integrating operations and culture to deliver that value. Throughout this book discussion of a company's excellence in fulfilling a particular marketing imperative has necessarily involved some discussion of its experience in fulfilling the other four imperatives.

•   •   •

Measurements that help set, implement, and adjust market strategy have been a crucial factor in the success of the companies we've considered so far. For example, Progressive's measurement innovation — exploiting a previously unrecognized link between customers' credit ratings and the lost costs of servicing those customers — transformed pricing throughout the U.S. car insurance industry. Despite copycat pricing from bigger rivals, the company sustains increasing market share and revenues by continually refining its pricing metrics and by offering best-in-class customer service, measured by the speed and ease with which customers can buy and renew policies on the phone, on the Web, or with independent agents, and by claims settlement that Progressive asserts is "fast, friendly, and fair."

•   •   •

The Home Depot's business strategy depends on accurately assessing the life-stage needs of homeowners and the demographic drivers that affect their purchases of everything from paint, carpet, and flooring to garden tractors, power tools, and new kitchens and baths. Operationally, The Home Depot practices a measurement-driven approach to serving customers, battling competitors, and adapting to changing market circumstances. The Home Depot told us that it monitored store associates' time and rescheduled tasks that took them away from customers — pretty basic, but it shifted to putting freight away at night, so that during the day associates could concentrate on helping customers.

The Home Depot knows the buying patterns for its various products — if it sells closet organizers mostly on Saturdays and Sundays, but sells pneumatic nail guns mostly on Monday and Tuesday mornings from seven to nine, it gets the manufacturers in to do demos and promotions when the highest proportion of interested customers is in the stores. The Home Depot closely monitors competition to meet the core challenge of being the low-price leader across the board. And when the market changes in important ways — like lumber prices hitting their lowest level in years or mortgage rates going down — The Home Depot reminds its customers that now is the time to build a deck or redo the basement rec room.

The Home Depot illustrates how a company's measurements must be focused externally on what is going on in the customer's world.

Target's emphasis on trend spotting, which we explored in chapter 8, points to the same moral: you will profit insofar as you monitor and assess circumstances—and then adjust operations—from the customer's point of view.

●   ●   ●

ESPN's enormous success shows how niche cable channel programming has changed the television industry. Niche programming enables a tighter company-customer link, supports deeper data mining, produces greater potential understanding of customer needs, and thus can pay off in a sustainable differential advantage for the company with the clearest understanding of this dynamic and the firmest commitment to serving customers.

ESPN's growth stems from the relationship it has nurtured with customers in the largest such niche, sports fans. Using ratings data, focus groups, and surveys, ESPN continually measures customers in a feedback loop with its programming. Accurate measurement of sports fans' enthusiasms and passions enables ESPN to evolve programming to capitalize on them, from its signature sports news show, *SportsCenter*, to the X Games, to movie biographies of sports figures and even dramatic series centered around sports. The popularity of that programming, which can now be recorded on a minute-by-minute basis, validates the measurement and contributes a new data set to ESPN's database of sports fan information.

The audience for ESPN's national and international cable television channels, its sports radio network, *ESPN the Magazine,* and one of the most heavily visited sites on the Web represents a sizable percentage of the total sports fan population. As such it commands the attention of cable system operators, advertisers, and all others interested in reaching or learning about sports fans. And because men make up the majority of its audience, ESPN can also exploit the value of male consumer data as distinct from sports fan data.

Note how ESPN's increasing ability to measure its sports-fan customers feeds into all the prior marketing imperatives. Knowledge of sports fans' behaviors, perceptions, needs, and wants clearly underwrites its ability to operate in a market that matters, sports entertainment, and has done so since ESPN's founder picked the sports market as the one for his new company to enter. Likewise, understanding sports fans and their needs supports ESPN's more venturesome programming decisions, as with the creation of the X Games or its running a scores-and-results line under commercials on certain shows, such as *Baseball Tonight.* The X Games exemplifies the value of keen segmentation, and the score line exemplifies ESPN's consistent drive to enhance customer value.

Intelligent measurement of sports fans underlies the way ESPN integrates its operations to serve customers. For example, the so-called shoulder programming that ESPN creates to support important programs such as Major League Baseball or NBA or NFL games caters both to end-customer sports fans watching their favorite sports and related programming and to the advertisers seeking to reach those fans. And the sense of shared purpose and understanding that ESPN employees have for customers as fellow sports fans sustains a company-wide marketing culture that is the most coherent, effective, and profitable franchise in cable television.

●   ●   ●

In considering all the examples of measuring what matters in this chapter, I think four lessons emerge as paramount.

1. Your measures must include a balance of input, intermediate, and output variables that capture essential monitor-and-control measures of current interactions with customers. But there should not be too many measures: generally, one measure is too few, but twenty-five is too many. You also need measures relating to customer and market insight that are crucial to setting strategy and reaching near, intermediate, and long-term goals.

2. You must make certain that you are measuring the *right* things. If you sell through distribution, you should be concerned with what the final customer buys, not just what you sell to your direct customers. If you're measuring customer satisfaction, don't let salespeople choose their best customers to survey; if you're measuring transportation time, don't let your traffic managers focus on rail yard to rail yard, instead of from your factory to the customer. Don't forget that its human nature to want to appear successful; if you're not careful, some people will try to game the system rather than focus on improving the firm's performance.

3. Your measures must have clarity and transparency. That is, they must produce a definitive enough answer for the circumstances, keeping in mind that it is not possible for a company ever to have the total of all relevant information at its fingertips. And the clear measures that you compile must be transparent to everyone who needs them to help meet customer needs. It is no good to measure the right things and then sequester the results from those who could put them to good use. Unfortunately, many dysfunctional companies are hobbled by precisely these sorts of blocks in information flow, created by officially sanctioned or self-appointed, turf-guarding gatekeepers who treat the information as part of their personal power base. The top marketing companies not only measure what matters, they also make sure employees know the results.

4. Compensation at all levels must be pegged to performance against fair, well-understood, customer-focused measures.

TEN

Conclusion: Sustaining Marketing Excellence

This book concludes a four-year study of marketing excellence. Its most important finding is that the world's leading companies all understand that customers are the firm's core assets. From the metals industry to consumer electronics and computer software, from cosmetics to health care, from business to business to retail, Marketing Mavens in the CEO's office and in the marketing department are focusing their companies on executing five customer-focused marketing imperatives. Through good times and bad, this keeps their companies at or near the top, and makes them better able to weather the inevitable bumps along the way.

A couple of years ago, Dell was on top of the world. Its stock price hovered around $40 per share, down from its peak in 2000, but showing steady upward progress from the difficult times in 2001. At the peak, twelve years following its initial public offering in 1988, Dell stock had appreciated 45,000 percent compared with 400 percent for the Dow Jones industrials. Accounting for splits, a share bought in the IPO at $8.50 was worth over $4,000 in 2000, constituting one of the greatest investments in modern business history.

A few years later, Dell's stock dropped to $20, and then began inching upward. At first I panicked; was this the performance I wanted to showcase? But then, as I looked across the business landscape, I saw that all companies, good and bad, have their stumbles and missteps. What distinguishes the good companies from the bad is their ability to limit mistakes and minimize recovery time. The companies we've looked at in this book exemplify this pattern, with those enjoying the greatest long-term success, and ability to ride out tough times, showing a clear commitment to fulfilling the five core imperatives.

Even at a relatively low point in the mid-2000s, Dell has maintained impressive market share and profitability, notwithstanding significant improvements at Hewlett-Packard (HP) and new challenges from Lenovo, the Chinese firm that acquired IBM's personal computer business. Dell continued to execute well in each of the five imperatives, as its recent experience in the Chinese market, product lineup shifts, and new internal controls exemplify.

Unlike its rivals, Dell held back from doing business in China until the mid-1990s, when the Chinese government eased rules requiring foreign companies to have local partners. Dell was thus able to maintain its policy of dealing directly with customers, and avoid the negative consequences for its business model of selling through distributors and retailers.

Remember that Dell has followed a single business model from day one: deal directly with the customer, manufacture every order to the customer's specifications, and beat all comers on price. This strategy defined Dell's core customer base as people who were sophisticated enough about technology to make telephone—and then in addition Web-based sales and service—efficient. When Dell thought customers weren't sophisticated enough technologically for the company to be able to deal with them profitably, it held back from entering that segment. But once Dell deemed a market segment ready for its direct model, it quickly came to dominate that segment.

Waiting until the moment was ripe to bring its direct model to China was characteristic of Dell's disciplined brand integrity and market selection. China was a market that mattered to Dell's long-term future, and it had the patience and savvy to pick the right moment to enter. Dell made its first gains in the Chinese market by doing what it has always done, segmenting for technologically savvy small business customers who can be sold and serviced most efficiently, and using them as a wedge to open up other market segments over time.

Naysayers predicted that China's lack of a nationwide landline telephone network would hamper Dell. But the company rightly counted on the ubiquitous cell-phone and Internet use among China's new middle and entrepreneurial classes.

As in the previous markets it came to dominate, Dell's adherence to its direct model means that it can create exceptional customer value and wield differential advantage on cost even over Chinese competitors such as Lenovo. That is truly something to marvel at. We live in a global business environment where companies in the United States and other developed countries constantly cry wolf about the lower labor and manufacturing costs of their competitors in China, Singapore, India, and elsewhere. Yet the *Wall Street Journal* reported, "Behind the scenes, Lenovo is struggling to cut its costs closer to Dell's level."[1]

Dell is now third in the China market, with over 9 percent market share. It is gaining ground on a slipping Lenovo, whose share remains in excess of 30 percent. In the global computer market, Dell is neck and neck with HP in market share with around 16 to 17 percent worldwide, and it is far and away the world's most profitable computer company, with an operating profit margin roughly double HP's because of its dominance in laptops.[2]

I have stressed the consistency of Dell's methods, but it is also important to note that the company knows when to be flexible and take a fresh tack. The consistent top marketing companies all adapt flexibly to changing market conditions.

As the market has matured, PCs have become an increasingly low-margin product. Dell has responded to this decrease in profitability in its core business in several ways. It has continually honed its core competencies to ensure that it can always sell its PCs on the lowest cost basis. It has steadily gained market share in servers for business computing. It has successfully expanded its product line into higher-margin laptops, printers (the ink and paper supplies are high margin, if not the printers themselves), handheld devices, and consumer electronics. It has steadily taken on and met challenges in new markets, as in China, following established success in Europe and South America. And in 2006 it finally joined the design sweepstakes, seeking Apple-style cachet and premium pricing with its launch of the XPS line of desktop and laptop/notebook computers.

The first XPS products have not become must-have designs, whereas Apple hit the design bull's-eye again with its MacBook line of laptop computers powered by Intel chips. But the XPS line shows that the company has its eye on the product-design ball.

The mid-2000s also brought Dell customer service and product quality problems. In 2006 the company received considerable media attention for a small number of fires in overheating laptop batteries. But Apple's iBook and PowerBook laptop computers were soon found to have the same problem, which ultimately lay at the door of the supplier of the batteries—Sony—and Dell also limited the damage to its reputation through a prompt, efficient customer recall of the affected batteries.

More serious were complaints about bad customer service in general. Much of this was owing to Dell's having cut customer service expenditures by outsourcing the function to a large degree, but there were also complaints about U.S.-based customer-service reps. Technology-related blogs created a buzz about an incident in which an unsophisticated customer who needed a router was up-sold a server, as well as about quality problems with new computers.

Dell responded by dramatically increasing customer-service spending and shifting much of the outsourced customer-service operations back to North America, with new quality control checks and training for customer-service reps. Within a month, Dell cut the response time to customers' calls by half.

To cite another small, but telling example of Dell's nimbleness, look at one of its China moves. Listening carefully to its new market, Dell discovered that its usual offer language, "direct sales," translated idiomatically into Chinese as a term used to describe crooked pyramid schemes. The company quickly switched to "direct orders," which Chinese customers found much more congenial in translation.

To take good aim on moving markets, Dell relies on a complete integration of its lowest-cost-basis operations and its company culture. Dell is noted for its "tight messaging," and industry observers find it "a little bit scary how everyone from the highest to the lowest employee is on message."[3] Dell seeks customer-focused measurement of everything at the firm, including the performance of senior Dell executives, who are regularly evaluated by those working under them.

Dell in China

IMPERATIVE	DELL ACTION
1. Pick markets that matter.	1. Identify China.
2. Select segments to dominate.	2. Enter China market only when core target market segment is ready, and only when prevailing infrastructure allows for direct interaction with the customers in that segment.
3. Design the market offer to create customer value and secure differential advantage.	3. Exploit efficiencies of the direct model to win on price/value.
4. Integrate to serve the customer.	4. Hone low-cost advantage over Chinese rivals; keep culture aligned with "tight messaging."
5. Measure what matters.	5. Measure market conditions accurately to enter at propitious time, measure operations to maintain low cost basis, and high product quality, measure senior managers as rigorously as line workers.

Business observers and Wall Street analysts quite rightly concern themselves with Dell's future. Certainly the PC market overall is maturing and Dell's performance in consumer electronics has been somewhat lackluster. But Dell's numbers only look slightly disappointing against the backdrop of its own meteoric history, and they remain the envy of the computer industry.

In early 2007, founder Michael Dell once again became CEO. As with Charles Schwab's move at the firm that bears his name, this was a clear signal to customers and shareholders that Dell would gather its considerable resources to focus on its newer challenges. Certainly it is safe to say that HP, Lenovo, and other rivals will not make the mistake of taking Dell lightly.

• • •

Dell's newfound emphasis on design was part of a clear pattern across the top marketing companies. As I observed in prior chapters, design excellence has become a difference maker in various ways for Nokia, Motorola, Apple, Alcoa, L'Oréal, Target, Samsung, Sony, and Toyota. And as we have also seen, companies that demonstrate excellence in fulfilling the five core marketing imperatives can leverage iconic product designs across the full range of their operations and customer engagements. The success of the iPod, and the boost it gave to MacIntosh's computer sales, depended not only on its design and ergonomic appeal but also on its seamless interface with Apple's iTunes software and its iTunes Music Store. It also gave Apple a parallel revenue stream in its share of the $.99 a song customers pay to download music from the iTunes Music Store, a nice complement to the sale of the iPods themselves.

Toyota's design advantage over other automakers meant that across its Toyota, Lexus, and Scion brands, it had eight of the ten fastest-moving cars on U.S. dealers' lots.[4] Typical rankings were:

RANK	MODEL	DAYS ON LOT	AVERAGE PRICE
1	Toyota Prius	9	$24,718
2	Scion tC	10	$18,262
3	BMW 7 Series	12	$80,572
4	Scion xB	13	$15,646
5	Scion xA	13	$14,392
6	Toyota Avalon	17	$31,578
7	Toyota Tacoma	18	$23,582
8	Lexus RX 330	18	$39,729
9	Honda Odyssey	18	$30,095
10	Lexus GS Sedan	20	$47,820

Note that only two other auto companies, BMW and Honda, have models that make the list. Also, Toyota's models cut across all price points and market segments, from first car to pickup, and SUV to luxury sedan. None of Detroit's vehicles make the list. Superior design and excellent overall value minimize Toyota's inventory and thus the need for margin-slashing incentives to move it. And while Detroit pushes gas guzzlers as though oil prices were heading south of $1 per gallon, Toyota's early bet on hybrid technology is already paying off impressively with the Prius, an advantage that will only increase as Toyota leverages this technology right across its product line.

As we saw in earlier chapters, Toyota's edge over competition is not restricted to producing the cars customers want most. It also includes superior dealer management, customer service, and communications—including cost-effective advertising. As with the other consistent winners in our study of Marketing Mavens, from Mayo Clinic to ESPN, Starbucks, The Home Depot, ExxonMobil, Progressive, and Prudential Financial, among others, Toyota's excellence in fulfilling one customer-focused imperative leads to excellence in fulfilling the others in a virtuous iterative cycle of linked processes. Designing and making cars better suited to customers' needs enables Toyota to promote the cars efficiently. This in turn enables the company to direct resources to maintain R&D capabilities in order to pick markets that matter and segment them well, as it has done with its Toyota, Lexus, and Scion brands; hone cost and quality manufacturing competencies, integrate operations, and foster the Toyota culture to serve customers; and assiduously measure what matters from defects on its high-quality production lines to customers' satisfaction with their ownership experience.

To sell their cars, Detroit automakers have boosted sales with employee-discount pricing for all customers. Because they offer less customer value, they have to spend three to four times as much in advertising and promotion costs to sell each heavily discounted vehicle as Toyota spends to sell its undiscounted vehicles. For example, as a single datum, in June 2005, for every vehicle sold in the United States, GM spent $4,458; Chrysler, $3,975; Ford, $3,855; Mitsubishi, $3,391; Hyundai, $2,894; Mazda, $2,200; Volkswagen, $2,201; Nissan, $1,880; Honda, $1,248; and Toyota, $1,090.[5]

• • •

Toyota can also stumble, as all companies do. In April 2006 Toyota passed DaimlerChrysler to take number three in U.S. market share, and in July it passed Ford to take the number-two spot. In August 2006

Toyota trailed number one GM by a mere 1.7% market share. But that same month, Toyota announced that it might delay new models to work on quality control.

Toyota's quality problems sent a rumble through the automobile industry in 2006. They were ultimately traceable to Toyota's having hired too few engineers to manage its growth in the 1990s. Toyota had been guilty of "Chainsaw" Al Dunlap behavior—overaggressive cost-cutting—and the Japanese police investigated three Toyota officials on suspicion of concealing vehicle defects for eight years.[6]

Toyota apologized forthrightly for these problems and backed its words by beefing up its Quality Control Division and tripling the hiring of engineers. For the first time it sought to hire midcareer engineers with experience outside Toyota as well as fresh engineering graduates. The company understood, one executive said that "[i]f we can't lick it [the quality control problem], we will have to slow down" in the campaign to acquire number one market share.[7]

At the same time, Toyota quality overall has remained high. In 2006 *Consumer Reports* continued to rate Toyota number one for build quality. In the June 2006 J. D. Power & Associates quality ratings, Toyota was number three, with Porsche in first place. Holding down the number two spot was South Korea's Hyundai, obviously harboring the same ambition to replace Toyota as the world's most respected automaker that Samsung has to replace Sony as the most respected consumer electronics brand.

We have not discussed Hyundai in this book, but the most notable element in its brand positioning has been its offering the longest standard warranty in the U.S. market. In other words, it made the same promise to customers—"Quality is Job 1"—that Ford did. But unlike Ford, it made good on the promise in the view of customers and benefited accordingly in increasing market share.

The lesson for Toyota, and for any leading company, is clearly that there is no resting on one's laurels. Whatever you do that pleases customers will eventually be duplicated by one competitor, if not another. To stay in the top spot, or return to it, you must focus, laserlike, on the five marketing imperatives. This is abundantly clear in the case of Sony, for which 2005 was an *annus horribilis* of bad results and worse press.

In 2005 the precipitous decline in the prices of Sony's consumer electronics products, its most important business, led to plunging margins. Declining prices demonstrated that Sony had lost its edge on the competition in technology, manufacturing quality, design, and product lineup. Committed to mature lines of cathode-ray tube televisions, for example, Sony missed the wave of customers' desire for flat-screen televisions that Sharp and Samsung both rode to new heights. And unable to keep its various functional parts working in concert, with marketing, sales, R&D, and all other operations focused on customer needs, Sony failed to meet customers' desire for digital portable music. Sony's Walkman had once owned portable music, but it suffered the negative public relations impact of a blizzard of news stories identifying Apple's iPod as "the new Walkman." Since its market peak in 2000, Sony had lost almost 75 percent of its market value.[8]

In response to these bad results and bad news, Sony adroitly formed joint ventures with rising star Samsung, "the new Sony" as it has been called, in both manufacturing operations and patent sharing. It did so, it is important to note, as merely an equal partner, and for the present the comparatively needier one. In a move once equally unthinkable, Sony named Sir Howard Stringer, head of Sony USA, as its first *gaijin* CEO, bypassing several Japanese contenders.

It's quite clear that Sony, a firm that for so many years did a great job with the five key imperatives, had taken its eye off the ball. Once it lost sight of its customers, it's scarcely surprising that interfunctional integration fell apart. Unfortunately for Sony, its 2005 *annus horribilis* concluded with perhaps the most egregious example of the company's failure to put the customer first.

Like other producers of entertainment content, Sony is justifiably concerned about music, television, and movie file sharing. This is not the place to argue whether the entertainment companies are fighting a losing battle and would benefit from treating file sharing more as a form of advertising rather than attempting to stamp it out. Regardless, Sony's approach to help stamp it out was unequivocally a bad idea. Determined to copy-protect its CDs and DVDs, Sony placed a "rootkit" in its software without informing customers. In some cases, this antipiracy software damaged customers' personal computer operating systems, and laid them open to attack by viruses, spyware, and the like. However angry or frustrated they may be with customer behavior, companies, like physicians, must first do no harm. Sony has every right to defend its intellectual property rights but not by attacking its customer's property. Never forget that businesses prime objective is to acquire, retain, and grow customers—Sony's actions undermined that objective.

Sir Howard Stringer obviously has his work cut out for him, but he has taken the reins of a company that for all its troubles is still financially sound. Sony has great technology and sufficient resources to invest in fulfilling the five core marketing imperatives. It will surely rediscover a customer focus and appropriately integrate its various functions to serve them. Sony is still capable of creating design and sales magic, as with its recent successful launch of the PlayStation Portable. In fact, critics of Sony for letting Apple's iPod become the new Walkman may have missed something: Sony's signature brand is no longer the Walkman, but rather the enormously popular PlayStation, and nothing will be so important to its fortunes over the next few years as the PlayStation 3, launched in fall 2006.

In recognition of this, as well as recent gains in flat-screen televisions, Sony's brand value remains high. It climbed two spots to rank twenty-six on *BusinessWeek*/Interbrand's 2006 ranking of the hundred most valuable global brands. It will be interesting indeed to see where Sony ranks in 2010, but as with Dell and Toyota, I would bet that Sony emerges from its troubles stronger than ever.

•   •   •

Sony stumbled and ran low on steam against the contrast of consumer electronics successes achieved by Samsung, Sharp, Apple, and Nokia. Pfizer's stock has been on a downward trend since 2002 and encountered special difficulties post-2004 in the midst of tough times for all big pharma. Here are several news stories that together and separately exemplify the state of the U.S. and global pharmaceutical industry in the mid-2000s:

1. "Article Says Diabetes Pill Would Increase Coronary Risks" reported an article and a prepublication online editorial from the *Journal of the American Medical Association* pointing to increased risk of heart attack and strokes with use of Pargluva, a joint venture of Bristol-Myers Squibb and Merck. The article asserted that the two companies "had been 'disingenuous' in

submitting data to the Food and Drug Administration that may have fostered an illusion of safety."

2. "Roche Agrees to Talks With Generic Rivals on Flu Drug" reported that the company was responding to intense political pressure to license its anti-influenza drug, Tamiflu, for generic manufacture, amid global worry over possible epidemics of lethal avian flu in human populations.

3. "Pfizer Profit Falls 5%; Outlook Uncertain" reported that the "news keeps getting worse for . . . the world's largest drug company."

4. "Lilly Profit Rises on Sales of Newer Drug" reported Eli Lilly and Company's 10 percent revenue increase in the third quarter, "led by a 13 percent increase in sales of diabetes products" but glimpsed trouble ahead in declining sales of the anti-psychotic drug Zyprexa and concerns about increased suicide risk associated with use of the attention deficit disorder medication Strattera.[9]

The bad news for Pfizer included the impact of safety issues in the arthritis market; the end of patent protection and generic competition for antidepressant drug Zoloft; generic competition for Lipitor in the anticholesterol category, caused by Merck's Zocor coming off patent; and cancellation of Torcetrapib, Pfizer's new drug for raising "good" cholesterol. Other problems cited were a "pipeline of new drugs [that] is also relatively bare," all in the context of "an industry wide slowdown in prescriptions of expensive branded medicines."[10] Concern over changes in prescription growth rates in key therapeutic markets and geographies, and other factors led Pfizer to withdraw its guidance forecasts on expected revenues and profits for 2006 and 2007.

Like all top marketing companies, Pfizer has responded to its pressures by refocusing on customer needs and communication. Incoming CEO Jeffrey Kindler began his tenure in late summer 2006 with a highly symbolic visit to Pfizer's R&D center in New London, Connecticut, and elevated the company's two chief medical scientists to the status of direct reports. This signaled a determination to harvest more medicines from the combined pipelines of Pfizer and its recent acquisitions. Pfizer marked the end of Merck's Zocor patent with full-page ads for Lipitor in major newspapers, clearly aimed at stemming potential switchers from Lipitor to Zocor generics. And Pfizer introduced a new *authorized-generic* strategy for Zoloft, aimed at blunting attacks from generic producers.

It is clear that Pfizer's troubles are part and parcel of industry-wide afflictions, including but not limited to the safety of new prescription medicines. Pfizer's response has been to refocus its resources on its core pharmaceutical business but also to reduce costs by cutting 20 percent of its U.S. sales force. In chapter 6, we saw how Pfizer recognized the potential growth it could achieve with Lipitor, previously Warner-Lambert's crown jewel, and with Celebrex that came along with its Pharmacia & Upjohn acquisition. In a very real sense, Pfizer's willingness to place big bets on markets that matter to the firm was complemented in 2006 by its decision to exit markets that did not matter. Pfizer added over $16 billion to its war chest by selling its over-the-counter (OTC) health-care business to Johnson & Johnson.

Until mid-2006 the OTC health-care area represented markets that mattered to Pfizer. But in refocusing on its core pharmaceutical business, Pfizer sold its OTC health-care division to J&J for whom OTC remained a market that matters. Markets that matter to your company at one point in time may not matter enough to retain at another. Likewise, markets you deem not worth pursuing may well become attractive to another firm. As with all things in business, market selection and deselection are moving targets.

Growth by acquisition dynamics are also at play for Alcoa. Under CEO Paul O'Neill, who left the company in 2000 to become President George W. Bush's first secretary of the treasury, Alcoa grew and profited in large part through such acquisitions as Alumax, Ivex Packaging, Fairchild Fastners, Reynolds Metals, and several Australian, European, and South American fabricators. In 2005 there was no acquisition target of significant size left for Alcoa or its main rival, Alcan. Alcoa remains the dominant player in the market but must now deal with the slightly larger Rusal, formed from the 2006 merger of two Russian aluminum producers, and run twice as hard as before to maintain growth and profitability that will impress Wall Street, with its "what have you done lately" mind-set. As we saw in chapter 7's look at its work with Airbus on the A380 jumbo jet, Alcoa can only keep moving forward if it effectively integrates its operations on behalf of customers.

Other top marketing companies for whom acquisitions loomed large are UnitedHealth Group and UPS. A salient difference between these two firms is that acquisitions represent a smaller percentage of UPS's growth, but both are participating in industry-wide waves of consolidation. UPS's two main rivals, FedEx and DHL, have engaged in similar acquisitions, for example, and UnitedHealth Group's competition with WellPoint in health insurance is being waged on both sides through acquisition.

Management researchers have known for some time that, on average, acquisitions are dilutive for the acquiring companies' stockholders. Did you own Time Warner shares before the firm was acquired by AOL? The problem with acquisitions is that they may occur for many reasons, not the least of which is CEO hubris. And, of course, they do bring value—notably to the investment bankers that promote them so assiduously. But not all acquisitions fail—certainly some that we observed have been highly successful. The critical issue is quite straightforward; as with iconic product designs, those companies that excel at meeting the five modern marketing imperatives in their acquisitions are best able to leverage any advantage an acquisition may bring across their operations. Acquisitions can be an excellent way for the firm to gain swift entry into markets that matter (Imperative 1), may in addition bring a sharp focus on desirable segments where the firm has a good chance of winning (Imperative 2), and bring with them in-place market offers that create customer value and secure differential advantage (Imperative 3). Where so many acquisitions fail, however, is in the fourth imperative, integrating to serve the customer. Make sure you have a well-thought-out integration plan before you take the acquisition route, as Pfizer wisely did before its Warner-Lambert purchase.

Whereas UnitedHealth (notwithstanding some difficulties with its Oxford purchase), UPS, Alcoa, and Pfizer (still the world's most profitable drug company) appear to have had good success with acquisitions focused around coherent customer needs, discount brokerage Charles Schwab provided evidence of the danger of acquisitions that are not so well focused. Schwab's expensive purchase of private bank U.S. Trust represents a form of buyer's hubris. Schwab was convinced it could migrate up the food chain through its baby-boomer customers to wealth management for the rich and also extract new fee-for-service business from the most affluent boomers. As we saw in chapter 5, this strategy diffused and dissipated Schwab's brand identity and value in the eyes of its most important customers, the broad demographic of upper-middle-class baby boomers it had served since its origin. Schwab got the segmentation right, but not the targeting. Just as success in fulfilling one of the five marketing imperatives gives impetus to fulfilling the others, so too failure in one all too quickly breeds failure in others.

A renewed emphasis on customer-focused marketing was paying off for Schwab in 2006, when annual profits reached $1.2 billion, up from $286 million just two years earlier. Crucial to Schwab's recovery was a return to its discounting roots in the form of lower trading fees, some 30 percent lower than in 2004.

The evidence from our study is that one important factor in the ability of top marketing companies to remain at the top is consistent brand positioning. Schwab ran into trouble when it diffused its focus on discount value for affluent baby boomers and began chasing the outright wealthy with its acquisition of U.S. Trust. After changing marketing campaigns like yesterday's clothes for much of the early 2000s, Schwab has steadied itself by bringing founder Chuck Schwab back as CEO, making him the centerpiece of its advertising, and concentrating on serving its core discount customers. The message to customers—and the Schwab value proposition—is clear: with Chuck Schwab back in charge, Schwab once more offers great service at a discount price, if not absolutely the cheapest one vis-à-vis E*Trade and other online discount brokers.

Schwab may well consolidate its recent recovery and go on to new success, if like SAP, as we saw in chapter 8, it remains true to its enduring brand identity and its continuing core customers.

Now consider the steadier brand positioning and customer messaging of Prudential, Progressive, Starbucks, UPS, Bloomberg, Mayo Clinic, Verizon, Virgin, ExxonMobil, Samsung, Nokia, L'Oréal, Oracle, Dell, and The Home Depot, the consistent big winners in our study of the top marketing companies. You might take it under advisement as an investing tip, to consider selling your shares whenever a company you hold starts shifting advertising campaigns and what it tells its customers too quickly.

Several times in this book I have quoted executives as saying that the impetus for customer-focused action "starts at the top" in the CEO's office. If there was any doubt of the importance of the CEO's commitment to serve customers, it was dispelled by the stumbles of two of our highlighted companies, Pfizer and UnitedHealth. When Pfizer replaced Hank McKinnell as CEO in 2006, his obscene $200 million golden parachute was a virtual announcement of a disconnect from the interests of customers. In seeking to reposition the company for future growth, new Pfizer CEO Jeffrey Kindler will have to lump that payout in as a lost resource along with the $1 billion or more in R&D on Torcetrapib, for which the company had great expectations until it was doomed by poor outcomes in patient trials.

At UnitedHealth, William W. McGuire was forced out as CEO when it was revealed that nearly all his generous stock options from 1994 to 2002 were backdated, leaving the company with ongoing legal issues to resolve with regulators. Although UnitedHealth grew enormously during McGuire's tenure, as Pfizer did during McKinnell's, the two executives' ousters demonstrate the danger to even the most successful companies when CEOs seem unable to distinguish between what is good for their company's shareholders and customers on the one hand, and what is good for them personally on the other.

Across the board, however, the top marketing companies tend to have stable management teams and consistent leadership performance from CEO to CEO. They do not need to pursue celebrity CEOs or shuttle back to the corner office a successful leader who has relinquished the post, like Chuck Schwab and Michael Dell. Our modern business memories are so short that we forget, for example, that GE's pre–Jack Welch CEOs were much admired star executives of their day, and that Mr. Welch took the reins of a hugely successful company. He deserves great credit for leading it to even greater success, and my point is not to slight the importance of exceptionally gifted leaders. Rather it is that the top marketing companies have a well-developed sense of direction, embodied in the five marketing imperatives, and manage their human resources well from top to bottom. In particular, they meet the recurring challenge of finding the right leader, and their performance and their market value are not dependent on celebrity CEOs.

• • •

However, the success of one of these companies, Bloomberg L. P., did make its founder, Michael Bloomberg, enough of a business celebrity to provide a platform for his successful campaign to be elected, then relected, mayor of New York City. To close this chapter and this book, and recalibrate the urgency of the five marketing imperatives for business now and in the future, let's revisit the Bloomberg company's business model and consider its likely prospects in the near, medium, and long term.

When we looked at Bloomberg in chapter 8, we saw that all the company's efforts, including its media business, are part of the company's single product, the Bloomberg Professional service, provided to users on a subscription basis that in 2005 cost its users $17,000 annually. We also saw that Bloomberg has continually added to the terminal features, now numbering in the thousands, only a fraction of which any one customer is likely to use for trading equities, commodities, or bonds, as the case may be, or for some other purpose. Finally, we saw that Bloomberg's hand-holding customer service is designed to support the customer as markets evolve and the firm adds new functionality to the Bloomberg service.

From the time he founded the firm, Mike Bloomberg saw the unique design of the Bloomberg system as a potential asset, as a way of locking the customer into Bloomberg because of its high data quality, and special "design language," and by making a Bloomberg subscription a badge of clout in the financial services industry. As another means of ensuring customer loyalty, the founder decreed that no Bloomberg service would be available separately, off the terminal.[11] Any service the customer needed would be right there at his or her fingertips, delivered by what had become a familiar system. In addition to its customer service, Bloomberg sweetened the deal for subscribers by massaging the financial data available on the terminal in useful ways. The subscription fee paid not only for a terminal but also for the quality of the information that could be found and manipulated on it, and for the support of an instantly available crack customer-service operation. The entire package added up to high customer value through simplicity—single interface, all-inclusive product, single price, and high-quality human customer service, and via the psychological value of prestige. In the latter regard, it is interesting to note that many

Bloomberg users stipulated in their employment contracts that a Bloomberg terminal would be a perk.[12]

While the people at the trading firms, brokerage houses, banks, and other companies who ultimately earn the dollars that pay for most of their firm's Bloomberg subscriptions demand the product, the administrative staffs such as IT departments have never been happy with buying more features and services than their employees actually need at any given time: Bloomberg's "one-size-fits-all strategy . . . run[s] the risk of alienating clients who feel that Bloomberg is force-feeding them an exorbitant goodie [and] [s]ome information technology mavens also say that the software architecture underlying the Bloomberg terminal is outmoded and that newer users find the Bloomberg screen too intimidating."[13] As a result, "firms have tried installing keystroke software to monitor employee usage and determine which Bloomberg functions are the most popular and which ones can be done away with— information that would be helpful when trying to negotiate price discounts."[14]

But Bloomberg does not discount its product, and statistics show that firms that remove Bloomberg systems often replace them within a year based on end-user demand. Also, during the market downturn at the beginning of this century, when customers were forced to choose one single system rather than several systems, Bloomberg grew market share in a flight to quality in the competitive financial markets.

There is plainly potential for change in customers' perceptions of value, however. As information technology advances, the opportunity for a competitor to unbundle the functions on the Bloomberg terminal and offer them in ways that are both cheaper and easier to use will also advance. How long a bundled "one-size-fits-all strategy" will enable Bloomberg to retain its leading share of the $7 billion industry in real-time market data is a question that should be keeping Bloomberg management awake at night. In 2005 Bloomberg was just ahead of Reuters with 43 percent versus 40 percent market share. Fortunately for Bloomberg, it knows this is an important question, with one senior executive acknowledging, "We live in a world in which the better you get the more you have to do, and we're constantly trying to figure out how to keep running on that treadmill."[15] By staying close to those end users who produce the bottom-line results, and by continually improving its product based on customer feedback, perhaps at the risk of alienating some corporate purchasing departments, Bloomberg again experienced double-digit sales growth during 2005.

To make the point more broadly, just look at the changes brewing in telecommunications for top marketing companies like Verizon and Vodafone. With eBay paying $2.6 billion for Skype, the Internet telephony service that allows two broadband computer users anywhere in the world to talk in pristine digital sound for free, and lets one person with Skype connect to a regular telephone user for only $.02 a minute, and with several competing free and fee-based Internet telephony options gaining customers worldwide, a new shakeout in the local and long-distance phone business is clearly not far distant, no doubt with a brutal thinning of profit margins.

We could sketch similar challenging forecasts in every industry. The fundamental challenge of business today is to serve customer needs amid continuous change. As the examples in this book demonstrate, the top marketing companies meet that challenge by fulfilling five core marketing imperatives:

1. Pick markets that matter.

2. Select segments to dominate.

3. Design the market offer to create customer value and secure differential advantage.

4. Integrate to serve the customer.

5. Measure what matters.

Nothing is certain and many decisions that you make on a daily basis are crapshoots. Nevertheless, by continually striving to achieve excellence in these five imperatives, you can tilt the odds in your favor, and earn significant rewards for employees and shareholders alike.

Appendix 1

Selecting the World's Best Marketers

The material in the book is based on transcribed interviews with executives from 40 organizations. In some cases several executives from a single organization were interviewed; some executives were interviewed on more than one occasion. Most interviews were conducted in-person, face-to-face; a few interviews were by videoconference, and telephone. To secure 40 cooperating organizations, interviews were requested from 56 organizations. These 56 were selected from 602 candidate organizations for the world's best marketers.

The process for selecting the world's best marketers comprised several stages:

- Identifying candidate organizations for the world's best marketers

- Constructing variables to rank candidate organizations

- Ranking candidate organizations

Identifying Candidate Organizations for the World's Best Marketers

Candidates for the world's best marketers included leading public companies, private companies, and individual brands, from a diverse group of industries worldwide. The candidate organizations were se-cured from numerous lists of leading companies and brands compiled for other marketing and financial performance research studies. All but a few candidate organizations were named in one or more of the fol-lowing lists[1]:

- *Forbes* **Platinum 400** The best large public companies based in the United States or overseas are ranked on five-year stock price changes. Included were thirteen hundred firms with annual revenues over $1 billion. The top twenty overall leaders were selected, and the top firm in each industry.[2]

- **New Market Leaders Study** DiamondCluster International's Center for Market Leadership contained over fifty-four hundred public companies worldwide.[3] Firms were ranked based on the previous five years' organic sales growth and market value-to-sales ratios, relative to their closest peers within their respective industries. The top hundred overall were selected, plus the top ten companies in each of twenty-four industries.[4]

- *Advertising Age*'s **Global World's 100 Biggest Advertisers** The top hundred firms by worldwide advertising expenditures were identified; ninety firms were selected.

- **World's 100 Most Valuable Brands** Interbrand's study, published annually in *BusinessWeek*, lists the world's one hundred most valuable brands. Candidates must have minimum annual revenues over $1 billion, 20 percent of sales outside the home country, and sufficient publicly available marketing and financial data to base a valuation. The valuation considers the brand's current and future projected earnings; all were selected.

- **America's Most Admired Companies** *Fortune* publishes results of an annual survey of two thousand U.S. businesspeople. It scores U.S. firms in eight categories, including management quality, innovation, product quality, and financial soundness. The top hundred leaders from the innovation and product quality categories were selected.

- **Global Most Admired Companies** *Fortune* publishes the results of an annual survey of executives and analysts. Nine attributes are surveyed but only overall firm scores are published. The top one hundred highest-rated companies were selected.

- **Winners of Significant Marketing Awards** Recipients from company and brand marketing awards were selected from several lists: *Advertising Age*'s 50 Most Powerful People in Marketing; *Advertising Age*'s annual Marketing 100 lists of America's best marketers,[5] and *PROMO* magazine's 50 Best-Promoted Brands.

This procedure produced 602 candidate organizations for the world's best marketers—316 public companies, 69 private companies, and 217 brands.

Constructing Variables to Rank Candidate Organizations

The candidate organizations were evaluated on three dimensions that we developed encompassing measures of success and influence on the practice of marketing:

- *Market leadership* focuses on marketing and financial performance.

- *Company/brand reputation* focuses on reputation.

- *Market power* focuses on influence among marketing professionals.

The variables constituting each dimension fulfilled two criteria. First, each variable had to relate primarily to the marketing function or department. In most cases, the same variables were used both for public and private companies and for brands. However, because data are generally more difficult to secure for private companies, some variables were constructed especially for these organizations. Second, the data had to be publicly available or otherwise relatively simple to obtain. The selected variables follow.

Market Leadership Six variables were constructed[6]:

- **Sales Growth Index (SGI)** The SGI was computed by dividing an organization's organic sales growth—actual sales growth, excluding the effect of mergers, acquisitions, and/or divestitures—by the average organic sales growth of the organization's twenty-one closest peers.[7]

- **Market Value Index (MVI)** The MVI was computed by dividing an organization's market value/sales ratio (MVSR) by the average MVSR ratio of the organization's twenty-one closest peers.[8] The MVI measures the market value of the organization's customer franchise.

- **New Market Leaders Overall Rank (NMLOR)** Companies were ranked by a calculation that took into account their sales growth, industry sales growth, market capitalization/sales, and the market capitalization/sales of the overall database.[9]

- **Percent Change in Brand Value (PCBV)** PCBV was simply the percentage change in brand value from Interbrand's brand valuation survey.[10]

- **Percent Change in Sales (PCS)** PCS was the percentage change in total sales.[11]

- **Net Margin (NM)** NM was simply the net margin.[12]

Company/Brand Reputation Eight variables were used:

- *Fortune*—**America's Most Admired Companies**—**Product Quality Score (AMAPQ)** AMAPQ is the product quality score on *Fortune*'s survey of America's most admired companies.[13]

- *Fortune*—**America's Most Admired Companies**—**Innovation Score (AMAI)** AMAI is the innovation score on *Fortune*'s survey of America's most admired companies.[14]

- *Fortune*—**Global Most Admired Companies**—**Overall Score (GMAO)** GMAO is the score on *Fortune*'s survey of the world's most admired companies.[15] Executives and analysts graded companies according to nine attributes, including management quality, product and service quality, innovativeness, and long-term investment value.

- **Harris Poll of the Best U.S. Brands—Rank (HPR)** HPR is secured from a nationwide online survey of 2,641 adults.[16]

- ***Advertising Age's* Marketing 100 List (AAM100)** *Advertising Age* publishes an annual list of the top hundred marketers in the United States, marketers that "get the big picture and run with an idea." AAM100 is the number of times a public and private company, and/or its brands appeared on five annual lists.[17]

- **Brand Equity Score (BES)** *Brandweek* conducts an annual survey on the U.S.'s top two thousand U.S. brands. Twenty-seven thousand consumers rated over a thousand brands on quality and salience; included are both public and private companies as well as brands. BES equals quality multiplied by salience.[18]

- **Normalized American Customer Satisfaction Index (NACSI)** The American Customer Satisfaction Index (ACSI) is a national economic indicator of customer satisfaction with the quality of goods and services available to U.S. consumers. NACSI is the organization's ACSI score divided by the average score for its industry.[19]

- **Number of Significant Marketing Awards and Keynote Speeches Delivered at Marketing Conferences and Seminars (MAKS)** Issues of *Brandweek, AdWeek,* and *Advertising Age* magazines were searched for mentions of major marketing awards received and keynote speeches given at marketing conferences or seminars.[20]

Market Power Five variables were used:

- ***Advertising Age*—50 Most Powerful U.S. Marketers (AA50PM)** *Advertising Age* publishes an annual list of the fifty most powerful people in marketing based on the editors'

assessment in three categories: advertising spending
(50 percent), charismatic marketing (30 percent), and hands-on
involvement in strategic decisions (20 percent).[21]

- **Global Media Spending Index (GMSI)** The GMSI is an
  organization's total global media expenditures relative to its
  competitors—specifically, the actual or estimated worldwide
  advertising (media) budget, divided by the average global media
  budget for all firms in its industry.[22] Data was secured as follows:

  - *Ad Age Global:* Total media spending for ninety public and
    private firms.[23]

  - *Brandweek:* U.S. media spending from the annual
    Superbrands survey of the top two thousand U.S. brands.[24]

- **U.S. Media Spending Index Score (USMSI)** The USMSI is
  the organization's total U.S. media expenditures relative to its
  competitors—specifically, its U.S. advertising (media) budget,
  divided by the average U.S. media budget for all firms in its
  industry. Data were secured using *Brandweek*'s annual
  Superbrands survey of the top two thousand U.S. brands.[25]

- **Brand Value Index (BVI)** The BVI is the organization's total
  brand value relative to its competitors—specifically, brand value
  divided by the average brand value for all firms in its industry,
  based on Interbrand's annual survey published in
  BusinessWeek.[26]

- **Most Recent 12 Months' Sales Index (12MSI)** The 12MSI was
  an organization's most recently available twelve-month sales
  divided by the average twelve-month sales for firms in its
  industry.[27]

Ranking Candidate Organizations

The process of ranking the candidate organizations required several
stages:

- Companies and brands that lacked sufficient data in one or
  more of the three categories were eliminated.[28] After this cut,

314 public companies, forty-one private companies, and
172 brands remained.

- It was evident that significant data disparities existed across
  public companies, private companies, and brands. For example,
  variables such as SGI and MVI applied only to public
  companies; other variables were unique to private companies
  or brands. Hence, organizations were separated into their
  respective groups for the remainder of the data analysis.

- Within each category, intercorrelations among variables were
  run to assess redundancy. There were no correlations greater
  than 0.5; hence, no variables were eliminated.

- All data for each variable were turned into ranks,
  notwithstanding the loss of information in the interval to ordinal
  transformation, for two reasons. First, several of the key variables
  were already ordinal. Second, scaling anomalies might have
  distorted the scores for many companies and brands. Overall,
  standardizing on ordinal data allowed for further analysis
  without forfeiting much precision.

- The average ranks were calculated for each public company,
  private company, and brand for each of the three variable
  categories—market leadership, company/brand reputation,
  and market power. For each organization, the sum of ranks
  was divided by the number of available variables.

- A weighted average rank was calculated for each public
  company, private company, and brand. For public and private
  companies, and brands with market leadership data, the
  weightings were as follows: market leadership—40 percent,
  company/brand reputation—30 percent, and market power—
  30 percent. For all other brands—the majority—the weightings
  were as follows: company/brand reputation—50 percent
  and market power—50 percent. This process resulted in
  separate rankings for public companies, private companies,
  and brands.

- We eliminated those organizations that performed poorly
  on these weighted average ranks. That left us with the top

150 public companies, one hundred brands, and forty private companies. These organizations spanned twenty-four industries.

- From this set of organizations, we selected fifty-six to interview. In general, we chose organizations that were leaders in their industries. In some cases, where an industry was very broad, we identified leaders in subcategories. For example, subcategories in the media, entertainment, and information industry included book publishing, cable TV, financial information, Internet service providers, media conglomerates, movie and TV production, music distribution, newspapers, radio stations, satellite TV, and sports leagues. Also, when we selected one organization, we deliberately omitted its close competitors.

- Interviews were requested with senior marketing executives from fifty-six great marketing organizations. Forty of these organizations were interviewed for the book. These forty organizations comprised a broad array of leading marketing organizations in a diverse set of industries. Specifically, the industries represented were as follows: automotive—1; banking, investment—4; business services—1; computer, communications products—3; consumer durables—1; consumer nondurables—3; energy—1; health-care services—2; industrial materials—2; insurance—2; media, entertainment, and information—5; pharmaceuticals and medical supplies—1; retail intermediaries—5; software and IT services—3; technology, other—1; telco services—3; and transportation and logistics—1. One firm, Virgin, was not classified by industry. Of the twenty-four industries, only six were not represented: automotive (*FT:* engineering); construction, services, public works; hospitality, food service; industrial, diversified; semiconductor; and utilities.

- Those industries providing the most interviewees were quite diverse. For example, organizations in the media, entertainment, and information were BMG, Bloomberg, Bloomsbury Publishing, ESPN, and the *Wall Street Journal.* Firms in the retail intermediaries category were Amazon, Target, The Home Depot, and Starbucks.

- These organizations are a broad representation of leading public companies, private companies, and brands. Twenty-eight organizations were public companies, seven were private companies, and eleven were brands. They differ markedly in organization size, from the world's largest firm, ExxonMobil, to Bloomsbury Publishing. Headquarters location also varied widely. Although the majority of firms were based in the United States, there is significant representation from Asia and Europe. Some organizations are global; others are distinctly domestic.

- Quite deliberately, we chose not to invite several high-ranking organizations. Rather, a significant goal was to secure organizational diversity and, hence, richer data.

- The organizations and the interviewees are listed in appendix 2.

Interview Procedure

The vast majority of the initial interviews were conducted face to face. Most were conducted in the United States, but several took place in London. A couple of interviews were by videoconference and one was by telephone. Extensive secondary research, which preceded each interview, provided an interview guide. The interview guide functioned as a loosely followed road map for the interview. In general, two interviewers conducted each interview. All interviews were audiotaped, and transcribed for analysis. Most follow-up interviews were conducted by telephone. Where the original interviewees had moved on, we talked with organizational members then in similar positions.

Appendix 2

Executives Interviewed for This Book[1]

Alcoa
Richard Melville Jr.
Vice Chairman, Aerospace Market Sector Lead Team

Amazon.com
Lance Batchelor
Head, Worldwide Marketing

Avon Products
Bob Bridden
Group Vice President, Global Marketing

Deborah Coffey
Executive Director, Public Relations and Promotion

BMG Entertainment
Stuart Rubin
Senior Vice President, Worldwide Marketing

Bloomberg L. P.
Judith Czelusniak
Head, Global Public Relations

Bloomsbury Publishing
Minna Fry
Director, Sales, Marketing and Publicity

Boise Cascade Office Products (Boise Office Solutions)
David Goudge
Senior Vice President, Marketing

Charles Schwab & Co.
Jack Calhoun
Executive Vice President, Advertising and Brand Management

Citigroup
David Bowerin
Chief Marketing Officer, Global Relationship Bank

Dell
Michael George
Chief Marketing Officer and Vice President, Corporate Strategy

Scott Helbing
Vice President, Global Brand Strategy

Kurt Kirsch
Director, U.S. Consumer Marketing, Planning, and Services

Steve Larned
Vice President, Marketing, Dell Americas

ESPN
George Bodenheimer
President

Edward Erhart
President, ESPN ABC Sports Customer Marketing and Sales

Rosa Gatti
Senior Vice President, Corporate Communications and Outreach

ExxonMobil
Hal Cramer
President, Fuels Marketing Company

Stewart McHie
Global Brand Manager, Fuels Marketing Company

Fannie Mae
Vada Hill
Senior Vice President and Chief Marketing Officer

GOJO Industries
Sandor ("Sandy") Katz
Vice President and Leader, Consumer Group

IBM
Gary Bridge[2]
Vice President, Market Intelligence and Marketing Management

L'Oréal Paris
Carol Hamilton
U.S. President, L'Oréal Paris

Michael Tangui
Senior Vice President, Marketing, L'Oréal Paris

Mayo Clinic
Steve Kopecky
Cardiologist; Chair, Rochester Marketing Committee, and
Foundation Brand and Marketing Group

Kent Seltman
Director, Marketing and Brand Team Leader

Microsoft
Mitch Matthews
Vice President, Marketing

Nestlé USA, Prepared Foods Division
Stephen Cunliffe
President

Nokia
Richard Geruson[3]
Chief Marketing Officer

Oracle
Mark Jarvis
Senior Vice President and Chief Marketing Officer

Pfizer Pharmaceuticals Group
J. Patrick Kelly
Senior Vice President, Worldwide Marketing, Pfizer Pharmaceuticals

Price Waterhouse Coopers
Michael Kelly
Partner for Advertising, Brand Management, and Markets

Rocco Maggiotto
Global Markets Leader; Head, Strategic Planning

Progressive
Dave Pratt
Direct Marketing General Manager

Prudential Financial
Michael Hines
Senior Vice President, Global Marketing and Communications

SAP
Marty Homlish
President and CEO, SAP Global Marketing

Chris Powell
Director, Global Marketing Operations

SBC Communications
Vicki Graves
Vice President, Marketing Integration

Samsung
Eric Kim
Executive Vice President, Global Marketing Operations

Sony
Ron Boire
President, Consumer Sales Company, Sony Electronics

Starbucks
Howard Schultz
Chairman and Chief Global Strategist

Target
Caroline Brookter
Director of Corporate Communications

Michael Francis
Senior Vice President, Marketing

Gerald Storch
Vice Chairman

The Home Depot
Mr. Richard (Dick) Sullivan
Senior Vice President, Marketing

The Wall Street Journal
Celia Currin
Director, Marketing Communications

Toyota
Steven Sturm
Vice President, Marketing

UnitedHealthcare
Jay Silverstein
Chief Marketing Officer

UPS
John Beystehner
Senior Vice President

Dale Hayes
Vice President, Brand Management and Customer Communications

Gary Maestro
Vice President, Brand and Product Management

Susan Rosenberg
Manager, UPS Public Relations

Verizon
Jody Bilney
Senior Vice President, Brand Management and Marketing
Communications

Virgin
Will Whitehorn
Director, Brand Development and Corporate Affairs

Visa
Bob Pifke
Senior Vice President, Marketing Services, Visa USA

Liz Silver
Senior Vice President, Advertising and Brand Management, Visa
USA

Vodafone
David Haines
Director, Global Branding

Endnotes

INTRODUCTION

1. Peter F. Drucker, *The Practice of Management* (New York: Harper & Row, 1954).

2. By coincidence, this book is being published a quarter century after the path-breaking Thomas J. Peters and Robert H. Waterman, *In Search of Excellence: Lessons from America's Best-Run Companies* (New York: Warner, 1982). The authors identified forty "excellent companies" that performed well on eight different characteristics: a bias for action; close to the customer; autonomy and entrepreneurship; productivity through people; hands-on, value driven; stick to the knitting; simple form, lean staff; and simultaneous loose–tight properties. Unfortunately, several "excellent" firms went out of business shortly after publication, and most of the others lost their positions as industry leaders. Time will tell about the success of the firms presented in this book. Other related books are James C. Collins and Jerry I. Porras, *Built to Last* (New York: Harper-Collins, 1997); Jim Collins, *Good to Great* (New York: HarperCollins, 2001), and W. Chan Kim and Renée Mauborgne, *Blue Ocean Strategy* (Cambridge, MA: Harvard Business School Press, 2005). Notwithstanding Rosenzweig's skepticism, these are all important books. Phil Rosenzweig, *The Halo Effect* (New York: Free Press, 2007).

CHAPTER 1

1. IBM's earnings for those years were $6.02 billion in 1990, $2.82 billion in 1991, ($4.96 billion) in 1992, and ($8.10 billion) in 1993.

2. Louis V. Gerstner, *Who Says Elephants Can't Dance? Inside IBM's Historic Turnaround* (New York: HarperBusiness, 2002); all quotes in this chapter are from chapter 6.

3. The intellectual underpinning of transactions cost analysis is found in the seminal article, R. H. Coase, "The Nature of the Firm," *Economica* 4 (1937): 386–405.

4. "High-Tech's 'Sweatshop' Wake-Up Call," *BusinessWeek Online*, June 15, 2006.

5. "Motorola's Modernizer," *Wall Street Journal*, June 23, 2005.

6. S. H. Haeckel, "Adaptive Enterprise Design: The Sense-and-Response Model," *Planning Review*, 23 (May–June 1995), 6(9).

CHAPTER 2

1. www.Amazon.com

2. Larry Bossidy, Ram Charan, and Charles Burck, *Execution: The Discipline of Getting Things Done* (New York: Crown Business, 2002), 15.

3. Ibid., 22.

4. Louis V. Gerstner, *Who Says Elephants Can't Dance? Leading a Great Enterprise Through Dramatic Change* (New York: HarperBusiness, 2003), 71.

5. Ibid., 231.

6. This is the essential message from W. Chan Kim and René Mauborgne, *Blue Ocean Strategy* (Cambridge, MA: Harvard Business School Press, 2005).

7. Personal communication with the author, November 12, 2006.

8. "Less Than the Sum of Its Parts," *Economist* (June 23, 2001): 73–74.

9. "The Big Surprise Is Enterprise," *Fortune* (July 24, 2006): 141–50. GE and other firms are focusing on the Net Promoter Score (NPS)—NPS = % of Promoters − % of Detractors.

10. After reaching a high of $354.94 on January 4, 1999, three months before the technology and dot-com stock bubble burst, Amazon split its stock three to one, which did not disguise its dizzying drop to a low of $5.97 on September 28, 2001. In early 2007 the stock price hovered around $40.

11. I take some vicarious pride that Jeff Bezos's first job out of Princeton was working for my Columbia Business School colleague, Geoffrey Heal.

12. *Amazon.com—Chairman & CEO Interview.* Maria Bartiromo, Tyler Mathisen, Joe Kernen. CNBC/Dow Jones Business Video. November 7, 2002.

CHAPTER 3

1. An interesting gauge of ExxonMobil's size and profitability is its relationship to Wal-Mart, the world's largest retailer. In 2006 ExxonMobil had total revenues of $377.6 billion and net income of $39.5 billion; Wal-Mart had total revenues of $348.7 billion and net income of $11.3 billion.

CHAPTER 4

1. "In Clean Politics, Flesh Is Pressed, Then Sanitized," *New York Times*, October 28, 2006.

CHAPTER 5

1. Of course, by the mid-2000s, environmental pressures had changed the supply-demand relationship and oil companies were being widely criticized for their high profits.

2. "Schwab Ousts Chief and Founder Steps In," *New York Times*, July 21, 2004.

3. "On the Sixth Day, They Published: Can a Saturday Paper Pull Up Profit at the Journal," *New York Times*, June 20, 2005.

4. "WSJ Weekend Disproves Critics, Attracts New Advertisers," *Advertising Age*, August 29, 2006.

CHAPTER 6

1. Interestingly, to direct its new branding efforts, Intel hired Eric Kim, our interviewee from Samsung.

2. In both 2004 and 2005, Mayo Clinic published almost four thousand articles, book chapters, and books and around fifteen hundred abstracts.

3. Centers for Medicare and Medicaid Services, Office of the Actuary. Expressed in 1980 dollars; adjusted using the overall Consumer Price Index for Urban Consumers.

4. Apple's financial year ends on September 30. Hence the first quarter of 2007 is October 1 to December 31, 2006.

CHAPTER 7

1. *Alcoa Annual Report*, 2004, 2006.

2. Ibid.

3. "A Way Cool Strategy: Toyota's Scion Plans to Sell Fewer Cars," *Wall Street Journal*, November 10, 2007.

4. By 2006 UPS was handling over 11.1 million ground pieces, and 2.2 million U.S. air express packages per day.

5. "New to the Starbucks Menu: Exclusive Dylan," *New York Times*, June 28, 2005.

CHAPTER 8

1. Interbrand is a division of Omnicon. Each year it produces a valuation of major global brands, published also in *BusinessWeek*.

2. For more on SAP's transformation, see "SAP: Building a Leading Technology Brand," Center on Global Brand Leadership, Columbia Business School, New York, NY, 2006.

3. CNN.com, March 22, 2007.

4. http://www.sap.com.

CHAPTER 9

1. "RAZR Sharp: New CEO Is Trying to Make Motorola Cool Again," *Wall Street Journal*, June 23, 2005. But more recently Motorola has slipped.

CHAPTER 10

1. "For Dell, Success in China Tells Tale of Maturing Market: Shoppers Prove Willing to Buy PCs Sight Unseen on Web," *Wall Street Journal*, July 5, 2005.

2. "Dell's World Isn't What It Used to Be," *New York Times*, May 13, 2006; "Dell Loses Lead, and Investors Can Take Heart," *Wall Street Journal*, November 10, 2006; "Popular Demand: Laptop Sales," *New York Times*, August 28, 2006.

3. "He Naps. He Sings. And He Isn't Michael Dell," *New York Times*, September 11, 2005.

4. "Hot Off the Lot," *Wall Street Journal*, August 11, 2005.

5. "Detroit Finds a Bandwagon in Employee Discounts," *Wall Street Journal*, July 6, 2005.

6. "Repairing Some Dents in an Image: A Rise in Defects at Toyota Puts Its Reputation at Stake," *New York Times*, August 5, 2006.

7. Ibid.

8. "Samsung Is Now What Sony Once Was," *New York Times*, March 10, 2005; "How the iPod Ran Circles Around the Walkman," *New York Times*, March 13, 2005; "Media Frenzy," *New York Times*, September 18, 2005; "The Financial Page: All Together Now," *New Yorker*, April 11, 2005.

9. "Article Says Diabetes Pill Would Increase Coronary Risks"; "Roche Agrees to Talks with Generic Rivals on Flu Drug"; "Pfizer Profit Falls 5%; Outlook Uncertain"; "Lilly Profit Rises on Sales of Newer Drugs," *New York Times*, October 21, 2005.

10. In 2006 Pfizer claimed an industry leading 154 compounds in its drug pipeline, an historic high for the firm.

11. "The Company He Keeps (for Now): Win or Lose at the Polls, Bloomberg May Sell Bloomberg," *New York Times*, March 20, 2005.

12. Ibid.

13. Ibid.

14. Ibid.

15. Ibid.

APPENDIX 1

1. Unless otherwise stated, all lists were for 2001. Annual revenues only factored into the identification process if it was a criterion for an individual list.

2. *Forbes* identifies twenty-six industries; http://images.forbes.com/lists/2006/88/htm/filter.html?sort=0.

3. DiamondCluster is an international management consulting firm based in Chicago. DiamondCluster helps clients develop and implement growth strategies via five hundred consultants working through eleven offices in the United States, Europe, India, the Middle East, and Latin America.

4. The twenty-four industries were advice and research providers; automotive; automotive (*FT*: engineering); banking, investment; business services; computer-communications products; construction, services, public works; consumer durables; consumer nondurables; energy; hospitality, food service; health-care services; industrial—diversified; industrial—materials; insurance; media, entertainment and information; pharmaceuticals and medical supplies; retail, intermediaries; semi-conductor; software and IT services; technology—other; telco services; transportation and logistics; utilities.

5. These *Advertising Age* lists comprised multiple years.

6. The first three variables—Sales Growth Index, Market Value Index, and New Market Leaders Overall Rank were calculated for public companies using data from the New Market Leaders database housed at DiamondCluster International's Center for Market Leadership.

7. For five years up to 2001.

8. The market value was assessed for June 1, 2001; sales were the previous twelve months.

9. DiamondCluster International's proprietary ranking for public companies based on data from the New Market Leaders database.

10. For the three available years of Interbrand's survey, concluding in 2001, for public companies, private companies, and brands.

11. For five years up to 2000 for private companies and brands. Sales data on private companies were estimates secured from *Hoover's* and *Forbes*. Sales data for brands were secured from investment analyst reports and various media publications.

12. For year 2000 for private companies. Net margin was actual or estimated data secured from *Hoover's* and *Forbes*.

13. Year 2000 survey, for U.S.-based public and private companies, published February 19, 2001.

14. Year 2000 data, published February 19, 2001.

15. Year 2000 data, for global public and private companies, published October 2, 2000.

16. For U.S.-based public and private companies; conducted from March 29, 2001 to April 2, 2001. Unranked companies were assigned an average rank according to the formula—sum of the total number of unranked companies divided by the number of unranked companies.

17. From five years up to 2001; http://adage.com.

18. Year 2000 data, published in 2001.

19. ACSI is produced through a partnership among University of Michigan Business School, American Society for Quality, and the CFI Group. An organization's score was for the most recently available quarter—2000 or 2001. ACSI now uses forty-seven industries; see http://www.theacsi.org/industry_scores.htm. In 2001, ASCI used thirty-nine industries; health and personal care stores, health insurance, wireless telephone service, computer software, cell phones, travel websites, search engines, and news and information websites were not used in 2001 and have been since added.

20. For private companies only.

21. Year 2000 data, for public companies and brands; *Advertising Age* did not select any private companies for this list.

22. For select public and private companies.

23. Year 2000 data, published November 2001.

24. Year 2000 data, published in 2001. Alternative calculations were made to deal with missing data:

- Global media spending known for the firm's brands: global media spending for a firm's individual brands were summed to secure a global company estimate.
- No global media spending known: the firm's U.S. media spending was factored by the U.S. percentage of global sales to secure a global spending estimate.
- No media spending known: the ratio of media spending to SG&A (selling, general, and administrative expenses) or revenues was calculated for a close competitor; this factor was applied to the firm to secure a global spending estimate.

25. Year 2000 data, published in 2001, for brands.

26. Published August 6, 2001, for public companies, private companies, and brands.

27. As of late 2001 for public and private companies; data for public companies secured from the New Market Leaders database housed at DiamondCluster International's Center for Market Leadership. Data for private companies were 2000 estimates secured from *Hoover's* and *Forbes*.

28. This rule was relaxed for brands as far as market leadership variables were concerned—these data were only available for a few brands. Enron was dropped.

APPENDIX 2

1. Indicated titles are those at the time of the first interview except as noted.

2. At the time of the interview, Gary Bridge was senior vice president, Marketing at Segway.

3. At the time of the interview, Richard Geruson was general manager and president of Global Services, Solutions and Alliances, Brocade Communications.

Acknowledgments

This book could not have been written without the generous cooperation of the executives at leading marketing companies. They gave freely of their time to my colleagues and me for the interviews that form the basis of this book. I am extremely grateful to them for their generosity, their openness, and their willingness to answer our questions. Since we first met with them, some have moved to different positions in their organizations; others have moved on to different organizations. They are listed in Appendix 2. I also thank their executive assistants for managing to find my team space on their bosses' busy schedules.

At Columbia Business School, my research assistants Russ Klein and Jeremy Gelbwaks rendered invaluable service on this project. Russ brought great energy and creativity to the challenge of identifying the world's top marketing companies, worked tirelessly to secure the interviews, and participated in the vast majority of them. Both he and Jeremy helped shape my thinking—including documenting the learnings from each interview—as the book took shape. Russ now is a director at American Greetings, and Jeremy is a private consultant. Don Pardew, adjunct professor of statistics at Columbia Business School and Principal of a New York City–based consulting firm, Cybernetica, was very helpful in developing the methodology for identifying the top marketing firms. It was a pleasure to renew a working relationship that commenced in the early 1980s.

Most important, I thank my colleagues at Columbia Business School, particularly those in the Marketing Division. Notwithstanding the fact that we are located in New York City, the world's financial center, the Marketing Division has long enjoyed a storied reputation as one of the world's leading Marketing departments. It has been a privilege to spend a quarter century as a member of the marketing faculty, and six years as its chair. From the time that I first arrived at Columbia as a student in 1969, the marketing faculty has helped shape my thinking about marketing and its role in the modern corporation. There are too many to mention them all, but I would be remiss if I did not note the roles played by the late Bill Brandt, John Howard, and Abe Shuchman, together with John Farley, Don Lehmann, and my longtime coauthor, Mac Hulbert.

But not all learning comes from colleagues. Over the years students have been especially important in challenging my ideas and helping to formulate my thinking. Not only MBA students from my early teaching years at UCLA and Harvard Business School, and at Columbia Business School, but also many executive MBA students at Columbia, and in Columbia's joint-venture programs with London Business School (EMBA Global) and the Haas School at the University of California at Berkeley. In addition, thousands of participants in nondegree executive programs at Columbia, other business schools, and in corporations around the world have provided contemporary marketing problems to test my understanding and sharpen my skills. I thank them all. Thanks also to my research assistant, Sumitra Lastkarthikeyan, who provided invaluable help in tying up loose ends on the book; to Chung Ho who provided many forms of administrative support; and to Grant Ackerman from Columbia Business School, Bob Shearer from Morgan Stanley, EMBA students Robert Chu and Andrew Randall, and Jonathan Copulsky from Deloitte & Touche who read earlier drafts and provided great feedback. Hilary Hinzmann provided editorial assistance. Jim Levine, principal at the Levine Greenberg Literary Agency was very helpful in steering me among potential publishers, and the editorial team at Crown Publishing was also extremely supportive. Frankly, it has been my observation that in this day and age, most book editors do very little editing! My experience with this book could not have been more different. Executive editor John Mahaney pushed and prodded as, like Jane Austen, I set about "lopping and chopping," to make this book the best it could be. I could not have asked for more informed editorial direction.

Finally, I thank my wife, Deanna, for providing the spirit of intellectual inquiry that forms the basis of our home life. As you well know, the camaraderie that comes from each of us pursuing our chosen fields in a similar fashion eases the burden that scholarship and writing can become.

Index

About the Author

NOEL CAPON is the R. C. Kopf Professor of International Marketing and past chair of the Marketing Division at the Graduate School of Business, Columbia University. Professor Capon is a highly experienced marketing and sales management educator and is widely sought after by major corporations and business schools globally. He is the leading expert on strategic and global account management. Professor Capon's next book, *Managing Marketing in the 21st Century*, designed to address the skyrocketing price of marketing textbooks, is available as print on demand and as a Web version at www.mm21c.com.